Last Woman Hanged: Roxalana Druse

Last Woman Hanged: Roxalana Druse

James M. Greiner

Last Woman Hanged: Roxalana Druse

By James M. Greiner

Published by James M. Greiner
Printed & Designed by Pumpelly Press
The self-publishing imprint of
Surry Cottage Books
800 Park Ave.
Suite 111A
Keene NH 03431

Additional copies of this book
can be obtained by writing to
Last Woman Hanged
318 Margaret Street
Herkimer, New York 13350

ISBN: 978-0-9829853-0-4

Acknowledgments

When it was over, some called it the trial of the century, and others claimed that it put the village of Herkimer on the map. In 1906 the public was transfixed by the events surrounding the murder of Grace Brown at the hands of her ex-lover, Chester Gillette, at Big Moose Lake. The trial was front-page news across the nation and the inspiration for Theodore Dreiser's classic, *An American Tragedy.* It made the rural county of Herkimer famous, or infamous, advanced the careers of some, and ended the careers of others. The same could not be said of the brutal murder that took place in the same county twenty-two years earlier.

The Druse murder has been largely overshadowed by the Gillette–Brown murder. Susan Perkins of the Herkimer County Historical Society notes that each year, the Society gets requests for information regarding the trial and its participants. She singled out the Big Moose tragedy as "the murder that will not die," and expressed concern that the horrific events that occurred on Hogsback Hill Road might someday be relegated to obscurity—garbled in folklore, fiction, or half-truths. Telling this story would have been extremely difficult without the cooperation, assistance, and suggestions of many individuals. High on that list is Sue Perkins. Every question I asked, no matter how trivial, became a high-priority item to Sue and her able staff at the Herkimer County Historical Society. Caryl Hopson, Dora Hendrick, and Betsy Cirelli were always ready and willing to search for bits and pieces of information, family histories, photographs and rural maps.

Information regarding the Druse murder is scattered throughout upstate New York. The task of assembling and discerning it would have been nearly impossible without the assistance of many librarians. James D. Folts of the New York State Archives made available all of the letters and petitions presented to Governor David B. Hill on behalf of Roxalana Druse. This collection of sympathetic correspondence, along with a number of less-sympathetic letters, remains the largest repository of Druse memorabilia. Dan Smith of the Onondaga County Public Library put his considerable detective skills to work collecting information about the elusive Mary Druse after her release from prison. The staff members at the Herkimer (Frank J. Basloe), Jordanville, Ilion, Richfield Springs and Utica Public Libraries, as well as those at the New York State Historical Association Research Library in Cooperstown, gathered old newspaper clippings and set aside rolls of microfilm of newspapers from the period for this project. Old Fulton NY Post Cards, a website organized by Thomas M. Tryniski, proved invaluable. Close to a dozen old newspapers from Buffalo to Syracuse to Utica are indexed on this site, and they helped me clear up a number of mysteries related to the Druse case. Pat DiTata and Tracy Smith of the West Canada Valley Central School library deserve special thanks for locating and obtaining a copy of the obscure booklet: *Mrs. Druse's Case, and Maggie Houghtaling, An Innocent Woman Hanged.*

Local historians too were extremely helpful. Marjorie Walters of Richfield Springs led me to the two known Druse photographs and Town of Warren Historian Cathy Hoke, who resides on Hogsback Hill Road, helped me understand the physical setting of her neighborhood and the changes this area has experienced over the years. Donna Dutton of Watertown collected information on Judge Pardon C. Williams, while Dennis Northcott of the Missouri Historical Society located and sent me the diary entries made by feminist Lillie Devereux Blake regarding Roxalana. Grace Farrell, author of *Lillie Devereux Blake: Retracing a Life Erased*, took time from her busy schedule to send me her research regarding the position Blake took regarding other women of that era who were sentenced to death. Jessie B. Ramey of the University of Pittsburgh and Annulla Linders of the University of Cincinnati offered their opinions on the gender inequity of this period. Kevin P. Mulcahy, Humanities Librarian, at the Alexander Library at Rutgers University, was most helpful in gathering information regarding the role of Susan B. Anthony in Roxalana Druse's final days.

I was most fortunate to have several members of the legal community take a special interest in this project. One of the greatest resources was Herkimer County and Surrogate Court Judge Patrick L. Kirk, who offered his advice and expertise not only from the standpoint of a district attorney but also as a county judge. His recommendations, guidance, and encouragement proved to be invaluable. Attorney Thad Luke was just as quick to step forward with his research regarding the New York Penal Code on murder, insanity, and on the rulings of the Court of Appeals for this period. Both deserve special thanks for guiding me through the somewhat confusing state of New York's health privacy laws in an attempt to obtain the psychological report on Roxalana Druse.

Retired English professor at Herkimer County Community College and longtime friend Dave Piwinski offered numerous suggestions and just as many corrections to the final draft. At the same time, Anne Eramo, the "queen of punctuation" and an English teacher at West Canada Valley Central School, put her red pen to work in much the same way. I can't begin to thank Dave and Anne for giving their time to review the manuscript.

Thanks go also to Craig Brandon—no stranger to a good murder story—for all his help and advice with this one and Elaine Ambrose for her many suggestions and corrections with the final draft.

Fay Cofrancesco put her talents to work and designed the cover as well as the rural map of Warren.

Finally, I wish to thank my wife, Teresa. Throughout exciting trips to libraries, tramps across rural cemeteries, and numerous visits to Hogsback Hill Road, she somehow managed to endure my singular obsession with this story.

James M. Greiner
Herkimer, New York

For

Mary and Beth

Introduction

The Mohawk River served as a water highway that brought the first European settlers to the vast wilderness of upstate New York in the 1750s. As time went by, succeeding generations continued to rely upon the river as a source of economic life in the Mohawk Valley. Packet boats and barges loaded with farm goods were a familiar sight. By the mid-1800s, the barges began to compete with the railroads for the business of shipping goods in and out of the valley. The Industrial Revolution introduced new businesses as well as new faces, and it didn't take long for valley towns to earn reputations as mill or factory towns. Immigrants sought work at the match factory in Frankfort and the gun factory in Ilion founded by Eliphalet Remington. Across the river at the county seat in Herkimer, there were small shops, knitting mills, and sawmills. Only the city of Little Falls was divided by the river, and it too had knitting and paper mills.

A mile or two north or south of the Mohawk River, dirt paths led to farms of all sizes. As the villages expanded, the rural areas remained virtually the same as they had been a generation earlier—the pace of life was a lot different from that in the valley towns. The land and the weather had a tremendous impact on life and what inhabitants there made of it.

Southernmost of all the townships in Herkimer County lies the town of Warren. By 1880 it seemed untouched by the passage of time. Scattered and sometimes clustered about the rolling hills were some 1,500 inhabitants who worked the land in much the same way their forefathers had. Country roads connected one hamlet to the next, all bearing the names of those who were the first to farm there. There were small hamlets like Cullen with 60 or so inhabitants, Crane's Corners, and Jordanville, the only village. The most unique feature of the region, two inland lakes, could be found at the southern tip of the town. Even today people have difficulty remembering which one is Weaver Lake and which one is Young's Lake, so they refer to the area as Little Lakes.

The lives of those who lived here were tied to the land. Apple orchards and fields of grain, corn, and hops were a common sight. Dairy farming was popular and profitable. Warren, with its eight cheese factories, helped make Herkimer County the largest cheese producer in the state. In the winter months, logs were dragged to sawmills over ice and snow covered roads.

Residents of the area attended steepled churches and sent their children to one-room schoolhouses. There were Grange meetings, harvest dances, and barn raisings. People worked hard, looked after their neighbors, and shared a bond that only farmers could appreciate.

When one farmer needed help, others pitched in, and when he had troubles, they showed their concern. In January 1885, many farmers in the area of Hogsback Hill Road became concerned about the disappearance of a farmer—Bill Druse.

Cast of Characters

ROXALANA'S FAMILY:

William (Bill) Druse, husband
Mary Jane and George, children
Lucy Teft Gates, sister
Charles Gates, brother-in-law
Effie, Idelia, Chester and Frank, nieces and nephews
Amon Teft, brother

HER HOGSBACK HILL NEIGHBORS:

Chester Crim, store owner
Jeremiah and Cordelia Eckler and their children: Delilah, Isaiah, Irving, William and Harvey
Will Elwood
Alonzo (Lou) Filkins
Clarence Marshall
Dan McDonald, Justice of the Peace
John Northrup
Charles Pett
Rudolph Van Evera

THOSE SHE MET AT HER ARREST AND TRIAL:

Pardon C. Williams, presiding judge
Abram Steele, district attorney and his assistant, William C. Prescott
H. DeWight Luce, defense attorney and his assistant, Amos H. Prescott
Valentine Brown, sheriff
Delevan Cook, sheriff
Dr. Irving O. Nellis, coroner
Dr. A. Walter Suiter, expert witness
Rev. George W. Powell, spiritual advisor

CHAPTER 1

"Is Bill at home ?"

The sharp breeze from the east seemed to add an extra chill to the morning air for the farmers on Little Lakes Road. Despite the cold and the snow, the morning chores on the Eckler farm were well underway. Sixty-year-old Jeremiah Eckler had just finished cleaning the barn stalls and was about to hitch a team of horses to a manure wagon when he noticed his son walking toward the barn. Stepping away from the wagon, Jeremiah suddenly stopped and stood in silence. Something was wrong. A foul smell permeated the crisp winter air. Slowly, father and son scanned the horizon in hopes of discovering the source of it.

Like his father, thirty-year-old William Eckler noticed thick, black smoke rising from the chimney of the Druse farmhouse over the hill, a few hundred yards away on Hogsback Hill Road. William thought this odd; neither their chimney nor any of the others in the neighborhood exuded smoke of this nature.

Jeremiah continued to stare at the smoke as it climbed into the winter sky and wondered what to make of it. What were the Druses burning? Each fresh gust of wind brought with it an awful odor of burnt wool or hair. There was no question that the Druses were different; no one knew this better than he did. The two families had been neighbors for thirty years but never became close friends.

Jeremiah would be the first to tell anyone that his success as a farmer was a combination of hard work and the support of his family, key elements that were sadly lacking on the Druse farm. Eckler had begun working on his family's farm at the age of twelve, and by 1851 had struck out on his own and rented a 250-acre farm on Little Lakes Road. It took him five years of hard work, but he was eventually able to purchase the farm outright. Here with his wife Cordelia, they lived and raised five children: Delilah, Isaiah, Irving, William, and Harvey.

It took almost two decades, but the Ecklers' place was firmly established as one of the premier farms in the town of Warren, and at the age of sixty, Jeremiah showed no signs of slowing down. Even the recent destruction of his cheese house by fire was regarded as only a minor setback. A new one, quickly built, was up and running in no time. If Jeremiah was one who always looked to the future, it was safe to say that William Druse just struggled to get past each day.

Whatever was going on at the Druse farmhouse would have to wait—Jeremiah had work to do. Besides, it didn't look as if the Druse family needed help. There was smoke but no fire. With the house and barn not appearing to be in any danger, Jeremiah climbed aboard his wagon and got back to work. Later that day when he returned home, he casually mentioned to his wife the strange, ink-black smoke he had seen coming from the Druse chimney. A bit more suspicious than her husband, Cordelia told him to remember the date, and he did. It was December 18, 1884.

Unbeknownst to Jeremiah and William, another Eckler was witness to the dense smoke and its noxious odor. Early that morning, twenty-five-year-old Harvey slowly navigated his horse-drawn wagon along Hogsback Hill Road. He was on his way to pick up a load of firewood from Alonzo Filkins when he passed the Druse farmhouse. Like his father and brother, he too felt that something was amiss. He would later describe dark, heavy smoke coming from the chimney, but there was something more: Harvey noticed that the windows of the house were covered with paper or cloth.

Like his father and older brother, Harvey had chores to do that day, and stopping at the Druse farm wasn't one of them. He put the matter out of his mind and continued on toward the Filkins farm. He was a little disappointed when he arrived since he'd expected Alonzo Filkins to help him load the wagon. Harvey didn't know it, but he narrowly missed seeing Alonzo at the Druse farm.

That same cold December morning, Alonzo, called Lou, set out on foot to pay Bill Druse a visit. Two days earlier, Bill had borrowed a hay knife from Lou, and now he needed it for his own chores. He walked up the driveway and immediately noticed, as Harvey Eckler had, that the windows of the farmhouse were covered with newspapers. This piqued his curiosity, and instead of going to the barn for his hay knife, he headed toward the house. His first knocks on the door went unanswered, though he distinctly heard voices inside. He knocked again, only to be greeted with silence. Filkins then walked to the east side of the house where he found the storm door unlatched and the main door bolted shut. He continued knocking, each knock louder than the one before. Whatever the reason was for covering the windows, Alonzo figured he wouldn't find the an-

This photo of the Druse farm on Hogback Hill Road was taken in January 1885 at the time of the Inquest.

swer this day. He turned away and headed to the barn to retrieve his hay knife.

Filkins was positive he had heard voices inside the Druse house, and it bothered him that no one answered his knocking. He made up his mind to pursue the matter. Instead of heading home, he walked up the hill to pay a visit to Charley Pett, whose farm was closer to the Druse farm than the Eckler place. Perhaps Pett knew something.

About a hundred yards from the Druse farm, on the same side of Hogsback Hill Road, was the farm of Charles Pett. Like Jeremiah Eckler, Charley had known the Druse family for a number of years, but unlike Eckler, he was more familiar with the family, especially the children. The Pett children, Mary, Howard, and Will, attended the same one-room schoolhouse as George and Mary Druse.

Charley Pett had just driven his wagon onto Hogsback Road when he noticed Alonzo Filkins. Both men were anxious to discuss the same subject. Pett surprised Alonzo when he told him that not only had he seen the thick black smoke, but five minutes earlier, he'd also noticed Alonzo knocking on the Druses' front door! Filkins told Pett he didn't know what was happening at the Druse house. He couldn't explain the smoke, the covered windows, or the voices he'd heard inside.

They cut their conversation short when both men noticed a lone figure walking quickly down the driveway of the Druse farm. While Filkins wasn't sure who it was, Charley Pett had little difficulty identifying the stranger. It was Will Elwood, an occasional part-time hired man at the Druse farm. Pett and Filkins watched

The scene of the crime

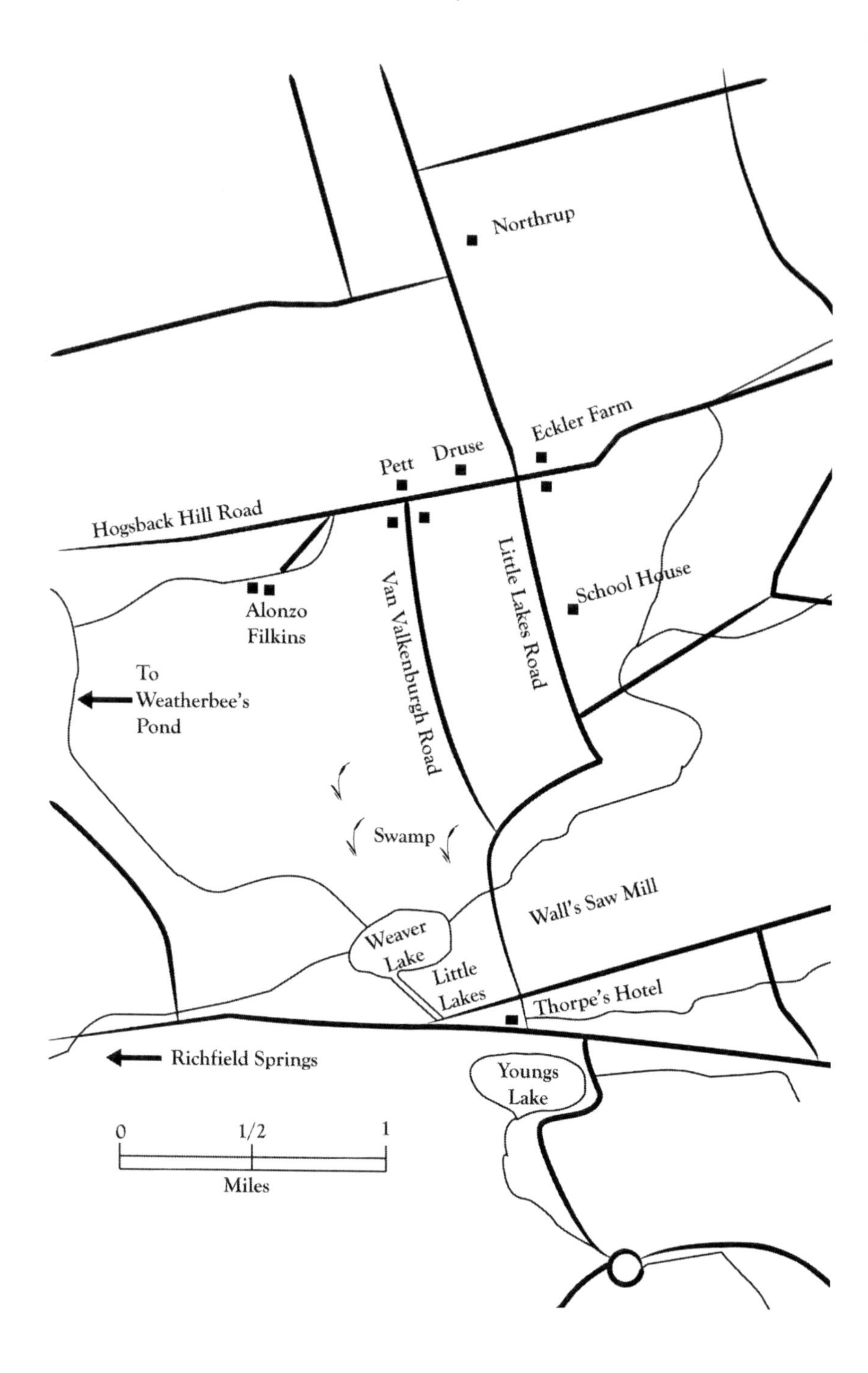

as Elwood crossed the road and began to traverse a snow-covered field. He was walking so fast that neither Pett nor Filkins had a chance to stop him and ask him about the mystery. With nothing more to be said or done, Filkins, hay knife in hand, walked home, while Pett took his wagon to Wall's Saw Mill at Little Lakes.

Will Elwood had arrived at the Druse farm just after Filkins left, and it was just by chance that the two never saw each other. When his knock on the front door went unanswered, Elwood knew that something was wrong. He was well aware of the sometimes volatile relationship between Bill Druse and his wife Roxalana. What's more, he knew that there were children in the house, and he feared for their safety. When Pett and Filkins noticed him crossing the field, Elwood had made up his mind to visit Roxalana's brother-in-law, Charles Gates.

It was late, almost 5 p.m., when Elwood arrived at the Gates house. Agitated, he wasted no time describing the covered windows, the bad smell, and the knocks on the door that went unanswered. "Either Bill killed them all, or they were all dead asleep," said Elwood.

Charles Gates was stunned and worried because his son Frank was staying at the Druse farm. A short while before Elwood's arrival, Charles's daughter Idelia had mentioned that her brother Frank and cousin George Druse hadn't been in school that day. This was a coincidence that Gates dared not ignore. He decided to go to the Druse farm and see for himself what was going on.

It was nearing six in the evening when Charles Gates arrived at his sister-in-law's house. Unlike the earlier visitors to the farm that day, his firm knock was immediately acknowledged. "Is Bill at home ?" he asked, walking into the house.

"No," replied Roxalana. She said that he had started out for Sabrina's and explained that he would not be home for some time as Sabrina, Bill's sister, lived five miles away in Van Hornsville.

Somewhat satisfied with this response, Gates looked casually about the small farmhouse. From the doorway he could see Mary Druse standing by the parlor door. The sight of his son Frank and George Druse sitting by the stove playing checkers put him at ease. Now, uncomfortable about making such an excited and, it seemed, unjustified entrance, an embarrassed Charles Gates knew he had to say something, so he scolded his son for missing school that day. The boy explained that they'd had to chop wood and there was no time to attend school.

Roxalana Druse -- There are no known photographs of her. This likeness appeared in the newspapers after she was executed.

Before he left, Charles Gates drew his sister-in-law aside and explained his impromptu visit. Not wishing to alarm the children, he spoke in a low whisper relating how Will Elwood had visited him in an excited, almost hysterical state. Covered windows, black smoke, a horrible stench, and unanswered knocks—naturally he was concerned. Roxalana seemed surprised; she had no idea what

Bill Druse -- After his murder, many neighbors came forward and suggested to artists that this was how he looked.

Will could be talking about. Why, a quick glance about the little farmhouse showed that everything was in perfect order. Satisfied with what he saw and reassured by Roxalana that there was no cause for alarm, Charles bid good-night to all and went home. Roxalana watched as he guided his wagon down the long driveway that led to Hogsback Hill Road. As driver and wagon disappeared into the night, she wondered how long she could conceal her dark secret from him and from her neighbors.

Half of Roxalana's life had been spent in this small farmhouse, and perhaps even she had difficulty explaining how it had all come to this. She was born in the town of Marshall, New York, in 1844. Her parents, Nathan and Maria Teft, were farmers who may have moved to upstate New York from Rhode Island to be near other family members. On May 28, 1835, Nathan Teft purchased a farm from Falls Teft for the sum of $1,600. Except for this lone transaction marked "hand paid" in a faded Oneida County deed book, little is known about the life Roxalana and her family led in Marshall. One can only surmise that for a time the farm was moderately successful and the children were afforded the opportunity to receive the basic "three Rs" education in a one-room schoolhouse.

What is known is that sometime after 1850, tragedy visited the family not once, but twice. Nathan Teft died, leaving his wife and five children to fend for themselves on the farm. His sixteen-year-old namesake, Nathan, and fifteen-year-old Amon worked the farm as best they could, while their sisters helped their mother. Eleven-year-old Maria and ten-year-old Roxalana helped cook, clean, and look after six-year-old Lucy. It was a difficult time, but the family managed to hold the farm together until the death of their mother that same year—an especially crippling blow to young Roxalana. The bond between them had grown very strong. She had tender memories of her mother and once said, "I used to mourn a great deal for my mother."

These were desperate times for the children, especially the girls. The boys could look after themselves as hired farmhands, but what would become of the three girls? They were too young to find work, not old enough to find husbands. The children were saved the fate of an orphanage when an uncle took them in, allowing them to finish school and work on his farm. Little is known about this arrangement, except that in a short while, Roxalana would make her own way in the world.

By 1860 the teenager had left her uncle's farm and her siblings. In the nearby town of New Hartford, she found work as a seamstress. It was about a year later that Roxalana suffered a near-fatal accident when an oil lamp broke. The particulars of the accident remain unclear, but what is known is that the young woman suffered burns on both hands.

Misfortune quickly turned to luck when Roxalana was brought to the home of Dr. William Griswold. The New Hartford physician examined her injuries and estimated that it would take a good six weeks for her hands to heal. The doctor and his wife took an immediate liking to the orphaned girl and made every attempt to include her as part of their family. She became a frequent visitor to their home, often accompanying them to church services. Once, when she fell ill, she spent four weeks convalescing at their house. When Roxalana had sufficiently recovered and found a job sewing at Williams Brothers in Utica, the Griswolds insisted she stay on with them.

In 1862, Roxalana either accepted an invitation or answered an advertisement to pick hops on farms in Warren, in nearby Herkimer County. A vital ingredient in beer, each year farmers increased their hop production to satisfy an ever-expanding immigrant population that loved its beer as much as its new country. For farmers, it was an excellent cash crop. However, hops had to be harvested quickly in a three-to-four week period from the end of September into early October. Farmers found it necessary to employ a large, temporary work force.

People from all walks of life and from across the county descended upon the small farms to pick hops and make a little money. For those who lived in cities or populous villages, this was an opportunity to enjoy the simple life and breathe country air. The work wasn't physically demanding, and for many, especially the women, picking hops constituted a pleasurable social gathering. "It was difficult to decide whether tongue or finger worked more rapidly," noted one observer of the banter that took place when a group of women gathered near the box tender to deposit the picked hops. For many a picker, it was a time to make new friends and renew old acquaintances. Many had not seen their fellow hop pickers since the last harvest.

Hop pickers lived with the farmers who employed them. Reputations were at stake as many a farmer's wife endeavored to produce the finest country cooking to feed their hungry workers. In time, an experienced hop picker knew which farms to pick as well.

This was the world Roxalana entered in the fall of 1862. When she arrived in the township of Warren in southern Herkimer County, she was hired by the Northrup family, and like her time spent with the Griswolds, this was indeed a fortunate arrangement. The Reverend Joel Northrup was sixty-one and still operated a farm with his sixty-year-old wife, Polly. Their oldest son, Chester, and his wife, Nancy, owned their own farm so were unable to help during hop season. Their youngest son, Bivaldo, was also absent; he had enlisted in the Union Army and was attached to an artillery regiment. So when Roxalana arrived at the Northrup farm, her services were in great demand and much appreciated. She worked alongside the other Northrup children, Mary and Julia.

For the second time in her life, she had found and—as she would later say—accepted by good people. Roxalana was so well liked by the Northrups that she was invited back the following year. It seemed like an ideal arrangement. However, instead of returning to the Northrup farm the following September, Roxalana went to work at the Druse farm.

The Druse family had been part of the farming community of Warren or just over the Otsego County line in Springfield for many years. Stewart Druse and his wife Dorcas managed their Springfield farm quite well with their four children: William, or Bill, the oldest, followed by daughters Phoebe, Rhoda, and Sabrina.

In time, however, a problem arose on the Druse farm. The relationship between father and son became strained; they could not—and would not—work together. The source of the bad blood between the two will never be known, but it's fair to say that they probably argued about work and money. On December 11, 1854, Stewart Druse deeded a tract of land to his son on Hogsback Hill Road in the town of Warren. William's absence on the farm was hardly noticed. Even as the health of his wife Dorcas failed, Stewart and his daughters worked hard and the farm prospered. Additional land was cleared, and by 1860, he had twenty milk cows, along with horses and other livestock. In that same year, Stewart claimed to have produced 5,000 pounds of cheese, and his kiln dried 8,000 pounds of hops. These, together with the crops he grew, placed his entire estate at a value of $14,000. Stewart Druse had every reason to be proud of his accomplishments, but at the same time, he must have been taken aback when he saw what his son Bill had done with the farm he had given him as a gift.

On the surface, Bill Druse's farm looked no different from any other medium-sized farm in Warren. There was a small house, a woodshed, and a large barn, along with cows, a few horses, sheep, pigs, and a farm dog. In addition, he had a small apple orchard and was trying to grow wheat, oats, hay, and buckwheat. Much of what he produced on the farm stayed on the farm. Milk, butter, and apples seemed to be his only cash crops, and the profit from these varied from year to year.

As the farm slipped slowly into debt, Bill Druse hit upon a plan that would free him from debt. On April 2, 1861, he signed an indenture with a neighbor. This was, in effect, a loan using land as collateral. Bill received $600 in exchange for allowing his neighbor to use twenty-three acres of his farmland. The money cleared up some debts and since he repaid it before the date specified on the indenture, he retained ownership of the land. For the next two decades, Druse would borrow against his land in amounts sometimes as high as $2,000 dollars, and then struggle to make payments on time.

An example of this occurred between 1864 and 1865 when Druse was forced to sell thirty-eight milk cows to meet expenses. This left him with only two cows, seriously reducing the farm's income as butter and cheese production effectively came to a halt. A short time later he signed another indenture, and soon there were more cows and an additional thirty sheep.

Stewart Druse and his son Bill were, by all accounts, a father and son with little in common. While one worked hard to achieve success despite hardships, the other never seemed to get ahead and oftentimes slipped behind.

Now the good fortune Roxalana had experienced with the Griswolds and the Northrups suddenly eluded her. When she arrived in Warren in the mid-1860s to pick hops, she chose the wrong Druse farm. Exactly how Roxalana and William Druse met and under what circumstances remains shrouded in mystery. There are several different stories. Did Bill Druse arrive at the train station in nearby Richfield Springs in a weathered black democrat wagon and brazenly announce to prospective pickers, "None but churchgoers need apply"? It seems unlikely, since he was not a member of any church in Warren. Did Bill dance a lively Virginia reel and take a shine to Roxalana at one of the barn dances that celebrated the end of hop-picking season? This may have happened since everyone knew that these dances were lively and fun. Or was Bill Druse, as some suggested, considered a good catch? Not likely, unless she considered a thirty-eight-year-old bachelor with a farm on the verge of financial ruin a good prospect.

Why didn't Roxalana ask her good friend Julia Northrup if Bill Druse would be right for her? Did she think that the difference in their ages, fifteen years, wouldn't matter? Maybe she was thinking of the past and her own parents. Her father Nathan was fifty-nine and her mother Maria just twenty-three when their first child was born. Or was Roxalana thinking of herself? At the age of twenty-two, she was considered old by the standards of the day. It was either marry Bill Druse, or face the possibility of spending the rest of her life as a spinster at the end of a needle and thread.

Finally, did she ever stop to consider what her life on a farm would be like? She may have harbored tender memories of her girlhood on her family's farm, but that was long ago. Except for picking hops a few weeks each autumn, she had not spent much time on a farm or endured the hardships of a farmer's wife.

For whatever reason, Roxalana Teft married William Druse at the Little Lakes Methodist Church on May 27, 1865. William Druse took his bride to the only home he had ever owned, the farmhouse on Hogsback Hill Road. Its location, set back off the main road, isolated them from the other houses in the area. It was a modest wood-framed building, but without the rustic barn-board interior common in that era. Wooden boards covered the floors, and the three downstairs rooms had lath-and-plaster walls. A small foyer led to the center room, with the kitchen and parlor to the left. A larger woodstove was in the parlor. The kitchen had a small cookstove and a basin sink, but water still had to be brought in from an outside well. Just off the kitchen to the right was the bedroom. During the winter months, it was often so cold the couple moved into the parlor to be closer to the woodstove and used the bedroom to store bags of buckwheat and other farm supplies. A set of stairs by the kitchen pantry led to the attic. Here a straw-tick mattress and a blanket on the floor were all that a hired man would need to be comfortable for the night. The house was set on a stone foundation with a small crawl space underneath that served as a root cellar. In all respects, it was a simple house for a couple with simple needs.

In the beginning, the two worked hard. Bill tended to a variety of farm chores, and Roxalana wasted little time securing employment. Recalling the kindness bestowed upon her by the Northrup family during her hop-picking days, she gladly accepted a job as their housekeeper. By this time, the aged Mrs. Northrup was widowed, had lost her sight, and needed assistance in her home. Her children were busy with their own homes and families, and Roxalana needed the work. She cleaned, prepared meals, and was a good companion to the lonely widow, and she worked for Mrs. Northrup until late fall when the weather turned bad and travel became difficult. For Roxalana, now pregnant with her first child, it was perhaps best to stay at home.

On February 22, 1866, barely nine months after her marriage, Roxalana gave birth to her first daughter, Mary Jane. Life now centered around the world that existed on the farm on Hogsback Hill Road. Caring for a newborn, keeping house, and cooking not only kept her busy but also isolated from neighbors for long stretches of time. When she did leave the farm, it was to go to the store where she purchased needed items on credit. Missing an opportunity to forge new friendships and become part of the community, she never made an effort (nor did Bill) to join a church where she could have escaped the tedium and loneliness of farm life.

A source of friction in the Druse marriage was the lack of money, evidenced not only by the store accounts that were in arrears but also, in time, by the rundown appearance of the house and farm. As the years passed, the small house offered very little in the way of creature comforts. It seemed that the only luxury it afforded was a sewing machine. Roxalana was a skilled seamstress; however, she never found time to finish making curtains for the windows. None of this seemed to matter to her husband, who was indifferent to the needs of the house and his wife. He never lifted a paintbrush or made any attempt to make life easier for his family, nor did he make any plans to add onto the house or make improvements as his family grew. The place on Hogsback Hill Road was never anything but a house to Bill Druse—it was never a home.

In 1869, Roxalana gave birth to her second child. She was christened Ellen, but Roxalana affectionately called her Nellie. Little is known about Nellie beyond a chilling entry in the local census of 1875: idiotic. A sickly child prone to fits, she required constant care.

The 1870s brought neither happiness nor contentment to the Druse family. Farmers throughout the state were experiencing the effects of low prices for their products. A slight dip in the economy wasn't necessary to underscore the hard times that already existed on the Druse farm. It was simply a valley of poverty between two hills of relative prosperity—the Pett farm on one side and the Eckler farm on the other.

By 1875 life on the Druse farm was a hand-to-mouth existence. Only four cows, the dog, and a few workhorses remained, and there was little income from the sale of sheep, swine, chickens, or apples. Bill Druse continued to use indentures as a quick fix to his financial woes. Gambling with the farm was no secret to Roxalana; she was fully aware of Bill's borrowing method and frequently signed the indentures with him.

These financially unstable times were made all the more difficult for the family by Bill's sporadic work schedule on the farm. He finished some projects, abandoned others, and in some instances, simply walked off, disappearing for days! Roxalana became accustomed to these sudden absences and rarely questioned her husband's affairs. Was he working as a hired man on another farm for a few days? Maybe he was trying to sell his idea of a new waterwheel to investors. He had spent many hours meticulously carving a wooden model of a waterwheel and was quite proud of his efforts, speaking often of wanting to patent his invention. Wherever Bill went or whatever he was doing, Roxalana could only hope that he would eventually return, ambitious and determined to get out of debt. Instead, he usually came back so far behind in his work that he had to hire extra help.

This was the case in 1875 when he hired Jan and Jay O'Brien. Their room and board was an additional strain on the family, which now included a baby boy. On December 8, Roxalana had given birth to William George Stewart Druse, named for his father and grandfather.

As the 1870s drew to a close, it was clear to most anyone who knew the couple that the farm, the family, and the marriage were all in trouble. Some problems were unavoidable, some should never have occurred, and others were simply tragic.

By the spring and summer of 1879, the biggest concern of Roxalana was the failing health of her daughter Nellie. One doctor after another was summoned to Hogsback Hill Road to tend to the ailing girl. As her seizures (which may have been epilepsy) increased, a frantic Roxalana called on her old benefactor, Dr. Griswold. But there was nothing either he or any of the other local physicians could do, and Nellie died just two months shy of her eleventh birthday and was buried on the farm not far from the house. Her friend Julia Northrup consoled the devastated young mother. Years later Julia recalled that Roxalana "treated [Nellie] kindly, always seemed to have a great deal of affection for [her] and I believe she loved [her] with a mother's love."

Another family tragedy occurred on December 2, 1879, when Stewart Druse died at the age of eighty-one. Although he had never filed a will with a lawyer, there was never any question as to who would inherit his estate: everything was left to his daughter, Phoebe. When Bill Druse learned of this, he flew into a violent rage. Stewart's only son made no attempt to hide his anger. He arrived at the home he had not inherited, glared at the body in the casket, and then ordered the undertaker to strip the suit off his deceased father and wrap the corpse in a shawl. He then had the audacity to wear the suit to the funeral. This brazen act of disrespect raised eyebrows in the small community.

Inheriting his father's farm would have given Bill Druse a new start in life. He could have sold the farm on Hogsback Hill Road and moved to an established, successful farm. It was his last chance to get ahead in life, and he knew it. Now he had to accept that he would never raise himself out of the poverty he had sunk to. Doctors' bills, land taxes, farm expenses, and overdue store credit never seemed to go away. And for the first time ever, Bill Druse failed to honor an indenture and lost sixty acres of farmland. Neighbors noticed that the farm looked worse than ever and some, like Charley Pett, thought Bill Druse looked just as bad. Pett said the man wasn't the old Bill Druse he used to know. Over the years he had noticed a change in his neighbor; it was as if he didn't care what he looked like or what others thought of him. His clothes, never neat, were rougher now, in need of mending and a good wash. He stopped shaving and cutting his hair. A long grayish beard now hid the handsome square jaw and his shoulder-length gray hair was topped with an unfashionable felt hat. His unkempt appearance made him look much older than his fifty-six years.

Bill Druse appeared tired and sometimes apathetic. It didn't seem to bother him that some projects were never completed and others never started. To many people in the area, he was a harmless character. Neighbors tended to tolerate his antics and poked fun at his ways. A few neighbors liked to tell the story of how Bill Druse would arrive unannounced at their homes. These visits always seemed to coincide with the arrival of the latest newspaper. Once welcomed inside, Bill would make himself comfortable by the fire and begin to leisurely read the paper. His timing was perfect; as he read, the dinner dishes would be set out on the table. Bill would be invited to have dinner with the family, and not one to ever refuse a meal, he always accepted. On one occasion, he shocked his host after dinner by glancing about the room and declaring, "You have all too many things here. If I were boss, I would set half of them outdoors."

Harmless encounters like these were amusing; however, some of the neighbors remembered a darker side to the feuding Druses. Bill and Roxalana were seldom seen together in public, but when they were, the verbal exchanges between the two were both embarrassing and frightening. Bill Druse frequently lashed out at his wife in the harshest language. She was a "damned bitch" or a

"Goddamned whore!" Roxalana could be just as cruel, calling Bill a "Goddamned cuss" and a "Goddamned son of a bitch!" And if that wasn't enough, he was also a "Goddamned *lousy* son of a bitch!" It is important to note that alcohol was never a factor during these shouting matches; these were not typical town-tavern arguments. Husband and wife apparently never displayed anything but blatant animosity toward one another.

The saddest part was that neither of them attempted to hide these vile comments from their children. "I heard him call mother a 'Goddamned bitch' a good many times," recalled George. Their nephew, Frank Gates, was more direct, remarking that he heard his uncle call Roxalana 'A damned bitch' by his judgment five hundred times.

Physical abuse probably accompanied the verbal abuse, or at least that is what Julia Northrup believed. She was convinced that Bill Druse was cruel not only to Roxalana but to the children as well. "There is reason to believe," she later recalled, "that William Druse caused the child [Nellie] to have fits by his brutality."

Some, like Dyer Lathrop, were witness to the abuse. Lathrop recalled a particular incident one spring day that shocked and scared him. He had been at the Druse farm for a few days helping Bill with a variety of chores. His last day at the farm was spent mending fences. Bill ordered him to "Go to the house and do the chores." It had been a damp and miserable day, and Lathrop was thankful that at least some of the outdoor chores had been completed. When he arrived at the house, he saw that most everything was in order and decided to go to the barn where there was always something that needed tending to. As he approached the barn, he was startled by a woman's scream. At the barn door, armed with a stick about three feet long, was Bill Druse, and cowering near the entrance was a terrified Roxalana. Bill had the stick raised and threatened to give his wife "a damned good thrashing!"

Lathrop rushed forward, placing himself between Bill and Roxalana. "You won't strike her tonight!" he said. Bill cursed at his hired man and demanded that he step aside, but Lathrop held his ground, shouting, "You damned son of a bitch—I ain't afraid of you!" Druse uttered a few more profanities but eventually backed down and walked away. Dyer Lathrop was stunned at what had transpired. He had known Bill Druse for thirty years and had never before witnessed this sort of Jekyll-and-Hyde behavior. He finished the chores in the barn, bid goodbye to a sobbing Roxalana, and returned to his home in Richfield Springs.

By 1880, the quarrelsome couple led separate lives. To many it appeared as if Roxalana led a friendless life on the farm while her husband wandered about the area content with a hand-to-mouth existence. Still, there were those who saw Bill as a down-on-his-luck farmer trying to make ends meet by selling buckwheat, apples, hay, and wood, and applying any money he made to the family's numerous bills. Bill Druse never paid off a single account, but as long as he made the effort, shopkeepers let him purchase on credit. Naturally, this shortage of cash made it almost impossible for him to employ a hired man for long. Not only did he have no means to pay him; he could never offer a hired hand room or board for more than a day. His last long-term help was a boy, Frank Gates.

The Gates family had lived in Warren only for a few years, having moved from Deerfield in Oneida County. George Gates, or Charles as he was referred to, was renting the old Rathbun farm, just south of the Pett farm on Van Valkenburg Road. His wife was the former Lucy Teft, Roxalana's younger sister.

Charles Gates was a hard worker, but he found it difficult to provide for his wife and four children. So when thirteen-year-old Frank went to live with his cousins in the first week of December 1884, it was one less mouth to feed at the Gates table. For the Druse family, Frank was a big brother who accompanied his nine-year-old cousin George to school and a live-in hired man who worked for his room and board; the simple arrangement suited everyone. There was no reason to believe that Thursday, December 18, 1884 would be different from any other day on the Druse farm.

On that cold December morning, Frank made his way downstairs and began to build a fire in the kitchen woodstove. No one else was awake, and he heard no sounds coming from the parlor where Mary and Roxalana slept. Upstairs , George was asleep, and as far as he knew, so was his uncle. Frank was cold and wasted no time filling the kitchen stove with dry wood shingles and kindling. Warming his hands before the blaze, he had already made up his mind to skip school that day. The snow and ice-covered roads made for near-perfect conditions for dragging logs to Wall's Sawmill at Little Lakes, two miles away. He knew it was a decision his father would not approve of, but there were plenty of chores to do on the farm, and school could wait.

A sudden knock at the door interrupted his thoughts. Leaving the warmth of the stove, Frank went to the door and was greeted by Irving Eckler. Having noticed the smoke from the chimney, Eckler inquired if Bill was there. Frank remarked that his uncle should be down at any moment. Eckler had come to retrieve an auger that Bill had borrowed; this didn't surprise Frank, as his uncle was famous for borrowing tools and not returning them. He didn't know where the auger was, and Eckler said it was not all that important. He would stop by later.

Frank returned to the stove and continued to put more wood on the fire.

"Goddamn you!" snarled Bill Druse. "What have you got such a hot fire for?"

The young boy turned with a start. He hadn't heard his uncle come downstairs. Aware of Bill's temper, Frank dared not answer the question; instead, he wisely decided to change the subject and asked if he should go to the barn and begin the chores before breakfast. Bill Druse had already finished lacing his boots and was just putting on his coat when he told Frank that he would rather do the work himself. Without even a "Good morning," Bill Druse headed out to the barn.

Roxalana and Mary could not help but overhear the early morning scolding that young Frank received. They emerged from the parlor only after Bill left the house. The late riser that day was George; he wasn't about to leave the warm blankets in the attic until the stove had made the downstairs comfortably warm. When he did come down, he made his way to the kitchen table, sat next to Frank, and waited for breakfast. It was then that the door suddenly burst open.

"You Goddamned bitch!" roared Bill. "You have been splitting up my board that I was to put on the barn door." Roxalana said she didn't know what he was talking about. "God damn you!" he screamed. "You lie!"

Roxalana began to sob and with each tear, Bill grew more and more angry. Seizing the axe near the stove, he raised it past his shoulders. "God damn you," he shouted. "If you don't keep still, I'll split your brains out!"

Frank and George sat at the table and didn't say a word as tempers between husband and wife escalated. This was just another day at the Druse house.

Bill set the axe aside and sat at the table with his back toward his wife. He wasn't ignoring Roxalana; he was getting ready to lash out at her again.

"God damn you, you have got a big bill up at Crim's," he accused.

Two days earlier, Bill had gone to Crim's Store for a gallon of kerosene. Store owner Chester Crim produced his ledger book and told Druse that he already had an outstanding bill of $20.48. Bill immediately questioned Crim about the account; he hadn't been in the store all summer. Crim pointed to an entry dated July 23 for $3.66, another on July 29 for $3.28, and another on October 20 for $2.95. Each charge was signed by Roxalana Druse. There was even a charge of $1.58 by Mary Druse.

Now, sitting at the kitchen table with the bill in his hand, Bill Druse wanted answers. He accused Roxalana of buying needless items and running him into debt. He reminded her that he had put $5.50 against this account, and he demanded to know what she had purchased.

For twenty long minutes the two screamed, argued, and swore at each other. Roxalana said that everything she charged was needed for the house. There were groceries, a dress for Mary, a suit for George. None of this satisfied her husband. He continued to badger her about the number of outstanding bills she had incurred. Neither of them wanted to back down, but Bill got in the last word.

"I'll have different arrangements before tonight," he warned.

It was an awful exchange, and more violent than what the children were accustomed to. George later recalled that the subject of the arguments was always the same —lack of food and lack of money. Only this time the intensity and volume were different. This was a bitter, heated exchange. On almost every other occasion, after such an argument, his father would simply storm out of the house, leave the farm, and disappear for a day or two, letting the family fend for themselves. This time Bill didn't leave; Roxalana did. As the screaming subsided, she slowly and silently slipped into the parlor and returned shortly to her place in the kitchen. Standing behind her husband, she motioned to the boys with a nod. Frank and George, who had been seated throughout the fight, rose from their seats. Roxalana drew them near and quietly whispered to them that they should leave the house for a bit, but not to wander too far. Neither boy noticed what Roxalana was hiding between the folds of her dress and apron.

Frank was a bit confused by his aunt's request but was nonetheless relieved to get out of the kitchen. She didn't tell him to begin any chores, and he was thankful that he didn't have to listen to the two scream at each other. As the boys walked from the house toward the barn, George suggested they get their sleds. The two had not gone thirty feet when they heard a gunshot. Both boys stopped in their tracks and stared at each other. There was another gunshot and another, followed by Roxalana's screams. Frank looked toward the house and could see Roxalana standing in the doorway. She yelled to him to get back to the house, and he did as he was told, with George not far behind.

Roxalana stood in the doorway with a loaded .22 caliber pistol in her hand. She thrust it into Frank's hand as he passed through the doorway.

"Take this revolver and shoot him," she screamed, "or I'll shoot you!"

Frank was terrified. Ten feet away, his uncle lay face down on the table. Writhing in pain, a wounded Bill Druse attempted to rise from his chair. Roxalana continued to scream hysterically, *"Shoot! Shoot!"* Standing behind his uncle and shaking with fear, he fired the pistol. *"Shoot!"* screamed Roxalana, *"Shoot!"* Frank shot his uncle twice.

She then took the weapon from Frank and fired it two more times. Frantic and out of bullets, Roxalana handed the gun to her daughter. Mary fumbled with it, trying to reload as her wounded father's groans filled the room. Even though some shell casings were jammed in the pistol, she managed to load several shells. When she attempted to hand the revolver to Frank, her grip on it remained so firm that she inadvertently pulled the trigger, causing the bullet to pass between her mother and Frank.

Roxalana never ceased screaming during the chaotic scene. She tried to push her husband from the table. Despite his wounds, Bill desperately held onto the corner of the table and resisted as best he could. Mary dropped the pistol, ran to the sewing machine, and returned with a rope used to tie up the dog. She put it around her father's neck and dragged him from the table onto the floor.

While Mary went for the rope, Roxalana went for the axe her husband had threatened her with moments before and raised it over her head. Writhing in pain from his wounds, Bill lay helpless on the floor. He looked at his wife, standing now above him with the raised axe.

"Oh, Roxy, don't!" he pleaded.

With a demonic look in her eye and all the strength she could muster, Roxalana Druse brought the axe down as if she was chopping firewood. Again and again she struck him as hard as she could. Blood sprayed across the floor, and finally the severed head rolled to one side. For a brief moment she stared at the corpse. Then, in an instant, she flew into a hysterical rage. Still clutching the bloody axe, she screamed at the children, telling each of them what to do.

Numb with fear, they did exactly as they were told. Mary gathered up papers and covered all the windows in the house while Frank went to the well for water.

The blood stains on the floor could be washed away, but how could Roxalana hide the body? It was December and the ground was frozen; tracks in the snow would lead to a fresh grave. There was another way. When Frank returned with a pail of water, Roxalana ordered him to the woodshed along with her son George and told them to bring in all the bundles of dried shingles they could find.

CHAPTER 2

The Neighborhood Detectives

If Charles Gates was satisfied with his sister-in-law's explanation of the events of that day, hired man Will Elwood was not. From that day until after the first of the year, Elwood never ceased to talk about the mysterious events of December 18. He was convinced that his former employer was dead, and he said so to anyone who would listen to him. He may have been overly dramatic in his accusations, but everyone he told agreed that something was out of place. Bill Druse was a familiar character in the area, and no one had seen him since that day.

Jeremiah Eckler remained suspicious of the dense smoke and foul smell he had witnessed. Something else bothered him as well. Later that December day, Frank Gates had come to his farm asking to purchase a box of matches. Young Gates hastily explained that the fires had gone out in both stoves over at the Druse farm. At the time, Eckler wasn't surprised—only the poor Druses would run out of matches in the middle of winter. He gave the boy a box and told him that payment wasn't necessary. Too busy working, Eckler didn't ask Frank what they were burning that caused both fires to go out.

Sometime after the first of January in 1885, Jeremiah Eckler made a trip to the Druse farm on the pretense of buying a load of hay. As he drew his wagon close to the barn, he was met by Roxalana and her daughter, Mary. They were happy to see him; Eckler was a well-off farmer who could have bought hay from anyone in the area, and money was always scarce on the Druse farm.

As Jeremiah loaded the hay into his wagon, he casually looked about and asked Roxalana if Bill was at home, mentioning that he hadn't seen his neighbor in quite some time. Roxalana replied that he hadn't seen him because her husband had taken a trip to New York City.

Bill Druse in New York City? Eckler had misgivings. It seemed quite out of character for a man like Bill to make a trip to the city. This was a man who had never been farther away than Little Falls or Herkimer, and where would Druse get the money to make such a trip? Eckler's suspicions grew.

Another neighbor anxious to receive some straight answers from Roxalana was Charley Pett. On January 6, he paid a visit to the Druse farm with another neighbor, Clarence Marshall. Pett got right to the point, demanding to know when he could expect to see Roxalana's husband.

Roxalana recited her lines to the two men as if she were performing in a well-rehearsed play. Bill left the farm before Christmas, she told them. He was on his way to his sister Sabrina's, and then he was going to Fayette Druse's house, then on to Little Falls where he would take the train to New York City. She carefully explained that he was wearing his old overcoat when she last saw him, but assumed that he would be purchasing new clothes for the trip when he arrived in Little Falls.

According to Roxalana, her husband had business to attend to in New York. Bill Druse fancied himself an inventor, and he had taken a wooden model of a waterwheel with him. Perhaps he planned to meet with potential investors.

She informed Pett and Marshall that she was as concerned about his absence as everyone else, and added that she was trying to get Bill to return as quickly as possible, as there were more important matters here at home. She proved her concern by producing a Western Union telegram:

Richfield Springs, N.Y.
Jan. 6, 1885

Amon Teft
Care J. J. Wignkoop
127 West Street, N.Y.

Your sister Lucy very sick, not expected to live, come immediately, have Mr. Druse come also. Answer. Mrs. Druse.

Amon Teft, explained Roxalana, was her brother, and she hadn't received a reply to this telegram yet.

Pett returned the telegram and reminded Roxalana that Will Elwood was still claiming that Bill was dead. This struck a nerve with Roxalana, who exploded in anger. It was a lie, she stated, and if Will Elwood did not cease spreading this rumor, she would have him prosecuted.

Their welcome clearly strained, the two men left the farmhouse agreeing that something was amiss. It was obvious to Pett and Marshall that Bill Druse was not home. His hat, coat, and boots were gone, and it bothered them that a family that could barely put food on the table had fresh paint everywhere. There were no curtains at the windows, but the sills, door, and ceiling had been freshly painted, and there was new wallpaper in the kitchen. Why, they had even painted the kitchen floor by the stove green.

If Roxalana breathed a sigh of relief at the departure of Pett and Marshall, it was short lived. Two days later Pett came back with Lou Filkins. This time it was Roxalana who asked the questions. She too had heard these vicious rumors spread by Will Elwood, and she wasted little time accusing Pett of doing the same. She demanded to know if it was true that he had told everyone he met that he had seen a bloodstained axe at the farmhouse on his last visit.

Pett wasn't intimidated by her outburst or accusations and remarked that the rumor may have started because an axe had recently been discovered.

Pett set the bait, and Roxalana took it. "Where?" she asked.

He told her an axe had been discovered a short distance from the Druse farm at Weatherbee's Pond. Pett went on to say that he had not seen the axe himself, but if she wished he would investigate the matter for her. Not only had the clever neighbor given himself an excuse for a return visit, he had also provided Roxalana with enough time to fabricate another story.

Still without real proof as to Bill Druse's whereabouts, Pett and Filkins left the Druse farm. Mentioning the discovery of an axe head at Weatherbee's Pond, however, seemed to unnerve Roxalana. Filkins, like Marshall before him, had said very little at the Druse house. While Charley Pett spoke with Roxalana, Lou Filkins glanced casually at the freshly painted windowsills and the wallpapered kitchen.

The next day, Pett made plans to return to the Druse farm; each new visit clearly agitated Roxalana. As he was about to leave home, he had a visitor—eighteen-year-old Sherman Bowen. His mother, Rhoda, was another of Bill's sisters. The boy said that his mother was upset by the rumors circulating about the fate of her brother Bill. Sherman asked Charley if there was something he could do to calm his mother's fears. Pett replied there was and suggested Sherman accompany him to the Druse farm.

When they arrived at the Druses, Pett got right to the point, putting Roxalana on the defensive. What kind of axe did Bill have, Pett wanted to know. How many did he have? Where were they? There were two, she told him. One was by the stove. Pett asked about the other axe. Roxalana said it had a round head, and added that her husband had carelessly left it in the woods. She'd sent the boys out to look for it earlier, but they couldn't find it, she told Pett.

Tired of this line of questioning, Roxalana changed the subject, once more accusing Will Elwood of being the source of all the rumors. She told them she was just as concerned as everyone else about her husband's disappearance and was doing all she could to locate him. As proof of this, she produced yet another telegram and presented it to Pett.

January 14, 1885
Mr. Cyrus Burns
East Shodac, via mail
Albany

Is William there? Mrs. Druse.

First, it had been a telegram to New York City addressed to her brother. Now it was one addressed to a cousin in Albany. Where next? Charley Pett had known Bill Druse for over twenty years, and in all that time he never remembered him going to any of these places. Pett wasn't disappointed, though, as Roxalana had come up with yet another story. He decided his next visit would need to be more forceful. She was hiding something, and he knew the only way for the truth to come out was to involve the authorities. He made plans to go to Herkimer and meet with either the sheriff or the district attorney.

After a long three-hour journey over snow-covered roads, a very cold and tired Charley Pett arrived at the law office of Abram Steele on Main Street in Herkimer. Frustrated after his interviews with Roxalana, he was relieved not only to find Steele in his office but also willing to listen to his story.

The chief prosecutor, who had never attended law school, had celebrated his fortieth birthday five days before Pett's visit. Admitted to the bar after interning for a year in his cousin's law office in Frankfort, Steele had been the district attorney since 1880. A workaholic by the standards of his day, Steele had a reputation for being knowledgeable, firm, and thorough in the way he prepared for and presented his cases—qualities Pett thought would be necessary for dealing with the alibi-prone Mrs. Druse.

Steele listened intently as the self-styled neighborhood detective described the mysterious happenings on Hogsback Hill Road: the black smoke, awful smell, newspaper- covered windows, and the oft-repeated phrase, "Gone to New York." Pett said he hadn't seen Bill Druse since mid-December, and he didn't believe anything Roxalana had said regarding his disappearance.

Steele shared Pett's suspicion that something was amiss; this didn't sound like a typical missing person case. He said that he would start out for Warren immediately and asked Charley to contact as many neighbors as he could who had been to the Druse house and have them meet at the Pett farmhouse. Steele said he wanted to interview them before he confronted Roxalana Druse.

Pett knew that he had to get Lou Filkins and the others to come to his farm to meet with Steele. When he arrived home, he couldn't believe his luck; in the distance Chester Gates, Frank's brother, was walking past the Pett farm. Charley Pett called out to Chester and explained that he had just been to see the district attorney about the disappearance of Bill Druse. He told the boy to go home and tell his father to meet back at his farm; the district attorney wanted to speak with him.

A somber crowd greeted Charles and Chester Gates when they brought their wagon to a halt by the Pett wagon house. Lou Filkins, Clarence Marshall, Justice of the Peace Dan McDonald and Charley Pett approached the wagon. The elder Gates knew all of these men, and he knew why they were here. When they told him that the district attorney was at the Pett house, Charles Gates stepped down from the wagon and told his son to proceed to the Druse farm and bring back his brother Frank.

Chester shook the reins, slowly guiding the wagon toward the Druse farm. He knew that his brother was involved in something. Frank had been home only once since mid-December, and that was only for an overnight because he was ill. He should have stayed at home for a few days to get better. Why did he have to rush back to the Druse farm? Chester didn't have a chance to ask his younger brother back then, but now he could—once he got him out of that house.

It was almost dusk when Chester arrived at the Druse Farm. His rap on the kitchen window brought a sharp response.

"Who's there?" asked Roxalana.

"Chester Gates," he responded.

This photograph of the kitchen was taken at the time of the Inquest. The ax stands out suspiciously at the stove, as if it were placed there by the photographer.

She demanded to know if he was alone. It was only after Chester said he was that she unbolted the front door. Chester walked into the house, ignoring Roxalana, and spoke directly to his brother. He told Frank that several men down the road wished to speak with him, and he felt it best that Frank come with him right away. Little George piped up and asked if they were at the Pett farm. Chester, hoping to avoid any further exchange with Roxalana answered yes, but was careful not to mention who they were.

As Frank gathered up what few clothes he had and prepared to leave, an irate Roxalana told him that if this meeting was all that important, these gentlemen should meet at her house instead of Pett's. She lashed out at Chester, demanding to know if Will Elwood happened to be one of the men. She then accused Chester of making up the entire story in order to get Frank out of her house. As a last resort, she said Frank could not leave the house.

"I am the boss of him now," she said in a firm tone.

This didn't scare Chester. "I told her I guessed he would go with me if I wanted him to," he later recalled.

Roxalana slammed the door behind the boys as they left the

farmhouse. They could hear her screaming as they climbed aboard the wagon and drove away.

As Chester guided the wagon onto Hogsback Hill Road, his brother told him what had occurred at the Druse farm on that fateful December day. Chester was stunned and begged his brother to tell the truth when they arrived at the Pett farm.

The adults at the wagon house were eager to hear Frank's story. While Marshall pressured the boy to tell the truth, Dan McDonald warned that if he didn't, he would probably be arrested. Frank looked at each of the men present, and then slowly told them what had transpired almost a month ago. All were horrified at what the boy related and agreed that he would have to repeat his story to District Attorney Steele, who was at the Pett house.

"Frank, are you willing to tell us all you know regarding the death of your uncle, William Druse?" asked Steele when the boy entered the house accompanied by the men.

"Yes, sir," replied Frank.

"Will you do so voluntarily, without any assurance of immunity from the counsel for the people?"

Frank looked about the room filled with men. At the wagon house, they had assured him that they would do all they could to help him if he told the truth. As if an immense burden had been lifted from his shoulders, Frank began to relate the details of that terrible December morning. When he finished, Steele was convinced that he had stumbled upon the most heinous murder in the history of Herkimer County and announced that they would all go to the Druse house to confront Roxalana.

Up to this point, some neighbors may have harbored suspicions regarding the whereabouts of Bill Druse, but few made a concerted effort to confront Roxalana directly. Jeremiah Eckler had been polite when he visited the Druse farm, while Charley Pett had made a nuisance of himself with repeated visits. All of this was about to change when four men led by District Attorney Steele arrived by wagon at the Druse farm.

Steele led the parade into the farmhouse, and before Roxalana could lodge a protest, he calmly asked to see Bill Druse.

"New York," said Roxalana, careful to add that she expected him home at any moment.

Aware of the rumors circulating in the neighborhood regarding his lengthy absence, Roxalana remarked that she didn't believe anything had happened to her husband. Steele wasn't surprised by her response or the fact that she didn't appear to be nervous. Her calm demeanor would soon disappear.

Leaving Roxalana, her daughter and the others in the kitchen, Steele brought Frank Gates and George Druse into the parlor. When asked where his father was, little George looked up to the ceiling, gave a little whistle and said, right on cue, "Gone to New York."

Steele then instructed Frank to relate the details of the murder that had occurred in the next room on December 18. Frank recalled the vicious argument, the shooting, and Roxalana beheading her husband as he lay helpless on the kitchen floor. He described how she disposed of the severed head by wrapping it in newspapers.

"That ain't so," interrupted George. "She wrapped it in her apron."

Next, Steele brought Mary into the parlor to join her brother and her cousin. After she too claimed that her father had gone to New York, Steele asked Frank to repeat his story. When he was done, Mary denied all of it and accused Frank of lying. Nervous and frightened, the girl didn't take long to recant—Frank had told the truth. When asked why she had denied Frank's version of the events, she replied, "Well, it's my mother, you know."

Satisfied with the information he had gathered from the children, Steele was now prepared to take on Roxalana. Speaking to her alone, he informed her that all of the children had given the same version of the murder, and it was now time for her to confess.

The charade was over at last. Steele listened intently as Roxalana, with very little coaxing, broke down and described every detail of the murder. Steele was shocked at how methodically she described the dismemberment of Bill Druse's body, and her attempts to hide her crime by burning parts of it in the kitchen and parlor stoves. Clarence Marshall, who had overheard some of the confession, later asked her why she did it.

"The devil must have been in me," she replied.

Abram Steele looked about the dimly lit farmhouse and announced that Roxalana, her children, and Frank Gates were all under arrest.

Roxalana's demeanor changed in an instant. The façade she had so carefully constructed suddenly vanished, and she seethed with anger. There was only one person to blame for the presence of the law in her house, and that was Frank Gates. His confession ruined everything, and Roxalana decided to punish her nephew in a unique way. She announced that Frank had not told the truth and that his father, Charles, had been in the house on December 18 as an active participant in the murder of her husband.

Before Charles Gates could protest the accusation, Steele placed him under arrest with the others.

It was late in the evening, well past 8 p.m., when Steele told his five prisoners to prepare to leave the farmhouse. At this hour, taking them to the Herkimer jail was out of the question; he had to find a place to secure them nearby, since the Druse house was deemed a crime scene. Either Marshall or Pett suggested that the closest farmhouse in the area that might be able to accommodate five additional lodgers was the Eckler place.

Steele told Roxalana and the children to collect whatever warm clothing they had and get into the wagon. Mary Druse seated herself next to her mother, while Frank helped George climb aboard. None of them would ever return to this house. In the darkness, the house faded quickly from view, but it would forever be etched into their memories.

The wagon full of prisoners slowly made its way up the slight incline of Hogsback Hill Road toward the Eckler place. When they arrived at the house, Steele introduced himself as the district attorney and apologized for the lateness of the hour. If Steele offered an explanation as to why he was there, it wasn't necessary—Jeremiah Eckler had looked out at the group in front of his house and knew instantly. Steele reassured Eckler that the county would compensate him for his inconvenience, adding that he hoped it would be only a temporary arrangement. In parting, he reminded Eckler that these individuals were under arrest and were to be treated as such. He asked that they be kept isolated from each other if possible. They had already practiced their alibis for weeks; he didn't want to give them any additional opportunities.

The next day Steele, in the company of Pett, Marshall, and McDonald, set out to find the remains of Bill Druse taking Frank Gates as their guide.

Leaving the Eckler house, the pair of horse-drawn cutters made their way along the frozen road past the Druse farm, turning onto Van Valkenburg Road. After a few minutes, Frank motioned toward the distance and the small column halted near a cedar swamp. He led the men to an edge of the swamp he had visited a month earlier. Approaching a mound of snow, he gave it a gentle kick. There, buried in the snow and ash, were a few bone chips and metal buckles—all that remained of William Druse.

The murder of Bill Druse. After the inquest, the *Utica Globe* published this drawing showing Mary dragging her father from the table while her mother shoots the pistol.

As they shoveled the evidence into a box, Frank recalled how, after the beheading, Roxalana ordered him and George to retrieve a bed tick from upstairs. The lifeless body was rolled onto it and dragged into the parlor near the stove. Roxalana then told George and Frank to go to the woodshed and bring back as many dried wood shingles as they could carry. Then, as the boys stood guard by the newspaper-covered windows, Roxalana and Mary chopped up the body and fed the pieces to a roaring blaze. A few days later, the stove was emptied and the contents brought to this spot.

When Steele asked if everything associated with the murder had been burned in the stove, Frank said yes. These included his uncle's overcoat, boots, and the model of the waterwheel. The only exceptions were the pistol and the axe head—these were disposed of at Weatherbee's Pond.

With the bones in his possession, Steele knew he had to contact the county coroner in Herkimer right away. He also needed the pistol and directed McDonald and Marshall to go to the pond with Frank Gates to retrieve it while he and Pett made their way to the nearest telephone in Richfield Springs.

When the trio reached Weatherbee's Pond, a boat was secured and Frank directed them to the approximate location of the weapon. Fortunately the pond was not frozen, and with the use of a garden rake, the men trolled the area and soon lifted the pistol from the water. Frank Gates recognized it immediately; the seven-shot .22-caliber pearl-handled revolver was still loaded.

Steele too had good luck. He'd contacted the county coroner, and now he and Pett were on their way back to the Eckler farm.

Twenty-nine-year-old Dr. Irving O. Nellis was the county coroner. An 1882 medical school graduate of the University of Vermont, he had graduated first in his class and had been practicing medicine in Herkimer for only two years when he was elected to the position. Receiving a phone call from the district attorney meant one of three things: either a homicide , an unattended death or unnatural death. In any case, the coroner, by law, had to take charge of the body and if necessary conduct an inquest into the cause of death. Steele told the young doctor to get to Warren as quickly as possible—a murder had been committed and an inquest was needed.

It was early Friday morning, January 16, 1885, when Dr. Nellis arrived in Warren. He guided his buggy down Hogsback Hill Road past the Druse farm and onto Little Lakes Road. When he noticed a small crowd gathered by the cheese house on the Eckler farm, he felt certain he was at the right place.

Nellis was anxious to view the remains of the deceased and was aghast when Steele presented him with a box containing, as the *Richfield Springs Mercury* observed, "an indistinguishable mass of dirt, ashes, and charred bones frozen together." Steele informed Nellis that this box, along with a few buttons and buckles, was all that was recovered. This certainly fit into the unnatural death aspect of his duties, but the real problem facing the coroner was that of positive identification. Could this frozen mass be human remains? Dr. Nellis told Steele that, in this particular instance, it would be most helpful to have the opinions of other medical men. Steele responded that he had already made inquiries and was expecting two physicians from Richfield Springs. His immediate concerns, however, were getting an inquest underway and controlling the small crowd gathered at the Eckler cheese house.

That same day, as Steele and Nellis interviewed potential jurors for the inquest, the press held interviews of their own. Reporters could not contain their zeal for presenting this story to readers. Aside from the misinformation they published (it was not Roxalana's second marriage in which her husband met an untimely end), the portrait they presented to the public was anything but sympathetic or flattering. The *Utica Sunday Tribune* called Roxalana a "sharp, hatchet-faced woman, with sandy hair; a disagreeable neighbor shunned by all." The *Utica Press* described her as a "calculating, malignant, and treacherous woman and from her looks and actions is perfectly capable of doing wickedness."

Nor were the children exempt from the harshness of the *Utica Press*. Mary Druse and Frank Gates were portrayed in a similar light as "miserable, wretched people who from their looks and demeanor would not be classified higher than savages," and the *Utica Observer* described George as "the son of the tigress, who was also compelled to assist in the butchery."

As the press began to relate the sordid details to an eager public, one reporter for the *Utica Sunday Tribune* remained skeptical, noting that "no one would dream, to look at her, that she was capable of such a fiendish act." It was a sentiment that was not shared by the district attorney; Abram Steele believed that she was quite capable, although he harbored doubts that she had acted alone.

Dr. Nellis had spent the better part of the morning interviewing prospective jurors for the inquest. Many of the nine jurors he impaneled knew the Druse family and, according to the local *Richfield Springs Mercury*, were "all intelligent farmers." He even managed to secure the services of a court stenographer. No stranger to the Druse affair, Richfield Springs resident James A. Storer was the Western Union Telegraph operator who had sent Roxalana's "urgent" telegrams to New York and Albany.

Once he had an impaneled jury and a stenographer, Dr. Nellis informed Steele that he was ready to begin the formal inquest into the death of William Druse. This was welcome news to Steele, for as each hour passed, more people were arriving at the cheese house to observe the inquest. Nellis began the proceedings with a formal presentation of the victim's remains to the jury. The nine-man panel stared silently into the box of bones and ash. It was difficult for any of them to believe that this frozen mass was once a farmer they had known. With this somber task completed, the first witness was called to testify.

Perhaps out of courtesy and respect, the first witness was Jeremiah Eckler, the owner of the cheese house. He told the jurors about his suspicions concerning the ink-black smoke he'd seen rising from the Druse chimney, and its accompanying repugnant smell. As for his personal observations regarding the relationship between Roxalana and Bill, the old farmer conceded that they were an argumentative, if not combative, couple.

Eckler's testimony seemed almost trivial in its content compared to what was to come. No one in the crowded cheese house was interested in what happened outside the Druse house—they wanted to know what happened inside. Steele didn't disappoint any of those present when he called Frank Gates to testify.

Without the benefit of council, Frank Gates was sworn in. He gave his name and age, and then promptly shocked the room full of spectators with his opening statement: "Last summer, Mrs. Druse and Mary tried to hire me to shoot William. They said they would give me a good many dollars for doing it."

This revelation sent shock waves through the small room. Everyone, including the district attorney, was stunned. Although Steele had wanted Frank Gates to recall certain events that had transpired before and up to the commission of the crime, he hadn't been expecting this. The statement in and of itself hinted not only of premeditation but also of a wider conspiracy on the part of Roxalana Druse. Was it possible that others were involved in the murder?

Young Gates informed the panel of jurors that he had refused Roxalana and Mary's offer, and that they never mentioned it to him again. He then proceeded to retrace his movements on the day William Druse was murdered. He spoke of the argument, the threats, the shooting, and the beheading.

Steele presented Frank with a revolver and asked him if he could identify the weapon. The nickel plated revolver, together with its pearl handle, left no doubt in Frank's mind that this was the same weapon that Roxalana had thrust into his hands on the day of the murder, and the same gun that was tossed into Weatherbee's Pond. Steele next asked if he had fired the gun at his uncle. Frank answered that he had, but only after his aunt had threatened him. Steele gave the boy a pencil and asked if he could demonstrate to the court his approximate distance from the victim when he fired the pistol.

Frank took the pencil and raised it toward Steele, as if it was the weapon and Abram Steele the victim. At such a close distance, many in the room wondered how he could miss.

After this demonstration, Frank Gates was dismissed, and Steele called on George Druse. Like his cousin before him, little George had no legal representation. He stated his name and told the panel that December 8 was his birthday. He was now ten years old.

Steele asked him if he could recall the events that led up to his father's death. The youngster looked about the room filled with adults and slowly began his story.

"Frank got up first," recalled George. "Pa slept upstairs, Ma slept downstairs with Mary. Pa and Ma never slept in the same bed that I know of."

The details of the murder were especially chilling coming from a ten year old. "I saw a rope around Pa's neck . . . . Frank shot three times, I think. Pa was on the floor with his head near the stove . . . Ma hit Pa on the head with the axe. Pa said 'Oh, don't.' Ma said nothing, but struck him again. Pa said nothing more . . . I did not hear him groan. Then Ma cut his head off with an axe . . . I did not cry any . . . I knew Pa was dead."

George then related how he went with Frank to the woodshed to get more wood shingles, and then to the woods to get the axe that his father left near a woodpile. George said that when he returned to the house, he and Frank were told to go upstairs.

"I heard pounding in the parlor," said George.

At the time, the youngster hadn't understood what this meant, but everyone at the inquest knew—Roxalana and Mary were chopping up the corpse and feeding the parts to the flames.

George continued, "We had no dinner that day . . . Ma told me not to tell . . . she said she would shoot me if I did. I believed she would . . . I am afraid now."

George told the truth. He was scared then, and he was scared now. Steele realized that the child was clearly a witness—not a participant in the horrible crime. To question him any further would serve no purpose.

Steele moved the inquest in another direction when he was told that the two physicians from Richfield Springs had arrived. Immediately, Dr. Albert Getman and Dr. W.P. Borland were sworn in and asked if they could positively identify the bones in the box as human remains. After a cursory examination, twenty-six-year-old Dr. Getman admitted that he could not be absolutely certain that the contents of the box were human.

"I do not find anything that I could positively swear were human bones," he told the jury. "I don't think any microscopic examination would reveal the identity of the bones as to whether they are human or not."

Dr. Borland agreed with his colleague, noting that the bones were small fragments. Their lack of size and shape made identification almost impossible. Steele was disappointed; this wasn't exactly the expert testimony he had hoped to hear.

"Supposing," asked Steele, "a man weighing 150 pounds, age 50, was placed in pieces in a stove, the area being two feet in length, two-and-a-half or three feet in height, and twelve to fourteen inches wide, in a fire built with wood shingles. How much time would it take to cremate the pieces?"

Drs. Borland and Getman could not answer this question. They were not experts on cremation, but common sense dictated that smaller, less dense bones would burn faster.

"Supposing," Steele continued, "that a fifty-year-old man, weighing about 150, was shot in the back two or more times, so that he fell to the floor. Then he was struck in the back two or more times with an axe. After the first blow, he was able to say 'Oh, don't,' and after that was struck on the head with the axe, and soon afterward, his head was severed from his body. What, in your opinion, was the immediate cause of death?"

"Probably the blows from the axe," replied Dr. Getman.

"Probably?" Steele would have preferred the word "definitely."

If the two Richfield Springs physicians could not make a definitive identification of the bones or impart any knowledge about cremation or whether axe blows could kill a man, Steele knew who could. He sent for Dr. A. Walter Suiter in Herkimer. He had worked with Suiter on previous cases, and Steele regarded him as an expert in the emerging field of forensic medicine.

Steele's next immediate concern was the growing number of Warren residents who wanted to witness the inquest. It was clear to Steele and Nellis that they had outgrown the confines of Eckler's cheese house. If the testimonies of Frank Gates and George Druse could fill the room with observers, how many more people would be there when Roxalana was called on? A larger and more comfortable location was needed, and Steele announced that the inquest would resume the next day at Thorpe's Hotel, a few miles south of the cheese house in Little Lakes. Following the change in venue, Steele wasted little time continuing his questioning. He called several witnesses to testify in quick succession.

The sworn statements of James Miller and Chet Crim both helped and hurt Charles Gates. Miller testified that he was with Gates the day of the murder, giving him a much-needed alibi. Store owner Chet Crim testified that he had sold a pearl-handled revolver to Gates. It certainly didn't look good to the room filled with Warren residents that Charles Gates had supplied a weapon to eighteen-year-old Mary Druse.

As the coroner's jury wrestled with the alleged complicity of Charles Gates in the crime, Steele felt it was time to call on his prime suspect. All heads turned as Roxalana Druse entered the room with her attorney, H. DeWight Luce.

With an air of self-confidence, she seated herself, and then looked at Dr. Nellis and boldly declared, "I do not wish to be sworn in or make any statements."

Steele wasn't surprised by this statement. Roxalana was under arrest and had the right to refuse to answer any questions. Still, he didn't want her to slip away that easily.

"Who, besides your family, was present?" he asked.

"I refuse to answer, by advice of counsel, as my answer might incriminate me," she responded.

Steele hesitated for only a moment. Up to this point of the inquest, he'd had little difficulty questioning anyone. Now it was clear to him that Roxalana's Richfield Springs attorney had prepared her. He tried one last time.

"Are you willing, Mrs. Druse, to tell us who, if anyone, was in the house when your husband died?"

"Yes," she responded. "Besides my own family?"

"Who was there, Mrs. Druse?" he inquired.

"Charles and Frank Gates, " she said.

Her accusation stunned everyone at Thorpe's Hotel, with the exception of Abram Steele. He was fully aware that Roxalana had lied. At the same time, her testimony contained some element of truth. Frank Gates had been in the house when the murder was committed, but his father wasn't in the house until after it was committed. The press, unaware of this, was quick to speculate about this latest revelation. "Mrs. Druse puts old Gates in a bad plight," declared the *Utica Daily Observer*, while the *Utica Daily Press* said that although Gates was "a common-looking fellow . . . a good many people are of the opinion that he had a hand in Druse's death."

Steele had no other option but to call Charles Gates to testify. Dr. Nellis reminded him that like his sister-in-law he was under arrest and could refuse to answer any questions.

"I don't know as if I can give any information concerning the cause of Bill Druse's death," replied Gates as he took the stand, "but I will answer any questions."

Charles Gates retraced his movements of that December day, being careful to add as many names as possible in an effort to add credibility to his story. He freely admitted that he had been to the house the day of the murder, but it was in the evening. Gates told the inquest that he went to the house after Elwood had told him about the newspaper-covered windows and the ugly black smoke rising from the chimney. As for the pistol, Gates admitted that he had indeed purchased the weapon from Chester Crim. The three-dollar revolver, which he described accurately to the jurors, was purchased at the insistence of his niece, Mary Druse. She had told him that her father was frequently away from the farm for long periods of time; a pistol was needed to protect their home. Mary also told her uncle that she was planning to take a trip and wanted a gun for her own protection. Gates told the jury he really couldn't argue with this; the Druse farm was set back off the main road, and it was true that Bill was away often.

However, he never provided her with cartridges for the gun, and when she reimbursed him for the cost of the weapon, Gates cautioned Mary not to hurt herself or anyone else with it.

"Up to that time," he said, "Mary said nothing to me of their having any problems at home."

When Charles Gates left the stand, the townspeople of Warren as well as the press were satisfied that he was a victim of a manipulative Roxalana Druse. The *Utica Daily Press* changed its tune in the very next edition. "He is a hard-working, accommodating, good-natured man," they reported. "His neighbors all like him and speak well of him, and when he was arrested as being one of Druse's murders the whole community was astonished. When he was on the witness stand and being questioned regarding his whereabouts on the morning of the murder, his answers were prompt and straightforward and had an air of truth....His statements were corroborated by several witnesses, proving unmistakably and thoroughly that Gates could not have been at the Druse house at the time Mrs. Druse charged him with being there, and that he could not have had any hand in the murder."

The exoneration of Gates by his own testimony as well as the statements made by others strengthened the public's perception of Mrs. Druse as a cold, calculating woman. Her comments, according to the *Utica Daily Press*, were simply "a shameless attempt to bring in Charles Gates as her accomplice."

For the moment, Steele too was satisfied. The forty-three-year-old farmer had answered every question in a straightforward manner, never once attempting to sidestep or evade any question asked. Although it appeared that Charles Gates had nothing to do with the murder, Steele believed that he knew about the horrible events of that December morning.

By now it was apparent to Steele that he would have to unravel a conspiracy of lies woven by Roxalana and added to by her daughter. Steele was aware of the fact that before Attorney H. DeWight Luce had been retained as counsel for the defense, Roxalana and Mary began telling stories about who was in the house on the day of the murder. Those assigned to watch the two women quickly relayed these stories to the district attorney.

Abram Steele also knew it would be pointless to call upon Mary Druse to testify. She too was represented by Luce and would no doubt behave in much the same manner as her mother if called to take the stand. Instead he called upon those whom she claimed were in the house when her father was killed. Convinced that Roxalana had not acted alone, Steele was eager to question the two men that both women claimed took part in the murder.

Will Elwood wasn't surprised to be called to testify. After all, he was the neighbor who convinced Charles Gates that something was terribly wrong at the Druse house. The one-time Druse boarder was stunned, however, to learn that he had been implicated as a participant in the crime.

"I left home at about eleven o'clock in the morning," recalled Elwood. "I had been nowhere that day. I was home taking care of a calf and a pig and talking to my wife . . . I live a mile and a half from the Druses."

Elwood nervously described his every move on the day of the murder and tried desperately to remember details of his activities before and after the crime. It probably didn't help his credibility as a witness when he admitted that Frank Gates had showed him Mary's revolver, or that he was aware that Roxalana and Bill had, "troubles."

"Do you know that Mrs. Druse claims you were there when William was killed?" asked the district attorney..

A simple "no" would not do for an answer. Elwood told Steele that not long after the murder, his own father had heard a rumor that Elwood himself had fired the first shot at Bill Druse.

"Do you know that she claims you cut Druse's head off?" Steele asked.

"I do not," replied Elwood.

"Also that you cut his arms and legs off and put them in the stove?" Steele persisted.

"I do not," Elwood repeated.

Was Elwood the accomplice that Steele was searching for, or was he—like Charles Gates—an innocent victim of Roxalana's vile accusations? Steele wasn't sure. Elwood wasn't as convincing as Charles Gates had been. His testimony lacked credibility, and until his alibi could be corroborated, Steele had no other recourse than to arrest the twenty-three-year-old farmhand.

Throughout the inquest proceedings, the press as well as the townspeople of Warren and Little Lakes had longed for a surprise witness. When Rudolph Van Evera walked into Thorpe's Hotel, many believed he was that witness. Rumors had raced through Warren that Van Evera was romantically linked to Mary or to her mother. His image as a drifter who liked his whiskey and his storytelling was made all the more interesting when his checkered past was revealed.

After giving a detailed account of every farm he had worked on during the previous three years, Van Evera candidly admitted that he had been sentenced to Randall's Island in New York City on a charge of vagrancy. He then proceeded to tell the audience at the hotel that the latest charge levied against him was false: "I heard they had a warrant out for me for the attempted rape of my sister. I am not guilty of this offense."

This statement prompted a *Utica Daily Press* reporter to quip, "While he is not an idiot, he is certainly below the average intellect. He has very little education or intelligence."

Like Will Elwood, Van Evera wasted no time in telling the inquest that he had nothing to do with the murder of William Druse. "Neither Mrs. Druse nor Mary ever tried to get me nor hire me to kill Bill," he said.

In fact, Van Evera claimed, on the day of the murder he had been home with his mother.

Steele had plenty of time to investigate Van Evera's alibi. For the time being, he was more interested in the drifter's relationship to Roxalana and Mary.

"I have stayed at the Druses when Bill was not at home," admitted Van Evera. "I was never intimate with Mrs. Druse or Mary. I was not engaged to Mary."

Van Evera said that this rumor probably began when he was joking with Elwood. "We were talking and fooling at Elwood's," he said. "I remarked that when they sent Bill up Salt Creek, Mary and I would run the farm . . . I told him [Elwood] I was going to marry a woman in Warren and run a farm there. I referred to Mary Druse. I was only fooling."

This testimony caught everyone's attention, and Van Evera

should have quit while he was ahead. Instead, he related that once he had carried Mary from the attic.

"I don't know what they were doing up there," he said. "They [Roxalana and Mary] were carrying on, and Mary asked me to carry her downstairs." Although this sounded innocent enough, he further complicated matters when he freely admitted that he had also carried Mrs. Druse downstairs.

"I never did it after that," he said, carefully adding that Bill Druse was not at home when any of this took place. This was terrific parlor gossip, but hardly the evidence Steele was looking for, and this colorful suspect was soon dismissed.

Despite the failure of Van Evera's testimony, Steele's diligence in pursuing any lead in the Druse case could not be denied by anyone. After sifting through the "I knew Druse . . ." or "The last time I saw Bill . . ." or the much repeated "I heard Roxy say . . ." it looked like the district attorney was running out of credible witnesses. The real question seemed to be whether the inquest should continue or conclude. The public was divided on the issue. Was Steele preoccupied with "innumerable, unnecessary questions . . . consuming a great deal of time," as the *Utica Daily Press* reported? Had the Druse case been "needlessly protracted" by the district attorney? Still, the paper praised his tenacity: "Mr. Steele has worked night and day and has left nothing undone that a good lawyer and a faithful, conscientious, hard-working officer could do . . . . He is entitled to the highest praise for his untiring efforts in the case."

January 28 was the last day of the inquest and attendance at Thorpe's Hotel was at its lowest. A recent snowstorm followed by below-zero temperatures prompted many of the hardiest inquest followers to stay home. Those able to travel to Little Lakes in their horse-drawn sleighs arrived at the hotel only to learn that Abram Steele did not plan to introduce any new witnesses. He recalled just two, and then asked the jury to render its verdict.

It came as no surprise to anyone that the jury not only reached a verdict quickly but also determined that Roxalana Druse did "feloniously kill and murder William Druse." Furthermore, it asserted that Mary, George, and Frank Gates were "feloniously" present and that Mary "did comfort and abet the said Roxalana Druse."

Some neighbors were overjoyed by the verdict. "Bill was the only decent one among them, and it does seem too bad that he was fated to undergo the life he led, and finally to come to his death at their hands," remarked one Warren resident to a *Utica Press* reporter. "And the more I think over the whole business, the more certain I am of the fact that they ought to have been lynched the day Frank Gates told his dreadful story."

Steele, however, was only partially satisfied with the verdict. Later that evening he too was interviewed by the *Utica Press* when a reporter caught up with him at the Utica train station. The district attorney had plenty to say about the verdict. He was disappointed that Mary Druse was not charged as a principal participant. He felt that the girl had materially assisted in the murder when she placed the rope around her father's neck and pulled him to the floor. As far as Charles Gates was concerned, Steele said he still wasn't convinced that he was not in some way involved.

"But," said Steele, speaking of the jurors, "if their consciences are clear, that is all that can be asked of them. It is no matter of mine. I have exhausted every line of evidence that seemed to throw any light on the case, and have done everything that I could to place the responsibility of the crime where it belonged. I have an idea that Charles Gates knows where the portions of Druse's body not recovered are, and he may yet be called in regard to it. I don't know why it is, but the people out there seem to think it impossible that Gates had anything to do with it. Many a man has been hanged on evidence weaker than that against him."

As Steele boarded the train to Herkimer, he had plenty of time to think about the past as well as the future. This was the second time in his career that he had been called to the township of Warren to investigate a murder. Many had forgotten that eleven years earlier in 1874, he had defended Alfred Travers on a charge of first-degree murder. In an old-fashioned lovers' triangle, Travers's affair with a married woman had been discovered by her husband. In the melee that followed, Travers beat the cheated husband with a large kettle and then fatally stabbed him. After two trials, Steele was able to get the sentence of death by hanging commuted to life in prison.

Steele also knew that although the Druse case was indeed bizarre, axe murders were nothing new in Herkimer County. In 1875, Orlo Davis from the town of Ohio was beheaded by Lodica Fredenburg with the assistance of her husband, Albert. The Orlo Davis murder was similar to the Druse murder. "Poor old Davis," lamented the *Utica Morning Herald*, "was hacked to pieces with an axe." As in the Druse case, an attempt was made to dispose of the remains, and also like the Druse case, many family members were implicated in the crime. After the trial was over, a key witness retracted his statement and the defense demanded a new trial. Governor Samuel Tilden of New York reviewed the case, denied a new trial, and commuted the death sentences to life in prison.

While the inquest was in session, Steele was aware that the public was speculating about the outcome of a murder trial. No one had ever been executed for a capital crime in Herkimer County.

"Is it time to begin?" asked the *Little Falls Journal and Courier* in an editorial as the inquest got underway. "The tragedy in Warren brings forward the question as never before. The county of Herkimer has never hung a murderer. . . . It seems to us that the time has come when the murderer of William Druse, woman though she be, if she shall, after full trial, be proved guilty, shall suffer the extreme penalty."

Steele had worked hard to save Alfred Travers from the hangman. Would he now work just as hard to send a woman to the gallows?

CHAPTER 3

"We have never been so comfortable...."

Travel arrangements for the Druses and Frank Gates were far different from those of Coroner Nellis and District Attorney Steele. Not wishing to traverse the snow-covered roads of southern Herkimer County, the two elected officials took the train from Richfield Springs to Utica. It wasn't the quickest or most direct route back to Herkimer, but it was certainly more comfortable. The accused were transported in an open sleigh drawn by a team of horses.

At the train station in Utica, reporters were eager to discuss the final moments of the inquest with Steele. This wasn't the case at Little Lakes. The standing-room-only atmosphere that had been regular fare at Thorpe's Hotel was gone. A reporter for the *Utica Daily Press* who was still at Little Lakes remarked, "They had only a few friends to bid them good-bye." He quickly added, "For cold-hearted, cold-blooded people, commend your friends to the Druse family."

It was half-past three in the afternoon when Sheriff Valentine Brown led Roxalana, her two children, and Frank Gates to the sleigh. The ride to Herkimer was long, cold, and uneventful. Sheriff Brown later recalled that Roxalana and Mary spoke very little, as if oblivious about what lay before them. The two boys were more talkative; every so often they commented about the places they passed.

By the time Sheriff Brown led the sleigh into Herkimer, it was 7 p.m. He could see that neither the cold nor the late hour had deterred the crowd of curious onlookers wanting a glimpse of the notorious Druse gang. Hoping to avoid a confrontation with the crowd, as well as any reporters among them, Brown quickly escorted his charges into the jail. This was not the time or place to grant an impromptu interview to the press or anyone else. It was late, and everyone was tired and hungry.

Inside the jail, the quartet was led to the sheriff's office and their names dutifully recorded in the daily logbook. It was a simple procedure and a necessary one, the sheriff being required to keep a record of each prisoner in his care.

Sheriff Brown instructed his deputies to house the new prisoners on the third floor—the attic—a space set aside for women, children, and other individuals deemed "less dangerous." This part of the jail was relatively new and in no way resembled the stark limestone cells on the floors below. The attic cells were constructed using lath and plaster and were a bit larger. In addition to a set of bunk beds, there was ample room for a table and chair. Roxalana and Mary were led to one cell and Frank shared a cell with George.

Concerning her new living arrangements, Roxalana was reported to have said that whatever the outcome—prison for life or death by hanging—she would never have to live with Bill Druse again. When the cell door slammed behind her, she quipped, "Well, I hope I may be able to procure tonight what I have not had before in two years . . . a good night's rest." Her first statement since the inquest quickly found its way into the *Herkimer Democrat*.

Remarks such as this made her attorney cringe—H. DeWight Luce had warned Roxalana repeatedly about making any statements. Some of her comments at the inquest had been disastrous. Luce was preparing for a high-profile murder case; the last thing he needed was for his client to incriminate herself further by having statements like this one find their way into the press.

A good night's rest is exactly what the weary prisoners from Hogsback Hill Road got. They spent two nights in jail before they were formally arraigned. On January 30, 1885, Roxalana and Mary were escorted from their cells by deputies and brought to the front entrance of the jail. Across the way stood the courthouse, an imposing brick structure with a large white bell tower. The deputies whisked their charges across the street to the courthouse past a relatively small crowd of spectators. Brought before Justice T. C. Murray, the two women, represented by their attorney, entered a solemn plea of not guilty. Given the severity of the crime, the courts established the bail at $2,000 for each woman, a sum their attorney did not protest. At the time of the arraignment, Luce didn't know how he would be paid for his services. For the time being, money was the least of his concerns.

With his clients secured in the county jail, Luce set out to do the impossible: build a credible defense for a woman already convicted in the hearts and minds of everyone who knew her. Aware that Frank Gates and George Druse were being tapped as key prosecution witnesses, Luce set out to prove that Roxalana had acted in self-defense. He did not have his client enter a plea of temporary insanity, something which at the time puzzled many people. He didn't register an insanity plea because he couldn't.

The Penal Code for the State of New York had been recently amended to address the issues of sanity and temporary insanity. Three years earlier, Section 20 of the code had been revised, reflecting the public's concern for the fate of the mentally ill charged with a capital crime: "An act done by a person who is an idiot, imbecile, lunatic, or insane is not a crime while he is in a state of idiocy, imbecility, lunacy, or insanity. . . ." As for temporary insanity, the revised code was clear: "A person is not excused from criminal liability as an idiot, imbecile, lunatic, or insane person, except upon proof that, at the time of committing the alleged act, he was laboring under such a defect of reason. . . ."

Almost from the moment the Richfield Springs attorney had been made aware of the vicious attack upon William Druse, the public and the press began to question Roxalana Druse's sanity. Did she commit this heinous crime while "laboring under such a defect of reason?"

The person who could best answer this question was near at hand. One of the most respected, although controversial, leaders in the field of criminal insanity was Dr. John Perdue Gray. A graduate of Dickinson College and the University of Pennsylvania, Gray had been the superintendent of the State Asylum in Utica since 1850.

The Druse case was not the first time Dr. Gray had been asked by the courts to determine the sanity of a murder suspect. In 1865 he interviewed Lewis Paine, one of the conspirators on trial in the Lincoln assassination. Years later he made a similar court appearance when called upon to judge the sanity of Charles Guiteau, the assassin of President James Garfield. Often criticized as pompous and overbearing, the portly Dr. Gray argued that Guiteau was sane when he shot the President. Ironically, a short time later, Gray himself became the victim of an assassination attempt. On March 16, 1882, Henry Remshaw, one of his patients, shot him in the face. Dr. Gray still suffered from the effects of this wound when he was called on to judge the sanity of Roxalana Druse.

Assisting Dr. Gray in the interview was Dr. A. Walter Suiter. No stranger to the court system, Dr. Suiter maintained a relatively low profile during the coroner's inquest. He was not called on to testify and spent most of his time sifting through the box of bones and poking around the Druse farmhouse. The two doctors conducted a brief interview with Roxalana. Not one local paper knew of their presence at the jail.

The Herkimer County Jail in the 1880s. Roxalana, Mary and George Druse, along with Frank Gates, were brought here in January 1885. Roxalana remained here for two years.

Drs. Gray and Suiter found Roxalana not only cooperative but also amiable. She spoke openly about her past, her marriage to Bill Druse, the birth of her children, and the hardships of operating a small farm with a husband who had a penchant for wandering. She expressed love and admiration for her children, but she carefully avoided mentioning any details of the crime. "I don't want to make any statement," she said, but candidly admitted that she was "under the influence of a certain man about the house, who obliged her to drink from a bottle. . . ." Roxalana declined to name this man but admitted that she was indeed afraid of him.

Throughout the interview, she never lost her temper, made any threatening remarks, or wallowed in self-pity. Her answers appeared to be sincere and honest. "Have never had much trouble . . . ," said Roxalana. "I happened to get with good people who took considerable interest in me. . . [I] always fell in good hands . . . always went in good society until I got to Warren. They were not refined, intelligent, or anything else. . . ." It was unfortunate that this disparaging remark eventually made its way into the *Utica Press*, for it widened the rift between Roxalana and the community. At the conclusion of the interview, Dr. Gray believed that she was sane before, during, and after the murder of her husband.

With his client declared legally competent to stand trial, M. DeWight Luce began to wonder if it was possible to conduct a fair trial in Herkimer County. The statements made by the "yellow press" during the coroner's inquest greatly concerned the Richfield Springs attorney. Roxalana was libeled a "modern-day Lucretia Borgia who," claimed the *Utica Tribune*, "made off with husband number one in a similar manner." The statement was blatantly false but never retracted, and a seed was planted in the public mind that Luce's client was a rural "black widow" murderess.

It wasn't just the *Tribune* that attacked Roxalana's character; all of the Utica papers were quick to condemn Roxalana and her "gang of killers." Given the testimony and evidence presented at the inquest, the *Utica Daily Press* went so far as to predict a fairly swift trial: "There is not much doubt that if Mrs. Druse and her daughter could be tried before any twelve men who have listened to the proof so far elicited, they would be convicted of the crimes they are charged with without a moment's hesitation." Readers were told that this was the sentiment shared by neighbors from the community in which the tragedy occurred. "The more I think of the whole business," remarked an anonymous Warren resident, "the more certain I am of the fact that they ought to have been lynched..."

Throughout the inquest, the *Utica Daily Press* never ceased its efforts to portray all those involved in the Hogsback Hill Road murder as cold-blooded killers: "The Druse women and Frank Gates display a recklessness of character that conclusively shows that they consider the killing of Bill as a matter of small importance and rather beneath their dignity as professional murderers....When one takes a good look at these monsters disguised as women and sees their nonchalant heartless behavior, he only wonders that they did not eat the body instead of burning it."

The power of the press and its ability to sway public opinion greatly concerned Luce in the closing days of the inquest. If coverage of this nature continued, he wondered if it would be at all possible to secure a fair trial for his clients in this part of the state. The

Herkimer Democrat reported that Luce was considering asking the court to move the trial out of Herkimer County. As February turned to March, however, and winter turned to spring, the Druse murder faded from the pages of the Utica newspapers. Luce never filed a motion for a change in venue; if he had, it would have been, in all likelihood, denied.

Of all the newspapers that covered the inquest, those closest to the murder scene were the least hostile. The *Richfield Springs Mercury* dutifully reported the activities of the inquest in transcript-style fashion. Initially, the *Herkimer Democrat* expressed shock and horror about the affair. "Murder in its simplest form is bad enough," it declared. "But when we hear [of] a woman killing her husband, chopping his head off, burning the body, and throwing the intestines to the hogs, we shudder at the thought."

A short while later the *Herkimer Democrat* too ceased all mention of the murder. The village newspaper was not going to be held responsible for having the most sensational trial in over a decade moved out of the county. In fact, the *Democrat* informed its readers that coverage of the upcoming trial would be far different from what they may have expected: "There has been a good deal said and published, well calculated to cause deep feeling. The press should always give the facts and allow the courts to administer the law. Purely sensational articles on either side do no good; they tend to mislead instead of giving light. The more of truth that appears in the public press - if read and considered by the intelligent reader—the better qualified is a juror for the discharge of his important duties after reading truthful articles relating to the subject. The evidence which is to be given to the jury under the oaths of the various witnesses, and the law as laid down by the Court, must settle the question as to the quilt or innocence of the accused."

With the Grand Jury scheduled to meet in April, and knowing that indictments for murder would be handed down, Luce needed time to build his case—what's more, now he needed money. He informed the court that he was not a court-appointed attorney for Roxalana; he had been retained by her. Since his client was penniless, who would pay for his services? There was only one way to obtain money, and that was through the sale of the Druse farm. After all, who would look after the farm while its former occupants were in jail? How would the taxes be paid? Who would look after the livestock, and most importantly, who would act as guardians for the children?

It took some time, but all of these issues were eventually addressed. Concerning the farmhouse, a few more months of neglect would hardly be noticed; it had withstood the elements this long. The farm animals were a different story. No self-respecting farmer would neglect the care and feeding of his livestock. Immediately after Roxalana's arrest, Jeremiah Eckler had taken it upon himself to care for the twenty or so animals left on the Druse farm. Although he billed the county for his services, he said that if the claim was denied, he was prepared to sell them.

Selling the property was the only logical way to raise money and satisfy creditors. By midsummer, Sheriff Valentine Brown had completed a detailed inventory of items on the Druse farm in preparation for a sheriff's sale. The list of farm equipment occupied two columns on two pages and described the farm in a way that seemed to underscore the poverty the Druses had experienced. Among the property listed were an old sleigh, an old carriage, an old mare, and so forth.

At first Roxalana scoffed at the idea of an estate sale. "We were not as poor as some people think," she said. However, sitting in her cell at the county jail, she quickly accepted the reality of her situation. Given her present circumstances, she was in no position to hire anyone to look after the farm while she awaited trial. Besides, she would have an equally difficult time trying to convince anyone that she wished to ever return to Hogsback Hill Road. Her comments about the hard life she endured there were common knowledge.

Roxalana didn't object to the sale of the farm, but she made it abundantly clear that there were certain items in the house that she did not want to see fall victim to the auctioneer's gavel. From her cell, she composed a list of items she claimed were her personal possessions and therefore should be exempt from the sale. It was as if she was trying to tell the residents of Warren that with these few material possessions, she could begin life anew. Her list included a table, a stand, a half dozen chairs, a bureau, a spinning wheel, and a sewing machine. The contents from the kitchen included an odd assortment of dishes: a dozen plates, forks and knives, with seven cups, four saucers, and a sugar bowl. The schoolbooks belonged to the children. There was no mention of clothing of any kind; however, she did want the Bible. She even included the stoves, unaware that one had been removed as evidence in her trial. She claimed that some of the livestock that Jeremiah Eckler was caring for were also hers and should not be sold, but she never offered any explanation as to how she would care for "a dark red cow, a sow, and a pig"

The Herkimer County Court House as it appeared at the time of the trial.

while incarcerated.

On June 6, 1885, a small crowd assembled at Thorpe's Hotel in Little Lakes for the auction. Charles Pett stepped forward and offered $3,700 for the sixty acres of Druse land that bordered his farm; Jeremiah Eckler offered $1,500 for the remaining twenty-seven acres, which included the house and barn. The only household item to survive the sale was a small box organ that belonged to Mary Druse. It seemed out of place at the rustic farmhouse and someone saw fit to bring it to her at the jail.

Many residents of Warren breathed a sigh of relief at the conclusion of the sheriff's sale. Not only did it ensure that, regardless of the outcome of the trial, Roxalana could never return to Hogsback Hill Road, it also generated money that could be used to satisfy the Druse's many debts.

Prior to the sale, the public had been told that if they had any liens against the estate of William Druse, now was the time to step forward. No fewer than twenty-seven people claimed they were owed money. Some merchants had ledgers to back up their claims; other liens were simply dismissed—it was too difficult to prove a transaction based on word of mouth and a handshake. Most of the claims were in the one-to-five-dollar range, and several individuals did not receive the exact amount they claimed was due them. The big winner was the law firm investigating all these claims. The Steele and Prescott law firm, the very same Abram Steele who was the district attorney, awarded themselves $125.00 for their services. Charley Pett received $25.00 for distributing the funds, while Charles Bell was awarded $25.00 for acting as "special guardian" for the children. What exactly a "special guardian" would be responsible for while both children were in jail remains a mystery.

In the end, Charles Bell's services were short-lived; a permanent guardian was needed for the Druse children, and it was not to be Bell or Charles Gates. Instead, the courts awarded guardianship to Charles Pett; the nearest neighbor to the Druse family seemed to be a logical choice. Pett was a family friend who had watched Mary and George grow up. They attended the same one-room school as his own children. Abram Steele could trust Charlie Pett to keep an accurate record of the money set aside for the children. That same trust could not be extended to Charles Gates. Although Steele was forced to release Charles Gates from custody after the inquest, he wasn't completely satisfied with the man's alibi. Gates may not have taken part in the murder, but Steele wasn't ready to dismiss him as someone who may have aided Roxalana in the cover-up. Besides, it would have been difficult to award custody to Charles Gates when his own son was in jail charged as an accessory to the crime.

H. DeWight Luce was by no means idle while the sheriff's sale of the Druse property was being planned. When the Herkimer Grand Jury met on April 16, Luce entered the courtroom with his assistant, Amos H. Prescott. The sixty-two-year-old Prescott brought to the defense team a wealth of knowledge and experience. A former New York assemblyman who had once been a Brigadier General in the National Guard, Prescott was one of the county's most prominent attorneys and had served for sixteen years as a county judge.

Roxalana and Mary's first public appearance was a public relations disaster. While anxious to appear dignified and somewhat refined before the large crowd in attendance, they were perhaps unaccustomed to wearing make-up. As one reporter from the *Herkimer Citizen* noted, "The Druses had their 'war paint' on as usual and their cheeks were a rich mahogany hue." Overly made-up women during those years were either actresses or prostitutes, and this comment was a sharp rebuke from the press—and one that was never repeated.

Upon hearing the evidence presented to them by the district attorney, the Grand Jury didn't take long to issue murder indictments against Roxalana and her daughter. Neither boy was charged with aiding or abetting, and eventually the charges against both of them were dismissed. Steele was already making plans to have them appear as principal witnesses for the people.

Luce and his assistant begged the court to consider a trial date in late September; they needed time to prepare adequate defenses for both women. As separate indictments had been handed down, it was decided that Roxalana would be tried first, then Mary. Luce then asked that he be allowed to examine the physical evidence of the murder that was now in the possession of the district attorney's office.

Steele objected to a motion to have the evidence taken from his office; he had told the Grand Jury that it was being examined by experts. Luce had the right, according to Steele, to cross-examine these experts properly when the case came to trial. As to the trial date being set for September, the court sympathized with Luce's plight but could do little to accommodate him. The court calendar was already full, and it looked as if it would get more crowded in the coming weeks.

Steele had already concluded his murder case against one Frank Mondon and was preparing to bring yet another murder case to trial. Frank Mondon, or "The Italian" as the press dubbed him, had been accused of murdering his father-in-law, John Wishart, in the town of Schuyler. Although two of Wishart's daughters had wed Italian immigrants, John Wishart vehemently opposed his youngest daughter's marriage to Frank Mondon. The ill will between Mondon and Wishart escalated from petty quarreling to fierce arguments and verbal threats. On April 17, 1884, Mondon savagely beat the seventy-year-old Wishart to death with a large club, and then tried his best to hide the body in a ditch near the railroad tracks east of Frankfort.

For Abram Steele, the Mondon case was unique. His investigation revealed that members of Wishart's immediate family tried to cover up the crime. Steele discovered that Wishart was a miserable old man, and that his widow, Nancy, aided and abetted Mondon in the bludgeoning death of her husband. Despite the fact that most of the witnesses at the trial couldn't speak English (interpreters were present), Steele was able to secure a murder conviction and Mondon was sentenced to hang.

At the conclusion of the Mondon trial, the county was shocked to learn that in addition to the Druse murder, another capital crime had been committed in the small village of Middleville. The same Grand Jury that heard evidence against Roxalana Druse now listened as Steele presented his case against the "Dutch Doctor."

Moritz Richter, the "Dutch Doctor," was a native of Saxony, Germany, who had resided in Middleville since about 1860. Dr. Richter had established a medical practice in the small community and was looked upon by villagers as a confirmed bachelor. It came as a surprise to more than a few residents when, in 1876, the fifty-one-year-old physician married thirty-six-year-old Eliza Ward. As it turned out, the union was brief. After less than a decade of marriage, Dr. Richter was convinced that his wife was on the verge of insanity. Her sometimes erratic behavior and an enlarged pupil in one eye suggested to him that she was in the early stages of madness.

Dismissing the marriage vow "in sickness and in health," the good doctor promptly left his wife on her father's doorstep. A year went by, and with no legal separation or divorce forthcoming, Eliza was a woman without any means. Not wishing to be a financial burden on her father, she decided to sell some of her personal belongings. This was a problem since all of her possessions were at her former home, and her husband was uncooperative. Nonetheless, Eliza was able to describe in detail all of her belongings, and she presented a bill of sale for $200.00 to S. Clark Smith, a professor at nearby Fairfield College.

On February 28, 1885, Smith, in the company of his brother-in-law, Malvin Getman, arrived at Dr. Richter's home. After examining the bill of sale, Richter led the men upstairs and pointed to a large trunk. A quick inspection of its contents revealed shoes, clothing, and a mink stole, as well as jewelry that belonged to Eliza Richter. When Smith and Getman carried the trunk to their sleigh and departed, Richter thought he had seen the last of them.

A short while later, however, both men reappeared and began badgering Richter about two mortgages Eliza Richter held on the property. An irate Richter told them to leave his house immediately; this was a matter for attorneys and was not in their bill of sale. The two left, but not for long. Returning a third time, Smith enlisted the aid of Fairfield Constable John Tabor and his brother Charles. Using the pretext that Richter had denied them items listed in the bill of sale, Smith convinced the Tabors to accompany him to the doctor's home.

When the trio arrived, Dr. Richter demanded to know why they were there. Constable Tabor produced the bill of sale and explained that the chamber set was missing. Richter glanced at the piece of paper and told them that the set was upstairs. Tabor proceeded up the stairs with Smith and the doctor following close behind.

Smith immediately recognized the chamber set, and just as quickly, Richter produced a .38 caliber revolver and shot him in the back.

"My God," cried Smith, "I'm shot!"

Smith reeled around to face his assassin only to be shot a second time in the chest. Mortally wounded, he managed to descend the flight of stairs, stagger past Charles Tabor, and make his way out the front door before collapsing twenty-five feet away in a snowbank.

Meanwhile, Richter leveled the revolver at Constable Tabor and attempted to shoot him. Tabor struggled to disarm him as he called out to his brother for assistance. By the time Charles made his way to the upstairs bedroom, his brother had wrestled Richter to the bed but still hadn't been able to release the doctor's grip on the pistol. Charles Tabor succeeded in wresting the pistol from him and Richter was immediately handcuffed.

With the Wishart murder and the gruesome details of the Druse case still fresh in everyone's mind, the Richter case sent shock waves not only through quiet little Middleville but also throughout the county. The day after the Grand Jury handed down indictments against Roxalana Druse and Dr. Moritz Richter, the *Ilion Citizen* expressed disparagement about these recent developments in a scathing editorial: "Under the light of existing facts it would not seem to be far out of the way to rechristen Herkimer County the "Heathen" County. Proof is not lacking to substantiate this statement.... Murder after murder, rape and robbery and all the way down even to cockfighting, go to give us a prominence among the headlines of modern sensational journalism as certainly anything but enviable."

It wasn't only newspapers trying to sensationalize this recent string of homicides. Hoping to cash in on the darker side of Herkimer County history, William Tippetts announced that he was writing a book that would chronicle all the murders of Herkimer County—from colonial times to the present. A self-described "traveling journalist" from Rochester, New York, Tippetts released his book in April 1885. Under the not-so-imaginative title *Herkimer County Murders,* the book was hailed in the local press as "an invaluable source of information for lawyers in this section of the state." At twenty-five cents a copy, the little book was a real bargain.

Most of the early murders described by Tippetts warranted only a few paragraphs, although he made every effort to mention all the participants of the previous murder trials. Tippetts reserved most of his ink and energy for the chapter entitled "The Druse Butchery: The Most Horrible Murder on Record—William Druse of Warren, Killed, Butchered, and the Body Burned in Stoves. The Wife, Daughter, Son, and Nephew Arrested for the Crime." Almost all of the information gleaned from the eleven-page chapter came word for word from the coroner's inquest testimony that appeared in the *Richfield Springs Mercury.*

Had Tippets been a little more patient, he could have added yet another chapter to his little book. In May 1885, a riot broke out in the railroad yard in the village of Frankfort. German workers had gone on strike in the hopes of raising their wages from $1.10 to $1.35 a day. Italian laborers, however, were satisfied with their wages and refused to cooperate with the striking Germans. The Germans attempted to coerce the Italians into joining their strike by confiscating their tools. Fisticuffs quickly followed verbal threats as the Italians attempted to reclaim their tools and return to work. In the ensuing riot, a shot echoed across the railroad yard and one of the Germans, Edward Heusoner, lay dead as the Italians fled the scene.

This bloody confrontation between the two immigrant groups sharply divided the community of Frankfort. "Some think the Italians were justified in their attack," claimed one editorial in the *Her-*

kimer Democrat, "while others are perfectly willing to rid the county of them. The Germans engaged in the riot have hereafter been known as peaceable citizens of good character."

In the investigation that followed the riot, seven Italians were arrested and escorted to the Herkimer County Jail. The unlucky seven joined Dr. Richter, Frank Mondon, Roxalana Druse, and her daughter, bringing the jail population to twenty-two. "We are like most summer resorts," quipped Sheriff Valentine Brown of these recent additions. "We always have rooms to let." Twenty-two prisoners was a relatively low number, compared to the seventy prisoners the jail was capable of holding.

Valentine Brown, Herkimer County's sheriff at the time, was a forty-four-year-old native of German Flatts, described by those who knew him as "a thorough Democrat." A cattleman by trade, Brown stunned the electorate by defeating a heavily favored Republican by a mere 499 votes in his first bid for public office. Brown seemed well suited for the job; he had an engaging personality, made friends easily, and was respected. For the remainder of his life he would be called "sheriff," as if the title itself was an honorarium.

Of the sheriff's many duties, the foremost was the operation of the county jail. The interior of the limestone structure had changed little since its completion in 1849. Fashioned after the Auburn prison, the cells lined the outside perimeter of the jail, leaving a large open center that provided for air circulation. Thick walls made for a secure environment; comfort was not an issue. Only recently had beds with straw-filled mattresses, some on planked sawhorses, replaced loose straw strewn about the floor. For many, life inside the six-by-nine foot cells constituted only a temporary inconvenience; anyone convicted of a serious crime was eventually transferred to the state prison. For less dangerous individuals, quarters were on the third floor or attic—the only way to isolate them from the rest of the population. It didn't matter what cell a prisoner was in; he or she could be moved to a different part of the jail at any time. A stickler for cleanliness, Sheriff Brown periodically had prisoners moved out so their cells could be whitewashed. Even the roughest character was entitled to a clean cell.

The sheriff's office, with its ceramic-tiled fireplaces and spacious rooms, was in sharp contrast to the Spartan atmosphere of the cell area. With tall ceilings, large windows, and hardwood floors throughout, this section of the building resembled a small mansion.

These comfortable surroundings were reserved for the jailer and his family, and one of Brown's first appointments as sheriff was to appoint his son Harry the new jailer. The only disadvantage to this living situation at the county's expense was the lack of privacy. It was a private residence for the Jailer Harry Brown, and at the same time, it was a public building. The jailer lived on the second floor and the sheriff maintained his office on the first floor. The kitchen was located in basement, as well as offices for the under-sheriff and deputies.

The jail was seldom quiet and busier than most people could imagine. The yearly operation of the facility required planning and attention to the most minute detail. Wary of expenses and a penny-pinching Board of Supervisors who questioned the least bit of extravagance, Brown endeavored to keep accurate records at all times. As the jail population increased, so did the food budget, and food and supplies were brought to the jail on an almost daily basis. In those days, neither refrigeration nor large storage facilities were available for keeping large quantities of food.

If Sheriff Brown was not in his office, he was either in the courthouse, out making an arrest, or traveling long distances to deliver a summons. In the Druse case alone, Brown personally delivered 54 subpoenas and logged close to 1,400 miles, a figure that didn't include a 476-mile round trip to New York City to subpoena Roxalana's brother, Amon Teft, to appear before the Grand Jury.

In addition to the daily operation of the jail, Sheriff Brown was responsible for the upkeep and maintenance of the county courthouse. While one contingent of deputies guarded the prisoners, another was sent to the courthouse. Armed with hammers and nails, paintbrushes, and ladders, they set about making improvements to the Supreme Court chambers. In addition to wallpapering and painting, the back row of bench seats was raised. Large crowds were expected to attend the murder trials scheduled for the fall of 1885.

Sheriff Brown was, in effect, a law enforcement official, county administrator, maintenance supervisor for the courthouse, accountant, and to some extent a public relations man. Hardly a day passed when he wasn't meeting with judges, lawyers, jail visitors, or the press. Aware that he had several high-profile men and women in his jail awaiting trial, Brown tried his best to placate the members of the fifth estate. As the jail population swelled that summer, the press found the inhabitants made perfect copy.

On one occasion a visiting reporter for the *Amsterdam Daily Sentinel* canvassed the entire jail population for readers. Dr. Moritz Richter, awaiting trial on a charge of first-degree murder in the death of S. Clark Smith, did not have the "look" of a murderer. "He wore eyeglasses," reported the *Sentinel*, "and looked like a minister on a poor charge." Frank Mondon, "the Italian," was "a young, thickset fellow, and of ugly disposition." As Mondon filled the air with the obnoxious odors emanating from his pipe, accused Frankfort rioters Alphonzo Dido and his cellmate serenaded the other prisoners. Dido teased Italian melodies from his accordion, while his one-legged cellmate accompanied him on a harmonica, completing what Sheriff Brown called his jail house orchestra. "Between the two," reported the *Sentinel*, "they produced a noise which the pen of man cannot describe."

The jail was also home to forgers, drunks, and two horse thieves—James N. Wheeler and Frank Elliot. Noted Little Falls pugilist Warren Shipman occupied another cell. Arrested for burglary, the paper described him as "a brutish-looking fellow with the top of his head running down to his eyebrows." Shipman loathed Mondon and told the sheriff that if the state failed to hang the man, he would do it for nothing. Another murderer, John Riordan, was describes as "a fat, chubby man with a heavy bristling moustache and a red flannel shirt." He was charged with the shooting death of Dan Healey.

When a reporter from the *Utica Globe* arrived at the jail on washday, he had no problem securing an interview with Roxalana Druse. She rolled down her shirtsleeves, unruffled her apron, and seated herself while Mary pulled the last of the laundry through the wringer. "Mary is a fine-looking girl," reported the *Globe.* "She is rather above the medium height, while her mother is shorter. Her hair is dark, her eyes have a mild and pleasant glance, her complexion is fair. . . . She wears glasses for nearsightedness. She is better looking and more modest appearing than one-third of the girls one would meet in a day's travel." Mary, added the reporter, seemed quite cheerful and did not appear to be at all depressed.

Her mother told the reporter that they both stayed quite busy sewing, washing, ironing, and reading. "As I said before," she remarked, "we are well cared for here. We couldn't have been treated better by our own people. We have never been so comfortable before in our lives as we have been here. We have enough to eat, and good food at that, and enough to wear."

The press and Tippett's book made murder and Roxalana Druse

famous throughout the region. The notoriety brought with it a great deal of attention in the form of visitors. As each day passed, more and more visitors could be seen lining the sidewalks and waiting their turn to enter the jail in hopes of getting a glimpse of the condemned as well as the accused. This carnival-like atmosphere did not go unnoticed by the jail's next door neighbor, Reverend Henry Cox of the Reformed Church: "It is sad enough to know that the most shocking crimes have become of late so prevalent among us; but that the criminals should be frequently exposed to public scrutiny, and that men, women, and even children, should be allowed to visit them, for no other object than to gratify a morbid and senseless curiosity, is an offense against good morals which ought not be tolerated. If the gaping crowd could be of any real service to the prisoner," he continued, "there might be some show of reason for the indulgence against which I protest."

Reverend Cox's sentiment was shared not only by Sheriff Brown but also by Brown's wife and staff. The sheer volume of daily visitors made it difficult to operate the facility. At one point, Brown posted a sign on the front door of the jail that read "NO VISITORS TODAY." Some, including the *Herkimer Democrat*, viewed the sheriff as a prisoner in his own jail: "We trust the people will cease to no longer impose upon the good nature of the Sheriff and his estimable wife. While the Sheriff is the people's servant, it is not right to make slaves of him and his family." The sign lasted a few days, after which the curious and the sympathetic returned in numbers as large as before.

Roxalana reveled in this attention. She received a steady stream of visitors, most of whom, it was noted, were women. How many of their working husbands were aware of their visits is not known. Always anxious to receive any news, Roxalana was particularly pleased when the press made favorable comments were about her. When the *Utica Globe* published likenesses of mother and daughter, she was quick to praise the image of her daughter as being a very good likeness. "Don't you think the picture of me is worst of all?" she said with a hearty laugh. Of her own likeness she exclaimed, "Why, if I looked like that I ought to be hung." The offhand remark no doubt horrified her attorney.

Her children, however, did not crave publicity. Mary was shy and said very little; George, prior to his release, was shielded from the public by the sympathetic sheriff. In a jail full of unsavory characters, Valentine Brown had a soft heart for the Druse children. Frank

Gates had his mother and father to console him, but the Druse children had no one.

It was Sheriff Brown who contacted the local merchants and had clothes brought to the jail. He made sure that George had shoes, pants, and shirts. When Easter arrived, he presented Mary with a new hat. Seldom locked in his cell, George became an unofficial mascot to the deputies; he ran for firewood and coal, and even collected dirty dishes for the staff. On the weekends he was a guest at the sheriff's farm in German Flatts, an arrangement that continued after George was released from custody on April 14, 1885. (Frank Gates was released on the same day.)

If the Druse children had a friend during this time, it was truly Sheriff Valentine Brown.

CHAPTER 4

The Expert Witness

Thirty-four-year-old H. DeWight Luce had been a practicing attorney in the village of Richfield Springs for more than a decade when he agreed to defend Roxalana Druse. One of only a handful of attorneys in the tiny village, Luce had studied law under the direction of Judge James S. Davenport in Richfield Springs and gained valuable trial experience in the nearby Cooperstown Courthouse. Married with two children, Luce knew that the Druse trial would be the turning point in his legal career. If he successfully defended Roxalana and saved her from execution, or if by some miracle she was found innocent, he would be the most celebrated defense counsel in the region. If he failed, she would be famous—and he would be relegated to obscurity, a minor footnote in the legal history of Herkimer County.

The first challenge facing Luce was seating an impartial jury. Finding twelve good men would not be easy, given the high-profile publicity Roxalana received from the press and from Tippetts' little book. When Luce arrived at the Herkimer Courthouse on September 21, 1885, he was informed by the judge that of the 360 drawn as potential jurors, only eleven failed to report to the courthouse. Four were excused because of illness, and another four were eliminated because they had moved out of the county. The remaining three were permanently eliminated when it was discovered that they had died the previous year.

It was well into the afternoon before the first of many prospective jurors was interviewed. Abram Steele reminded each candidate that this was a capital punishment case. All were asked if they had any personal or religious convictions that would prevent them from being impartial jurors. Just as important, he asked each one if he could be impartial given the immense amount of coverage the case had already received from the press. Steele and Luce questioned candidates for several hours that afternoon and stopped only once, when sheriff's deputies escorted the accused and her daughter into the court chambers.

The room fell silent as Roxalana and Mary were led to their seats. Luce turned and nodded with approval as mother and daughter seated themselves across from the jury in the prisoner's box. Both wore plain black dresses, and except for the tiny gold locket about Mary's neck, there was little to indicate that they were anything but simple country folk. A reporter from the *Utica Daily Press* noted that Mary, who was wearing her eyeglasses, "looked like a demure country schoolteacher [rather] than a person charged with the highest offense known to law."

Many in the court chambers that day, and this included a dozen or so women, noted that Roxalana observed each potential juror carefully, looking intently at each as he was accepted or rejected. Mary, by contrast, avoided eye contact with anyone in the room. Seemingly indifferent to her surroundings, she seldom lifted her head, instead staring at the floor. After all, she did not have to be there—the jury selection was for her mother's trial. Her own trial had yet to be scheduled.

Steele and Luce interviewed jurors late into the day and well into the afternoon of the next day. The excuses they heard were as varied as the occupations of the men. Some claimed that no amount of evidence could change their minds about the guilt of the defendant.

Then Gideon Farr stepped forward to be interviewed. The twenty-seven-year-old farmhand from Wilmurt, in northern Herkimer County, claimed he had absolutely no opinion about the case because he hadn't read a single newspaper. Could there really be someone in the county who had not heard of this crime? It came as a surprise to everyone in the room, and even prompted a smile from Roxalana Druse. As promising a truly impartial juror as he appeared to be, Farr was dismissed when it was discovered that he did not own property in the county, a prerequisite for jurors in those days.

Three days later, Hiram Johnson, a farmer from Schuyler, became the 133rd—and final—juror interviewed. He and nine other farmers, a cheese maker, and a sawyer would decide the fate of Roxalana Druse. Those remaining in the jury pool were dismissed and told they would be recalled at a later date and interviewed for the Moritz Richter trial.

The presiding judge remanded the Druse jurors into the care of the sheriff's deputies for the evening. It was well past 6 p.m. when they were escorted to the Waverly Hotel on Main Street. Many were hungry, some were tired, and probably all wondered how long this trial would last, a concern shared by the defendant.

Early the next morning, Roxalana and Mary were awakened by the jail's matron. They ate breakfast and had plenty of time to prepare themselves for what was expected to be a very long day. As they waited in their cells, Sheriff Brown grew concerned as he watched the crowd gather in front of the courthouse. Shortly before 9 a.m., Brown and his deputies led the women from the jail to the courthouse. They passed the waiting crowd without incident, making their way inside and up the spiral staircase that led to the Supreme Court chambers on the second floor.

When the large, dark-stained double doors of the courtroom opened, Roxalana and Mary beheld a room full of strange and unfamiliar faces. Sheriff Brown slowly led his charges down the center aisle to the prisoner box. There was not an empty seat or space in the room. By horse, carriage, foot, or train, people had come from near and far to observe the proceedings. The *Utica Daily Observer* noted that there appeared to be more women than men in attendance that day: "What any lady can find interesting in the recital of the details of one of the most horrible crimes ever committed is difficult to imagine." Even more disturbing to this reporter was that some parents had brought their children, a decision he said "is to be regretted."

The trial judge was forty-three-year-old Pardon C. Williams of Watertown, New York. His legal career was similar to those of Steele and Luce; like them, he had never attended law school. In 1862 he studied law and interned with the Hammond and Bigelow law firm in Watertown, and the following year he was made a partner when he passed the bar exam. Williams quickly earned a reputation as an aggressive attorney, and those talents were put to public use when he was elected district attorney for Jefferson County in 1868. In 1874 he was elected judge of the Fifth Judicial District of New York and as such was no stranger to the courthouse in Herkimer. When Steele obtained a guilty verdict in the trial of Frank Mondon, it was Judge Pardon C. Williams who sentenced him to death.

The spectators that day may have been a bit disappointed when the trial eventually got underway. It took a while for Judge Williams to address the jury, and even longer for William C. Prescott to deliver the opening statements for the prosecution. Steele remained seated while his esteemed assistant, himself a retired judge, droned on for over an hour and a half, outlining the prosecution's case

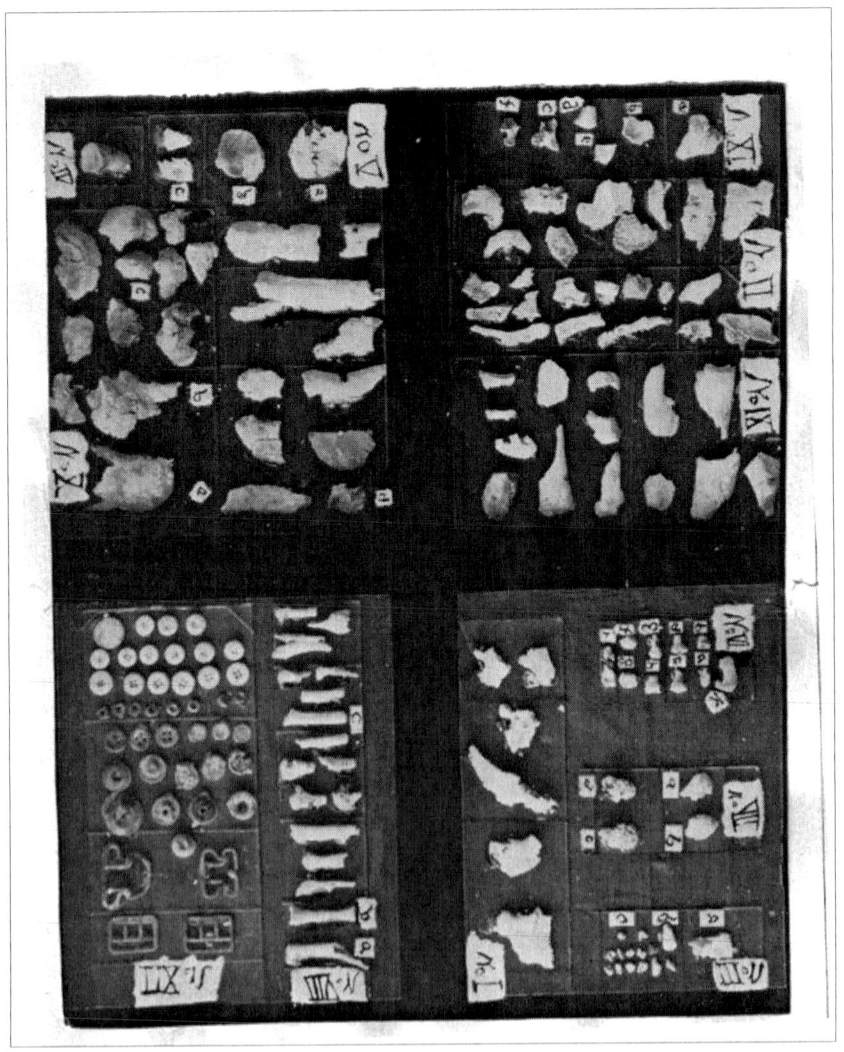

The forensic evidence - the bones of Bill Druse.

against Roxalana Druse. Prescott's dissertation was so boring that not a single reporter in attendance (and there were many) recorded any of his comments for the papers. No one wanted to hear about the murder from him—the press and the public were waiting to hear the details from those who were at the scene of the crime.

The crowd's anticipation turned to frustration once more when Abram Steele called as his first witness Zenus Green of Herkimer. A surveyor with over fifty years of experience, Green displayed a map of the Druse property, and with Steele's prodding, went on to explain to the jury where other farmers lived in relation to the Druse farm—informative but not exciting testimony. Green also had a wooden model of the Druse home built to scale. The Hogsback Hill Road farmhouse, he explained, with its three downstairs rooms, was thirty-six feet long and half as wide. Few present realized that the entire house could have fit easily inside the same courtroom where they sat.

When Green stepped down and returned to his seat, Steele turned and called for Frank Gates. "A buzz of excitement went through the courtroom" was how the *Richfield Springs Mercury* described the calling of the prosecution's star witness. This excitement heightened when, after giving his name, age, and relationship to the Druse family, his testimony was suddenly interrupted.

"We object to his being sworn and to his giving evidence in this case," declared H. DeWight Luce.

The objection was overruled as quickly as it had been introduced. The defense counsel never had the opportunity to explain to the judge or the jury why he objected to having Frank Gates being called as a witness. In due time, when he cross-examined this witness, the details of his objection would be known to all. For now, all Luce could do was listen patiently to the testimony of a fourteen-year-old boy.

Slowly and methodically, Frank Gates recalled the details of that December morning at the Druse farm. He told how he was the first to rise that morning, and that he started the fire in the kitchen stove. He went on to tell how his uncle scolded him for making the fire too hot, and that he was sent outdoors when his aunt and uncle began to quarrel.

"Then I heard a noise," he said. "Mrs. Druse called me to the door and handed me a revolver and told me to shoot or she would shoot me. . . .When she said that to me, she placed it to my nose. I took it. I fired it at Mr. Druse. He was sitting at the table with his back towards me. . . . After I fired, Mrs. Druse took the revolver and shot it off at Mr. Druse."

"Then what, after she did that?" asked Steele.

"Mary took the revolver and tried to load it," Frank continued.

He recalled how, amidst Roxalana's piercing screams and the mournful groans of a wounded Bill Druse, Mary attempted to reload the revolver. Trembling with fear, she inadvertently jerked the trigger, causing the gun to discharge. At that moment, Roxalana grabbed the axe that was near the stove and moved toward her

Dr. A. Walter Suiter

husband, now lying helpless on the floor.

"Mrs. Druse took the axe and hit Mr. Druse in the head with it, and he said, 'Oh, Roxy, don't.' Then she hit him again," said Frank.

"Then what?" asked Steele.

"Then she chopped his head off."

Gasps of disbelief filled the air of the crowded courtroom. An angry Luce was on his feet in an instant.

"We object to that. Move to strike it out!"

"We ask to have it stand," said Steele.

"He may describe this," replied the judge.

"What was done?" continued Steele.

"Is that retained?" asked Luce.

"I will see, after he has described," said Judge Williams, adding, "He may describe, particularly what he meant, how it was done."

This was exactly what Steele wanted. He wasted little time having Frank Gates describe to the jury just how his uncle met his death, even if it meant repeating his testimony.

"What did she do with the axe?" asked Steele.

"Hit him on the head with it," the boy answered.

"We object to the answer," said Luce.

"Overruled," said the judge.

"There was blood on the back of his neck and on the floor," said Frank Gates. "I saw him blowing blood out his mouth and nose."

"What did you notice with reference to his breathing?" asked Steele.

"We object to that," said Luce.

Judge Williams agreed with him on this point. "He must not give an opinion, but simply state what he saw."

"His head was near the stove hearth," recalled Frank. "Then she hit him on the head."

"Then what?"

"Chopped his head off, rolled it up in a newspaper, and carried it into the parlor, then she sent me and George upstairs."

"We object to that answer," said Luce.

So it went for the remainder of the morning. As determined as Steele was to get Frank Gates to relate what had transpired on that fateful December morning, Luce was no less determined to prevent this graphic testimony from being introduced. When Steele had Frank repeat the details of the shooting a second time, with particular emphasis on, "She chopped his head off," Luce voiced his objection in the strongest tone possible. "He has been all over the transaction and told it all," said Luce to Judge Williams, regarding this oft-repeated statement.

"I will overrule the objection," declared Judge Williams. "Let the boy tell his story. Now I will permit him to call his attention to details, so far as he thinks necessary, without leading of course."

A frustrated Luce sat down, knowing what lay ahead. First, Abram Steele asked Frank Gates to describe the kitchen and its surroundings after the beheading of William Druse. With remarkable attention to detail, the fourteen-year-old witness went on to describe the entire contents of the parlor, even going so far as to describe the differences between the parlor stove and the kitchen stove. Then, with the image of the stoves fresh in the jurors' minds, Steele subtly asked, "Did you see anything with reference to a large bone that afternoon?"

Abram Steele

"We object to that portion of the question," declared Luce.

"He may answer it," replied Judge Williams.

"We object to his characterizing anything he saw about the bone also as incompetent and immaterial. There is no evidence in the case that he had any knowledge upon the subject."

"Unless it appears on the examination that there is some doubt about what it was, so it may be regarded as an expression of an opinion. I don't see any objection to it," said Judge Williams. "Of course, he should not be allowed as an expert to tell what it was; he can't judge as to that. You may proceed a little further, and if it turns out there is any question of an expert to it, I will strike it out."

The objection overruled, Steele went ahead and simply asked him to describe what he saw that afternoon.

"I saw a large bone," said Frank Gates, "about that long, with a little meat on one end."

This drew a sharp objection from Luce. That the witness used his hands to describe the approximate size of the bone was "incompetent." Judge Williams agreed with him on this point and agreed that the comment should be stricken from the record.

Somehow, Steele had to introduce testimony regarding the disposition of William Druse's body. With Luce objecting to every statement made by Frank Gates, Steele tried a different approach. He asked Frank if he saw Mary Druse that morning, and if so, what she was doing in the kitchen. Luce knew what was coming next, and he voiced his objection to this line of questioning.

The judge turned and looked at Frank Gates. "At that time you saw something, did you?"

Steele could not believe his luck. The same question he had been asking, to Luce's objections, was now being asked by the judge. This was a major turning point for the prosecution; nothing could stop Steele, and he knew it. He no longer had to carefully rephrase each question he asked the witness. He could proceed, knowing that the judge would overrule any more objections.

"Give us a description of it," said Steele.

The boy hesitated, and then drew both hands together indicating the approximate size of the bone. "About so big around," he said, clarifying his description by pointing to the table near the district attorney. "Almost as big around as the top of that goblet."

"Move to strike it out!" cried Luce.

"It may stand," declared the judge.

"About two feet long, with something on the end . . . color, kind of brown . . . ," Frank went on.

"Was there anything said by Mrs. Druse as to what she had done, or what had been done with his body?"

"She burned it up," the boy continued. "She said she burned all of his clothing, that she burned his overcoat so they would think he wore it when he went away. His model was burned . . . she said she burned it up so they would think he took it with him. It was a model of a steamer wheel. She said she burned up the jackknife so they would think he had taken it with him. She said she burned up the rope so no one could see it. She said that if anyone asked where Mr. Druse was, to say he was gone to New York. She said if we told what actually became of William she would do the same to us . . . I mean kill us."

It was as if a dam had been let loose. With no interruptions from Luce, Frank Gates described how the kitchen was transformed after the murder. Fresh paint covered the bloodstained floor by the stove, and the walls were later repapered. He also described the carriage trip they all took to Richfield Springs to send the telegram to Roxalana's brother in an effort to establish an alibi. It was convincing, as Amon Teft surprised Roxalana a few days later when he appeared suddenly at the farm. Frank said that Teft remained at the farm for the night and returned to New York City unaware of what had happened. Finally, he described how key pieces of evidence—the axe, pistol, and bones—were discarded about the countryside.

It had taken the better part of the morning, but Steele had extracted the information from Frank Gates. With no further questions, Steele knew that the cross-examination of his star witness would be intense. Throughout the testimony, Roxalana had remained calm. Except for the icy stare transfixed upon her nephew, she displayed little emotion. Mary, seated next to her mother in the prisoner box, was clearly uncomfortable. Still avoiding eye contact with anyone in the courtroom, she continued to stare at the floor.

After a brief recess, Luce began his cross-examination of Frank Gates. Thus far, the boy had recalled his actions of that day for the jury not once, but twice at Abram Steele's insistence. Now he was asked to repeat his testimony a third time. The defense counsel wanted to compare the statements the boy had made at the coroner's inquest. Was there a chance that he could have omitted some details or somehow twisted a few facts? If there were discrepancies, it would be Luce's only chance to discredit the star witness for the prosecution. He had to shift some of the guilt for the murder of William Druse to the fourteen-year-old.

"I fired at Mr. Druse," said Frank Gates, "[but I] did not intend to hit him. I pointed the revolver that way. I could not tell as to whether I hit him or not. . . . I don't think I hit him . . . I don't believe I did . . . can't say how many shots I fired. I don't know whether the pistol was pointed at him or not because I was so scared on seeing Mr. Druse there and seeing the blood. I recollect testifying before the coroner's jury upon that subject."

At the coroner's inquest, Frank Gates had testified that his aunt must have struck her husband with the first shots, and that he too may have struck him when he fired the pistol. Later he recalled how he inspected the floor and walls to see if there were any bullet holes.

"Mr. Steele—at the coroner's inquest—gave me a pencil, and I indicated precisely the way in which I held the pistol when I fired. I pointed the pencil at Alonzo Filkins, directly at him. . . . I pointed the pencil directly at Filkins, indicating that I pointed the pistol directly at Mr. Druse when I shot. I remember that—it is true."

This was the moment Luce had been waiting for—did Frank Gates carefully aim the pistol or simply point the pistol in the direction of William Druse?

"Why did you say so before the coroner and deny it here?" demanded Luce. The question stunned and confused the boy, his pause interrupted when the judge demanded he answer the question.

"Come witness, any explanation you see fit, if you did testify so before the coroner and now here deny it. What do you say about it? Why do you do it?" asked Judge Williams.

"Because I don't remember."

"Don't remember what?" Luce asked.

"Whether I pointed it directly at him or not . . . I now say I pointed it towards him. When I fired, I was about ten feet from Druse, and Mrs. Druse was standing near the door. She was excited . . . she appeared just like a crazy person."

Luce pressed on, having the boy recall the events that led to his arrest.

"I first had a talk with Dan McDonald and Clarence Marshall. They told me that they wanted me to tell my story. They said it would be best for me. McDonald said he would help me all he could. Marshall said he would help me. McDonald or the other man told me that if I didn't tell, I would be arrested for the crime, but if I did tell they would protect me."

Luce made it clear to the crowded courtroom that the boy was indeed protected. It didn't matter if he aimed the pistol toward William Druse—he had shot a defenseless man in the back. He then helped drag a headless corpse into a parlor. For all of this, he was granted immunity from prosecution by the district attorney.

As difficult as this cross-examination may have been for Frank Gates, Steele wasn't concerned. The boy may have fumbled a few facts and details, but the macabre aspect of the murder and its aftermath was firmly planted in the jurors' minds.

The next witness caused as many heads to turn as the first. "He is a short, stubby little fellow of ten," observed a reporter for the *Richfield Springs Mercury* who watched George Druse seat himself in the witness chair, "with an intelligent face and bright, mischievous eyes. He is neatly dressed in a grey suit, with calico shirt and collar."

George Druse was understandably frightened and nervous that day. In a room filled with strange and unfamiliar faces, he glanced across the courtroom and looked briefly at the prisoner box. Kept incommunicado at the jail, this was the first time George had seen his mother and sister since they were all arrested nine months earlier.

"My name is George William Stewart Druse. I will be eleven years old on the eighth day of next December. I have a sister Mary, older than I. My mother's name is Roxalana and my father's name was William Druse. He was fifty-six. I don't know how old my mother is. I went to school last winter at Castle Corners. I lived in the town of Warren on my father's place, near Mr. Petts."

H. DeWight Luce

Abram Steele questioned George Druse in much the same way he had questioned his cousin. He wanted the ten-year-old to tell the court his account of that December morning. With very little coaxing and an occasional reminder to speak up, the boy reconstructed the events that led to the murder of his father. Luce, as if on cue, raised objections each time George mentioned that his mother "cut the head off from father." Each time, the objection was overruled.

Many in the courtroom were quick to notice that the testimony given by George was almost identical to that given by his cousin. "It is remarkable," noted a reporter for the *Herkimer Democrat*, "how well Gates and young Druse remembered dates, times, and minute particulars."

Throughout George's narrative, several new details of the murder came to light. It was Frank, he said, who removed the rubber boots from his father's body before helping drag the corpse into the parlor. And when Mary was unable to extract the empty shells from the pistol, it was Frank who assisted her. He also said that his father's head was rolled up in a skirt and brought into the parlor. He told Steele how he and Frank were sent to the shed repeatedly to fetch dried shingles so his sister and his mother could stoke the fires. He himself brought in water from the cistern to wash the blood off the floor. He then described how his father's remains were brought to Wall's Swamp.

Luce was fairly conservative in voicing his protests of George

Druse's testimony. While he raised four objections—all overruled by Judge Williams—there was no verbal sparring like what took place earlier when he had lodged fourteen separate objections to Frank Gates's testimony. Luce had been firm in cross-examining Frank Gates, but he was prepared to be gentle in his questioning of George Druse. How would it appear to the jury if he ruthlessly attacked the testimony of a ten-year-old boy who had witnessed the brutal murder of his father? Instead of hammering away at the few inconsistencies in the boy's statements, Luce preferred to concentrate on certain details that could implicate others in the crime. This was easy to do, given the parade of neighbors who happened by the Druse farm that fateful day.

"It wasn't a great while after Pa was killed that day that I seen Elwood," said George. "He was going from our house to the back end of the wagon house. The cloth that Elwood carried under his arm looked like Ma's dress. I know it was Elwood—I could see the scar on his head."

Luce had inadvertently raised a critical point. William Druse's head had never been recovered. Had Elwood disposed of it? Should he too be considered an accomplice to the murder?

Luce spent the remainder of the cross-examination trying to get George to describe the harsh physical conditions that existed on the farm. Roxalana, who had maintained a certain degree of self-control throughout the testimony of Frank Gates, now wept openly as her son described his life on the farm.

"I can remember about matters at home for the last five years," he said. "There was trouble between Father and Mother every two or three weeks—quarreling about store bills. When quarrels occurred, I heard him call Mother a 'Goddamned bitch' a good many times. I have heard him wish she was dead. There was only one occasion that Father drew the axe and threatened to knock Mother's brains out. I do not remember any other.

"There wasn't enough to eat," he continued. "Father was generally helping some of the neighbors from week to week. He was a great deal away from home . . . sometimes two or three days, and when he was gone there was nothing to eat."

The testimony that George offered aided not only the prosecution but also the defense. Newspaper reporters were impressed by the way he remembered certain details of the murder, and everyone in the courtroom felt sorry for the boy, who obviously led a miserable life on a destitute farm. For Abram Steele, the entire case was without parallel. A ten-year-old boy had given evidence against his own mother in a capital murder case. And it wasn't necessary to remind Steele that at no other time in the history of the county had a murder case been brought to trial without a corpse. The testimony of the next individuals would be crucial if he was to obtain a conviction.

Steele began carefully and methodically. One by one, the neighbors who had suspected something was wrong at the Druse house were called to testify. Harvey Eckler recalled the thick, heavy smoke rising into the winter sky, and his brother William added that it carried a foul odor, unlike the wood-smoke smell coming from the other chimneys in the neighborhood. Alonzo Filkins said that he had gone to Wall's Swamp with four others to retrieve the ashes and bones, and Charley Pett testified that he saw the same bones given to Dr. Irving O. Nellis, who in turn told the court that the bones were then given to Drs. Borland and Getman.

It was only after the two Richfield Springs physicians took the stand that Steele asked any relevant questions regarding these crucial pieces of evidence. "Were these indeed the bones of William Druse?" Dr. Getman admitted that he wasn't sure what to make of the frozen mass of ash, bones, buttons, and buckles. "We only made a casual examination," he noted.

His colleague agreed, adding that the bones he examined were very small. "Some," said Dr. Borland, "were two and a half inches long, by an inch and a half wide . . . I cannot say that they were part of the human skeleton."

Abram Steele did not expect anything more from either doctor. If they had suddenly admitted that these were indeed human remains, Luce could have asked why they were certain now, when at the coroner's inquest they were unsure. Steele had the physician who would make this claim, and his name was A. Walter Suiter.

Like his colleague Dr. Nellis, Suiter was a graduate of Fairfield College. From this rural campus, he had continued his education at the University of Michigan, and then transferred to the College of Physicians and Surgeons at Columbia University, where he graduated in 1871. Dr. Suiter returned to his hometown of Herkimer where his medical practice, as well as his financial portfolio, flourished. By the time of the Druse trial, his investments in stocks, bonds, and village real estate had left the thirty-four-year-old bachelor in comfortable semi-retirement. When not tending to his finances, Dr. Suiter worked in his laboratory at the rear of his office in his Queen

Anne style brick mansion, diagonally across from the jail on Main Street. Specializing in pathology and microscopy, he was obsessed with hygiene and sanitation. Convinced that germs spread disease and were everywhere, Suiter never touched a doorknob without first covering it with his trademark white handkerchief.

One subject above all fascinated Dr. Suiter, and that was forensics. Time after time he was called upon by the courts to offer his opinion on a variety of cases. His image as a consultant to the courts brought him notoriety, and often his testimony was not for the faint of heart. A year before the Druse murder, Dr. Suiter was called upon to assist in the investigation of an apparent murder–suicide.

On March 25, 1883, the village police of Herkimer were called to the Prospect Street residence of Mrs. Eugenia Parkes. Alerted by neighbors who had heard the muffled sounds of gunshots, the police entered the house and discovered a gruesome scene. In the upstairs bedroom, the body of Mrs. Parkes lay across the bed. Lying on blood-soaked pillows on either side of the deceased woman were her two children. Both were wounded and neither survived the night. The three deaths stunned the village. Mrs. Parkes's husband, absent from the house when the police arrived, was the prime suspect and was later arrested on suspicion of staging the murder.

At the coroner's inquest, Dr. Suiter testified that although Mrs. Parkes had no history of depression, she may have suffered a "temporary mental aberration." An autopsy showed that the angle of the bullet into her skull indicated that her wound was self-inflicted. Dr. Suiter surmised that the distraught Mrs. Parkes had shot her two children before taking her own life.

Law enforcement officials respected the expertise of the eccentric Dr. Suiter and were eager to involve him in the Druse investigation. It was a decision they would not regret. The coroner's inquest was in its third day when the doctor arrived at the farm on Hogsback Hill Road. There were only a few locals on the Druse farm that day; most everyone else was at the Eckler cheese house to watch the inquest. A sheriff's deputy soon arrived with Frank Gates, and the trio entered the abandoned farmhouse.

Dr. Suiter glanced casually about the kitchen and walked into the parlor. For the moment he said nothing, preferring instead to record his observations in a notebook. Then turning to the deputy, he asked that the door be secured to prevent anyone else from entering the house.

"I proceeded to make an examination of the premises, with a

view of ascertaining what, if any, evidence of a scientific character I might obtain," Suiter recalled later.

As every member of the house was under arrest, he was not hampered by a search warrant and got right to work. Removing a penknife from his pocket, he gently scraped off a small piece of wallpaper that looked as if it had been stained with blood. He placed the specimen in an envelope and after making a few notations on the envelope, he reentered the parlor to examine the stove. In his notebook, he recorded its height, width, and shape. Using another envelope, he carefully scooped out a sample of ash from the stove.

Walking back into the kitchen, Dr. Suiter approached Frank Gates and asked him to indicate approximately where his uncle was in the kitchen before he was murdered. Perhaps remembering the advice of McDonald and Marshall, Frank was all too willing to cooperate. He showed the doctor where his uncle was sitting when his hysterical aunt called him into the house, and where the body was when it was dragged to the floor.

Suiter knelt down on the rough kitchen floor and ran his hand gently across several of the boards. The fresh paint covered an assortment of grooves, gaps, and indentations. One sharp V-shape in a board was no doubt made with an axe, but this was not proof that a beheading had taken place there. After all, this was a country kitchen, and axe marks such as this one near a woodstove were common. Not the marks in the wood, but the paint on the floor was what intrigued the doctor. If there were bloodstains here, but they had been washed away before they were covered with paint—or had they?

Dr. Suiter looked up from the floor and asked if the house had a basement. Frank told him it did, but it wasn't an actual basement, but rather a crawl space under the house that was used as a root cellar. Procuring an oil lantern, Suiter made his way under the section of the house directly beneath the kitchen. By the lantern's faint light, he could make out dark stains of dried blood between the cracks of the kitchen floorboards. Hoping that some of the blood had dripped onto the dirt floor below, he slowly scanned the area beneath the boards with the light. There was no blood, but there was an empty shell casing from a small-caliber pistol.

Dr. Suiter emerged from the crawl space and asked the deputy on guard to summon a carpenter or anyone else who could lift a few of the floorboards in the kitchen. This was easily accomplished, as several neighbors had gathered outside the farmhouse in hopes of seeing what evidence was being collected. A few of these onlookers were ushered inside the farmhouse, and Dr. Suiter pointed to the boards he wanted removed. In a few places, the fresh green paint had not seeped between the cracks in the floorboard, and dried blood was clearly visible. When one board was lifted, the dirt and sand between the boards did not reveal blood, but instead another shell casing.

The floorboards were placed in Dr. Suiter's wagon. The only other piece of physical evidence he required from the farmhouse was the parlor stove. With the assistance of neighbors, this too was loaded into the wagon. Satisfied that he had obtained as much evidence from the farmhouse as possible, Suiter made his way to the Eckler farm, where Abram Steele presented him with the frozen mass of bones and ash recovered from Wall's Swamp. Wrapped in a white towel, the remains were placed in a tin box, which was secured with a padlock. Dr. Suiter bid good-bye to Abram Steele and returned to Herkimer to begin his scientific investigation.

Eight months later, in the third day of the trial, Dr. Suiter was sworn in as a witness for the defense. Educated and articulate, he needed little coaxing from Steele to tell of his findings at the Druse house. From "a woodstove of an oval form, part iron, part sheet iron" to the most trivial details—"pictures on the wall, several brackets upon which pictures and ornaments were placed"—it seemed as if nothing had escaped his observation. Perfectly at ease before the crowded courtroom, Suiter proceeded to relate how he was called to the Druse residence by the district attorney, and how he had collected the various types of evidence now displayed on the table in the center of the room.

"What did you do with the bones that you received from Mr. Eckler and the ashes that you received from the district attorney ?" asked Steele.

"I searched those bones carefully over several occasions, both alone and in the company of Dr. Deecke, and discovered certain fragments which were portions of . . ."

"To that we object!" cried H. DeWight Luce. "If he proposes to state that these bones are part of the human skeleton, we object to it. In the first place, they have lost the benefit of this evidence by reason of allowing the bones to be out of their possession, these bones must be in their possession continuously, and from the evidence in this case, there was a certain time, I don't say how long, but for a certain time, they were out of the possession of the people."

Having failed in an earlier attempt in June to examine the bone fragments himself, Luce had few options available. He had to try to get the bones deemed inadmissible evidence. They were the most important piece of evidence in the trial, and if he succeeded here, there would be no need of the expert witness, Dr. A. Walter Suiter. Luce had in effect raised a very serious question that caused the judge to turn and address the district attorney: "I don't recollect what the coroner swore to the reference to his taking possession of these."

"He swore that he received them from these doctors," said Steele. "He met them on the stairs, as they say, and they said they had got through with them, and he went up and took possession of them."

An elated Luce was on his feet in an instant to voice his objection. "They swore they left them in charge of a constable."

"I am not assuming for the purpose of this ruling that one witness has sworn to the truth, and the other has not," said Judge Williams. He then informed Luce that there was a fairly simple solution to this problem. "If there was any real question as to who had the evidence, the minutes of the coroner's inquest would have to be consulted. If there is any dispute about the evidence, then it is a question for the jury."

Luce was not satisfied and pointed directly at Abram Steele: "He said that these doctors were examining, and they were upstairs and he was downstairs, and as they got on the stairway, coming down, he didn't say exactly what place [on the stairway]."

It did seem odd that Steele would have omitted this piece of information. Could anyone have had an opportunity to tamper with the evidence, or was this a trivial misunderstanding? Abram Steele attempted to stress the latter: "We think if your honor will refer to the evidence of Dr. Getman, you will find that he said in substance, that he did not personally deliver the bones to Dr. Nellis."

Luce hadn't finished. Not only had this crucial piece of evidence been transferred from person to person—no one knew for sure what Dr. Suiter could have done with it. "We wish to include in the objection so that the court may have the whole of it, the fact that in the meantime, and without the knowledge of this man [Dr. Suiter], these bones and ashes, whatever they were, have been washed in hot water, three-quarters of a pail being used, and they didn't see the manner of their being done, or have any knowledge of the remains of the water afterward."

Judge Pardon C. Willams listened to what Luce had to say, and then repeated what he had said earlier on the subject: "In the absence of any authority you may have on the subject, I think it is a question for the jury."

Abram Steele assumed that the entire matter was resolved and resumed his questioning of Dr. Suiter.

"I discovered on making certain comparisons that a number of fragments were human bones," noted the doctor.

"Your honor," cried Luce, "What has become of the objection?"

Judge Williams leaned forward and glared at Luce. "The objection made is overruled; it seems to me from the evidence, *it is a question for the jury!*"

Luce had gambled and lost. Nothing could stop the expert witness from presenting his findings to the court. Dr. A. Walter Suiter stepped down from the witness chair and walked toward the evidence table; he had taken center stage. With the bones as his props and his notes as a script, he was at last ready to present his monologue to an eager audience.

"I found that a number of those fragments were fragments of human bones," he stated.

Directing everyone's attention to the table, he explained that the bones in question were on display here and scientifically catalogued. Dr. Suiter stressed that these were exactly the same bone fragments presented to him in January by the district attorney. He told the court that after he returned to his laboratory in Herkimer, he began his scientific analysis of the material. After thawing the evidence, he rinsed the material through different-sized sieves, thus separating the bone fragments from the ash. This done, he used ceiling wax to affix the fragments to large glass slides. When he was finished, he had a total of 126 bone fragments on eleven glass slides.

For the most part, he continued, the bone fragments displayed were just that—fragments. All were characterized by what Suiter testified as irregular shapes that were no doubt caused by some sort of sharp instrument. For the remainder of the afternoon, he slowly and methodically explained the contents of each slide. At times he used indecipherable medical terminology, once referring to a small skull chip as "the left mastoid process of petrous portion of temporal bone." For the most part though, the expert witness used general terms before he delved into specifics. There were fragments from the jaw and teeth, along with fragments identified as pieces of bones from the hand, foot, femur, and tibia. Many observers were impressed with the effort Dr. Suiter made to describe how each bone was part of the human skeleton. The last plate displayed four buckles, one of which bore the inscription "Paris" and another with "patent 1855." There were also twenty-seven buttons and a silver ten-cent piece that may have been used as a lapel pin.

When he had concluded his presentation, Abram Steele asked, "You say these are human bones?"

"I do," replied Suiter, "with the single exception of those that are marked 'probably,' I will swear positively to these being human bones."

With this affirmation on the part of the expert witness, Steele confidently announced that he had no further questions. As it turned out, Luce didn't either. Having sparred with Dr. Suiter and the judge and lost, Luce preferred to wait until the next expert, Dr. Theodore Deecke, presented his testimony. A pathologist at the state lunatic asylum in Utica for the past twelve years, Dr. Deecke testified that he had assisted Dr. Suiter in examining the evidence that had just been presented to the court. The German-born physician said that he and Dr. Suiter had spent sixteen days in their study of the bone fragments, and that he had reached the same conclusion as his colleague: "They are human bones, without any doubt."

When cross-examined, Deecke proved to be just as precise as Suiter. He had no problem identifying several of the bone fragments on display, flatly refusing any suggestion by Luce that they could be animal bones. "I have made other examinations similar to the ones here in question," claimed Dr. Deecke. "The bones may be similar in their composition, but they are different in their shape and form." Dr. Deecke concluded his testimony by stating that material from the floorboards removed from the Druse kitchen clearly displayed bloodstains when viewed under a microscope.

In light of both doctors' testimonies, it seemed that only one question remained unanswered: Could a woodstove such as the one in the Druse house produce enough heat to reduce a human body to ashes? At the inquest, Drs. Borland and Getman were somewhat hesitant to state for an absolute fact that a 150 pound body could be incinerated in such a short amount of time. Dr. Deecke offered his own opinion.

"Heat can destroy only the organic matter, and if the bone is untouched, it will remain in its original form. When hot, bones can be easily reduced to ashes, but on cooling they become hard. The heart, lungs, and abdominal organs would be nearly destroyed by burning. I think a temperature of 1,000 degrees on the centigrade scale would easily destroy all the organic matter, or a lower degree if the heat were continued."

Dr. Suiter not only agreed with Dr. Deecke but also, when recalled to the stand, offered proof that it was possible. Having access to the Druse stove, he claimed to have conducted his own experiments.

"Dry pine shingles," he said, "and thoroughly dried sticks of pine wood were used as fuel in imitation of the alleged cremation, and human and animal bones were burned. The amount of wood used was carefully weighed for each experiment and compared to the weight of animal tissue cremated."

According to Dr. Suiter, a 150-pound body could be incinerated in eight hours using one-and-a-quarter pound of fuel for each pound of animal tissue. Suiter never said where he conducted these experiments, but his comments did draw a response from the *Herkimer Citizen.* While praising the doctor's diligence, the press couldn't help but add a little dark humor to an otherwise solemn subject. "People having dogs," quipped the *Citizen*, "had better keep them where the doctor cannot get them."

After four days of testimony, Abram Steele believed that he was building a solid case against Roxalana Druse. The graphic testimony presented by her nephew and son, together with a detailed description of the fragmentary remains, proved that a brutal crime had taken place. Now the only thing that remained was to prove how Roxalana Druse attempted to cover up her misdeeds. For this he had to rely upon neighbors, family, friends, and anyone else acquainted with the accused. Although Steele felt confident that his case was strong, he was apprehensive about a few of these local witnesses. Could they withstand cross-examination by a persistent and aggressive H. DeWight Luce?

Initially, Steele was successful. Charles Pett had little difficulty identifying exhibit 4, the axe blade recovered from Weatherbee's Pond. Bill Druse, he recalled, had brought the blade to his farm that December to be fitted with a hickory handle. James Storer, the shopkeeper from Richfield Springs who had acted as the stenographer at the coroner's inquest, identified exhibits 7 and 8 as the Western Union telegrams Roxalana had sent to New York City and Albany. When her sister-in-law, Phoebe Chamberlain, took the stand, she vividly recalled the conversation she had with Roxalana at the county jail.

"I asked her if she killed William. She said no . . . that two men came and killed him . . . that she had nothing to do with it."

According to Phoebe, Roxalana then told her sister-in-law that the same two men had taken the body to Little Falls and thrown it into the Mohawk River. This seemed highly unlikely, but Steele never questioned her about any of the details. H. DeWight Luce would no doubt resurrect this story during his defense of Roxalana.

What concerned Abram Steele at this point was not so much the direction the trial was taking, but the possibility of introducing a potentially hostile witness. Having established that the axe head recovered from Weatherbee's Pond was the murder weapon, Steele now concentrated his efforts at placing another weapon—the pistol. Still harboring suspicions regarding the credibility of Charles Gates, the man who had purchased the weapon for Mary Druse, Steele had no other recourse except to call upon Rudolph Van Evera.

The itinerant day laborer and farmhand for Bill Druse had no love for the district attorney. At the coroner's inquest, Steele had placed Van Evera under arrest and all but accused him of being a paramour of Mary Druse or her mother. Although he flatly denied this allegation, the tabloid press couldn't resist this juicy piece of gossip.

"There is nothing in their looks to attract a wayfaring man," reported the *Utica Morning Herald*, "though a tramp like Van Evera might think otherwise."

Released from custody due to a lack of evidence, the nine months that had elapsed since the inquest had not soothed Van Evera's wounded feelings. He hadn't forgotten how ruthlessly Steele had treated him.

Steele too was on his guard. He considered Van Evera as perhaps the weakest witness—but one of the most dangerous. Steele proceeded cautiously, and Van Evera responded to his questions in much the same way. When asked if he could identify the axe, Van Evera merely glanced at the exhibit table and pointed to the round-headed axe blade. Asked if he had ever seen a pistol in the Druse house, he replied that on one occasion he had.

"Did you see it anywhere else?" asked Steele.

"Yes," answered Van Evera.

"Where?"

"Mary had it in her hand."

On this point, Luce raised a stern objection. Mary was not on trial at this time; the fact that she held a pistol in her hand had no relevance to the case against her mother. Luce, who had objected very little during the testimonies of the last handful of witnesses, was surprised when the judge actually agreed with him on this point. It was now useless to ask Van Evera any further questions regarding the pistol, so Steele changed direction and asked the witness if he had ever heard any verbal threats by Roxalana toward her husband. Van Evera was a little vague as to the exact time, but he said that perhaps sometime last winter she had made what he considered to be a threatening remark.

"If William kept on carrying on and raising the old Harry [the devil], as he had done, much longer, he would be a dead man."

This was the statement Steele had been searching for.

It didn't take the district attorney long to discover that Van Evera's testimony could also aid Roxalana's defense. When Luce began his cross-examination, he casually asked the young farmhand to describe what he had observed of the relationship between the husband and wife. Van Evera was more comfortable with Luce and spoke freely and clearly about what he had observed at the Druse farm. According to Van Evera, Bill Druse wandered away from the farm any time he chose and was usually found at a neighbor's reading the newspaper and taking advantage of a free meal. Roxalana, on the other hand, never strayed too far from the farm.

"Mrs. Druse did the work," he said. "She cooked the victuals and prepared the food as best she could."

As to her temperament, Van Evera stated that he could recall only a single instance when Roxalana initiated a quarrel with her husband. When one of the barn cats tipped over a pail of milk, Mrs. Druse called her husband a "Goddamned fool." When questioned further about the incident, Van Evera said that Bill Druse was capable of almost any kind of verbal abuse. "Goddamned bitch" and "Goddamned whore" seemed to be particular favorites of the foul-mouthed farmer, but Van Evera was quick to remind Luce that Roxalana herself could be quite feisty with a "Goddamned son of a bitch" here or a "Goddamned cuss" there.

"Were there quarrels of words alone," asked Luce, "or did they have blows?"

"No, they didn't have blows, but quarreling," said Van Evera. "I mean talking bad. I didn't hear anything else . . . only swearing."

"What, if anything, do you know of his cruelty to his animals?"

Now it was Steele's turn to raise an objection. "I don't see how that is competent [relevant]."

"We offer to show right here that he was cruel and unkind to his beasts," replied Luce. He tried desperately to explain to the court that if Druse was indeed cruel to his animals, he was just as cruel to his family.

"I don't see how this is competent," said Steele.

The argument between the two reached such intensity that Judge Williams pounded the gavel to restore order. This was the most serious flare-up between the two attorneys since Luce had tried to get the bones dismissed as evidence. He had failed then, and he failed now. The judge ruled that the question was not only irrelevant, but "immaterial and improper" as well.

Not wanting to end his cross-examination on such a sour note, Luce thought it best to revert to questions regarding the quarrels between husband and wife. He hoped that the swearing and death threats Van Evera recalled would impress the jury. With such hateful and spiteful rhetoric within the home, one juror raised his hand—which would never be allowed in a courtroom today. He asked if there wasn't a single instance when they were pleasant to one another.

"They were friendly when he gave her money," Van Evera said, and then went on to add that despite all Bill Druse's faults, he was a temperate man. "When I went away from the Druse farm, they had in the house potatoes, flour, beef, butter, and sugar. I don't know of anything that was not there, that was not really necessary, unless one has a great hand to drink."

Apparently, many things had changed on Hogsback Hill Road in the year that had passed since Van Evera was the hired man. Little George Druse had testified earlier to the impoverished conditions that existed on the farm just prior to his father's death. There was no food, no money, and plenty of quarreling. Van Evera's testimony reinforced the opinion held by many that this was not a match made in heaven.

For his final witness, Abram Steele called on Justice of the Peace Daniel McDonald. A life-long resident of the town of Warren, the forty-four-year-old father of five testified that he had been led to Weatherbee's Pond by Frank Gates and had assisted in the recovery of the pearl-handled revolver. He had no problem identifying the weapon now displayed on the evidence table, and he told the court that the weapon was loaded when it was retrieved from the pond. He also stated that after everyone was arrested and before the start of the inquest, he'd had an opportunity to speak with each of the suspects. Without the benefit of counsel (Luce didn't arrive until the next day), McDonald questioned Roxalana about the events leading up to the death of her husband.

"I did not tell her that she had better tell what there was of it," recalled McDonald of this interview. "I did not tell her anything on that subject. I did not threaten her if she did not tell, and I did not hear anyone else threaten her. At that time, I had the first conversation with her. I said to her that George, Frank, and Mary had told us all about it, and she might as well tell us too. I didn't add that it would be better for her."

"We object to the witness giving this conversation," said Luce. "First, because it was made while the defendant was under arrest. The statement that Frank, Mary, and George had told all about the transaction was an inducement for her to tell was unfair and unjust, and the very evidence he states was calculated to lead her to believe that it would be [in] her favor to tell."

Judge Williams felt the same way about this issue as he had earlier regarding the introduction of the bones as evidence. Despite the fact that Roxalana had no lawyer present, he saw no reason why her statement could not be entered into the court record. The ruling was yet another disappointment to the defense team.

According to McDonald, most of what Frank Gates and George Druse had stated under oath was essentially true. Roxalana did send both of them out, and it was only after the first shots were fired that she called for them to return to the house. She said that Frank had shot at her husband and that she cut up and burned the body.

"I think I said to her, 'Why did you do it?' and she said, 'To get rid of him.' I said to her I think there could have been a better way than this; you might have left him. I said, 'Why should you do it?' She said she 'thought she was possessed with the devil.' I asked her if anyone else was implicated except them that were there. I told her there was a difference of opinion; some thought someone else had a hand in it."

"What did she say when you asked that question?" Steele asked.

"She said that Charles Gates was there. She said that he was there and helped her that day and night. She said she wasn't sure if it [the body] wasn't all burned up. He was there and helped in the evening. He might have carried part of it off. She said she thought perhaps he might have put it in the barn and carried it off in the swamp and burned it."

If no one else in the crowded courtroom understood what had

just transpired, H. DeWight Luce did. McDonald's testimony served a dual purpose. Not only had she confessed to the crime she was accused of, Roxalana tried to implicate others as well. How many more times would the story about Charles Gates 'aiding and abetting' be told? McDonald's testimony underscored the impression of many present that the murderess was also a liar.

Steele returned to his seat and announced that he had no further questions. He was satisfied that he had presented the best possible case for the people of Herkimer County against Roxalana Druse. Between the physical evidence, especially the bone fragments, and the testimony of two eyewitnesses, Steele believed he had built a solid case against her.

CHAPTER 5

"Her life had been a hell on Earth."

The crowds that gathered by the courthouse steps were rarely disappointed during that September of 1885. Whether arriving at the courthouse or returning to the jail, Roxalana Druse greeted all with a pleasant smile. She reveled in the attention and was eager to show those who greeted her that she was not the vile monster portrayed in the press. She and her daughter were no longer the rough-hewn backwoods characters plucked from Hogsback Hill Road nine months earlier. Although isolated in the Herkimer County Jail, they were well taken care of; they wore clean clothes and, for the first time in many years, were afforded three good meals a day.

H. DeWight Luce was pleased with the demeanor and appearance of both women, especially Roxalana. He was relieved that she had not been goaded into making any comments to the local citizenry and especially the press. With the trial entering its sixth day, there was no shortage of reporters both in and outside the courthouse. His greatest concern had been Roxalana's explosive temper. A slip of the tongue or an offhand remark was just the kind of material that reporters would hasten to print.

Luce began his opening remarks for the defense of Roxalana Druse by retracing the life of this much-maligned woman. For over an hour, he described a Roxalana Druse that neither the press nor the prosecution knew.

"The prisoner," began Luce, "was born to poor but honest parents in the town of Marshall in 1842. At an early age, she was compelled to leave home by the death of her mother. She lived with relatives and friends until she was able to support herself. She reached womanhood without any blemish on her character and became a member of the Baptist Church in New Hartford. About 1861 she went into the town of Warren to pick hops . . . went three years in succession to pick for the same man, Mr. Northrup. She finally formed an association with William Druse and married him in 1864. Since then her life had been a hell on earth." Luce characterized Roxalana as an abused woman who carried the physical as well as mental scars of a loveless marriage. He told the court that there was abundant evidence to suggest that his client had feared for her life.

"Mrs. Druse was acting in self-defense," said Luce. "The Gates boy fired the fatal shot, and in that moment of frenzy, Mrs. Druse chopped his head off."

Luce cautioned the jury not to be overly impressed with the forensic display presented by Dr. Suiter. Denied access to this crucial evidence by an earlier court ruling, Luce claimed to have new evidence. Furthermore, he would prove that his client was a good person until her doomed marriage. "Bill Druse," said Luce, "demoralized [her] and made her what she is."

Luce began his attack on the prosecution's case by calling Glenville, New York, resident William Haselo to the stand. Five months earlier in May, the fifty-one-year-old farmer had made a gruesome discovery on his farm.

"I found part of a body," he told the court. "The head and arms were gone." Haselo told the court that he had seen something peculiar wash ashore near his farm on Viele Island in the Mohawk River. Horrified at the sight of the decomposed remains, Haselo immediately contacted the Schenectady County coroner. For a time, it appeared as if he was more concerned about the discovery than the coroner was.

"The coroner told me to bury the body on the spot where it lay, as not to make much expense to the county," continued Haselo.

From the time of the inquest at Little Lakes to the present, there had been a persistent rumor that the headless corpse of William Druse had been thrown into the Mohawk River. Luce certainly wanted to pursue this theory and now called on his own expert witness, Schenectady physician Lewis Faust.

"The arms, head, and neck were missing," said Dr. Faust, who was present when the body was exhumed three or four days later for an inquest. "I can't say whether the head had been cut off. If it had been cut off, it must have been by someone who understood anatomy pretty well. It might have been cut off by a heavy blow from some sharp instrument."

Surely his words conjured the image of an axe—an image that couldn't have been clearer to the jury. Dr. Faust said that the body discovered by William Haselo had been in the water for several months and was that of a male, approximately five-feet-eight or -ten inches tall. Faust admitted that a positive identification of the corpse would be impossible due to its advanced state of decomposition.

Luce proposed that the Viele Island corpse was indeed that of William Druse, and that a much wider conspiracy existed, one which the prosecution had conveniently set aside in its rush to judgment. How could a frail woman, weighing less than 100 pounds, wield an axe with such fury as to reduce a corpse to bone chips? Others had to be involved, notably Will Elwood and Charles Gates.

The introduction of this new evidence may have startled a few in the courtroom that day, but it did little to stir Abram Steele. He knew all about the discovery of the headless corpse, and how it could be linked to the Druse case. Faust may have testified about his observations at his own inquest, but he failed to mention that Dr. A. Walter Suiter was also there. Suiter went to Viele Island and later reported back to the district attorney's office that the corpse was indeed unidentifiable. He brought a portion of the clothing and the body back to his laboratory in Herkimer for, as he later said, "Repeated scientific examinations with a view of determining the identity of the same for the purpose of giving expert testimony in court."

Luce had raised an interesting question, but credibility was the deciding factor. It just didn't seem possible that a headless corpse could be transported from Hogsback Hill Road to Little Falls, fourteen miles away, tossed into the ice-clogged Mohawk River, and then drift to Viele Island over sixty miles away. Granted, at no time did Dr. Suiter ever claim that the bones discovered at Wall's Swamp were those of William Druse—but it was no coincidence that Frank Gates led the district attorney to them.

The second phase of the defense strategy began when Luce called upon Dr. William Griswold and his wife. The sixty-six-year-old physician from New Hartford had vivid memories of his former houseguest. Roxalana was a young lady, perhaps in her twenties, when she arrived at his house. Griswold told the court that the burns to her hands were serious and demanded almost constant care. For this reason, he invited her to stay at his home where she was welcomed as part of the family. The doctor stated that as far as he knew, her reputation was good in the community. After she left his house, he didn't see her again for almost eight years.

"State how she looked, acted, and appeared," Luce requested.

Steele objected, and before he was able to go any further, Judge Williams intervened and asked what Luce was trying to prove. Luce said that he was trying to show that her physical appearance had changed since leaving New Hartford.

"Do you propose to prove insanity?" asked the judge.

"No, sir," replied Luce.

Roxalana's sanity at the time of the murder had been firmly established; this was not the issue. Luce simply wanted the court to understand that her general condition had changed since she had left the Griswold home.

"What change do you offer to show in her condition; that she did not dress as well or looked careworn or what?"

"Yes, both," replied Luce.

Judge Williams ruled that the entire line of questioning was immaterial to the case. Having the doctor give his opinion on her physical appearance might lead some to believe that she had also changed mentally. Insanity, Judge Williams reminded Luce, was not an issue.

Having failed at this line of questioning, Luce called upon Mrs. Ann Eliza Griswold. As expected, the sixty-five-year-old wife of Dr. Griswold corroborated much of his testimony and painted a very favorable picture of Roxalana.

"I knew her then," said Mrs. Griswold. "I know her well . . . she bore a good reputation as any girl for aught I knew."

Mrs. Griswold couldn't say enough nice things about the girl they had welcomed into their home so many years ago. Not only was her disposition good; she regularly attended their church. Years later, Roxalana remembered her benefactors by paying them a visit. "She was a good girl. I did not notice any difference from her and other girls," she added.

Luce was pleased with the impression the Griswolds made on the court. How could anyone find fault with a respected physician like Dr. Griswold or question the sincerity of Mrs. Griswold? Luce needed another dozen witnesses like these to prove that his client was indeed a virtuous woman.

"I live in Warren. I know the defendant. I first became acquainted with her about twenty-one or twenty-two years ago," said Nancy Northrup. The Griswolds represented Roxalana's past, but Nancy Northrup was from her present; it was her family that had hired Roxalana to pick hops. Like the Griswolds, Nancy was quick to vouch for the good character of the woman who had worked temporarily at their farm some two decades ago.

"I never heard anything against her character. I should say it was good." she continued.

Abram Steele had been gentle when cross-examining the elderly Griswolds. Nancy Northrup would not be so fortunate. Tired of hearing repeatedly about the accused's "good character," Steele changed course and questioned the character of his witness.

"Where is your husband?" he inquired of Nancy Northrup.

"I am not living with my husband," answered Mrs. Northrup in a low tone. "He lives about two miles from me. I concede that he left me."

This admission on the part of Mrs. Northrup surprised many in the courtroom and gave some the impression that the Druse family wasn't the only one experiencing marital strife in Warren. Steele, discovering a weakness in this witness, moved in quickly to exploit it.

How can Roxalana Druse be of such sterling character, asked Steele, when rumors have circulated about the town of Warren regarding her penchant for stealing?

"I heard that she had stolen several things from a peddler who stopped overnight," said Nancy Northrup in a direct about-face, adding she had also heard that Roxalana had stolen butter, candles, and a gold ring from a neighbor who was now deceased. "I should say her general character, from the speech of the people, was not very good."

In a trial where one could not afford the slightest of errors, Luce had seriously blundered by not objecting to Steele's line of questioning. Mrs. Northrup's marital status was immaterial and should never have been entered into the record. More importantly, Luce never objected to the hearsay evidence that Roxalana had stolen from a peddler and a neighbor. Now she was portrayed as a petty thief as well as a murderess.

Completely unnerved by Steele's cross-examination, Nancy Northrup proved to be a very disappointing witness. The defense team fared better when Chester Crim took the stand. The proprietor of the general store that the Druse family frequented had no trouble remembering business transactions but experienced a lapse in memory when it came time to identify his own goods. When Luce presented him with exhibit 10, a copy of the store bill that had caused so much friction in the Druse household on the day of the murder, Crim recognized it immediately as the bill he had presented to Druse. Crim read it aloud, naming all the items Roxalana had charged and the lone gallon of kerosene her husband had paid for in cash.

In September of 1884—he couldn't be sure of the exact date—Crim said he sold a revolver to Charles Gates. "It was a pearl-handled seven shot .22-caliber," he stated.

Luce walked over to the table, picked up exhibit 3—the pearl-handled revolver that was recovered from Weatherbee's Pond—and presented it to Crim.

"I do not recognize it," said Crim. "I could not say that is the revolver; it looked about like that."

With no store ledger introduced as evidence and only his memory to rely on, how could Crim be so certain that he'd sold a revolver to Charles Gates?

"He paid me $2.95 . . . the price was $3.00. He was five cents short."

Steele couldn't believe that Crim was unable to recognize the weapon. Under cross-examination, he asked if this wasn't the same weapon purchased from his store by Charles Gates.

"I kept a good many revolvers like this one," said Crim, "and sold a good many different ones. I can't tell to whom now."

The fifty-eight-year-old shopkeeper was a far better witness than Nancy Northrup. Not intimidated by Steele, he refused to change his story. Unable to break Crim, the district attorney could ask only if Roxalana had made any additional purchases at his store. Crim recalled that Roxalana and Mary came to his store on December 22, 1884, and purchased wallpaper and an oilcloth. Ever the entrepreneur, Crim went on to say that wallpaper was not an unusual purchase at his store, and then took the opportunity to promote his establishment shamelessly by informing all in attendance that his inventory also included the very best in women's apparel, groceries, family items, and farm supplies.

This was a far better performance than Luce had expected. Crim had not only withstood the cross-examination but also inadvertently helped Roxalana by stating that she and her daughter arrived at his store on December 22 to purchase wallpaper, four days after the murder. This was a minor victory for the defense team and a small setback for the prosecution. Luce, who maintained all along that Roxalana had acted in self-defense, now knew that whatever happened, Steele could not prove that this was a premeditated act. His luck continued when an even stronger witness than Crim took the stand.

If any neighbor could elicit sympathy for the plight of Roxalana Druse, it was Dyer Lathrop. He had witnessed firsthand how miserable Bill Druse could be and minced few words when he told his story to the court. The forty-six-year-old farmhand and drover was quick to recall the time he had prevented Bill from striking Roxalana with a large stick.

"He was abusive a good deal of the time," he said. "I heard him fretting, scolding, and abusing Mrs. Druse considerable. She didn't used to say but very little—if anything she would cry." In addition, Lathrop scoffed at the idea that Bill Druse was a good provider: "If I had to say, there was no providing at all."

Despite the fact that this was the most compelling testimony thus far, Steele had to remind the court in his cross-examination that the incident recalled by Lathrop had not happened several months ago, but fifteen years ago.

What the defense needed was not a singular instance of abuse but an avalanche. Luce took the ultimate gamble with his next witness.

"I am nineteen years old, will be twenty the 22nd of February. I am the daughter of the defendant. William Druse was my father."

Everyone was anxious to hear from Mary Druse. Hers was the most eagerly awaited testimony since that of Frank Gates. Unable to produce more than a handful of neighbors who could testify to the abuse in the Druse household, Luce staked all he had on Mary's testimony. He skillfully asked questions that he knew would produce the most sympathy. If what Mary said under oath was true, then the Druse home surely was, as he had claimed, "a hell on Earth."

Over and over again, Mary recounted tales of abuse at the hands of her father. It appeared that no incident, great or trivial, escaped his wrath. Once, when a few cows made their escape by way of an unmended fence, the blame was shifted to her mother.

"He struck her in the head and choked her," recalled Mary. When a lame colt got loose, she said that her father became just as violent. "He took the horsewhip and hit mother four or five times over the head and back." Another incident prompted her father to strike her mother six or seven times with his fists.

It was a crescendo of domestic violence, the number of beatings increasing with each new story. From "four or five," it rose to "six or seven" times that Bill Druse had struck Roxalana. These stories were curious when one stopped to consider that young George Druse had testified that he'd never witnessed his father strike his mother. Mary was quick to point out that the verbal abuse was just as frightening.

"Once, we had a can of honey on the table. The cover to it had been broken and put back on. George had broken it and laid it back on the can. Father noticed it and asked her 'how in the hell she broke that cover?'" Mary related another occasion when her father grasped a pitchfork and warned her mother, "I will run your damned guts out with it!"

In one of her most harrowing tales, Mary vividly described how her father had put the entire family in danger. The family had been visiting the Northrups on a wintry Sunday afternoon, Mary recalled. As it became apparent that a storm was underway, Roxalana begged her husband to take them home while the roads were still passable. He refused to leave until he had finished reading a newspaper article about California. Mary said it was almost midnight when they finally left the Northrup home. It was a harrowing journey in a blinding snowstorm. About an hour away from their home, the sleigh skidded off the road and overturned.

"Mother had to carry George and set him down aways, and then go get Nellie and carry her," said Mary.

The sleigh mishap enraged her father, she said; he seemed to be more concerned about the horse than his children.

"By God, if you had stayed home, you Goddamned bitch, I would not have had to bother with you," she recalled her father saying.

In seventeen stories, Mary never missed a chance to quote a curse or describe a beating. Her eighteenth story was the one that would matter the most. She was asked by Luce to recall the events of that fateful December morning. At first there were only minor discrepancies: Frank and George were not asked to leave the house, claimed Mary, but left of their own accord to go sledding. Soon it became apparent that Mary had an entirely different story to tell.

It was after Roxalana had put the kettle on the stove for tea that the argument regarding the bill at Crim's store commenced. Mary said that her father grew enraged, rose from the table, and attacked her mother, beating her about the head and face with his fists.

"Then he grabbed hold of her and took his knife and said, 'By

God I will cut your damned throat right here.' I turned around to call the boys and heard a pistol shot."

This testimony recounted a decidedly different story from the one related by Frank and George, who swore that it was only after they heard what they believed were shots that Roxalana, not Mary, called them back to the house.

Conveniently forgetting to mention that she saw her mother fire the pistol, Mary did state that her mother gave the weapon to Frank Gates as he entered the house. She said that her cousin shot the weapon at least three times, and her father slumped to the floor.

"I ran into the parlor," said Mary. "I had no rope around father's neck—had no rope in my hand. I stayed in the parlor five or ten minutes after father was shot. When I came out, mother had fainted away. I got the camphor and some water and wet her face."

Mary told the court that her father had threatened her mother with the axe in much the same way the boys had testified, but said that she did not see her mother behead her father.

"I didn't look that way . . . I didn't want to see him." She also said that she took no part in dismembering the body. "I had no bone in my hand that day," she said in an effort to dispute her brother's testimony.

She then tried to distance herself from the crime by implicating others. Mary told the court that Will Elwood arrived at the house as her father's corpse was dragged into the parlor.

"Mother spoke to him. I don't know what she said. . . . I saw Elwood frequently after the killing. On one of these occasions he told me what had been done with Father's body. Charles Gates was also at our house frequently after the tragedy and had consultations with mother."

Mary's efforts to throw suspicion on both men fell flat. It was a well-known fact that Charles Gates had been exonerated by the coroner's inquest. It was Will Elwood who had a difficult time convincing the authorities that he had nothing to do with the murder. Elwood never denied seeing the newspaper-covered windows or the thick black smoke that filled the winter sky. His problems began at the inquest when Roxalana accused him of beheading her husband. If that wasn't bad enough, she further stated that Elwood had cut his arms and legs off and stuffed the limbs into the stove. A very nervous and fearful Will Elwood tried to explain his movements on the day of the murder, but it wasn't enough to convince

Abram Steele that he was completely innocent. At the conclusion of the inquest, Steele had him arrested, charging him with accessory after the fact, and had him remanded to the county jail.

Fortunately for Elwood, his stay there was brief. Two weeks after his arrest, sympathetic neighbors in and around Warren obtained his release by posting $2,000 bail. Later, when more details of the crime came to light, Steele had the charge against Elwood dismissed.

That both Charles Gates and Will Elwood were innocent mattered little to the nineteen-year-old girl in court that day. Mary had presented a vivid and disturbing reminiscence of her childhood.

"Father was not kind to his children or his wife. He went away from home most every day and sometimes stayed away several days. He was very slack about his work, generally left his farming implements on the lot, and usually they laid out all winter."

H. DeWight Luce returned to his seat. He could only hope that this narrative of domestic abuse would impress a jury comprised of family men. If the jurors were swayed by Mary's remarks, the effect didn't last long. Abram Steele stepped forward and set the tone of the cross-examination with one question.

"Do you know what you were arrested for?"

"Yes, sir," answered Mary.

Luce objected to this question immediately, and before Judge Williams could speak, Steele quickly rephrased it and asked if Mary understood why she was arrested, to which Luce objected again. The rap of the gavel ended the sparring between the two attorneys.

Mary hesitated to respond to the question and said quietly, "I don't know." Timid, shy, and frightened, she was no match for Steele.

The cross-examination of Nancy Northrup was nothing compared to what Steele had in mind for Mary Druse. He would be as ruthless as the court would allow.

When asked about her arrest, Mary told the court that neighbors were at the farmhouse questioning her and her mother. Steele thought that this was interesting and asked Mary if she could recall the specific details of these conversations. At this, Mary became very forgetful. Steele wondered how this could be. Just a short while ago, she had claimed that she could recall details of her youth since, as she said, "I was five years old." Now specific details regarding a conversation about a murder that had occurred the previous December were met with "I don't know" or "I don't recollect."

Anxious to get to the bottom of the Charles Gates controversy, Steele asked Mary for specific details regarding her uncle's visits to the farmhouse on the day of the murder. Mary claimed that not only was he at the house that morning but also that he had plied her with liquor before the shooting! When asked why she didn't mention this at the inquest, she answered that she "didn't think it was that important."

"I don't recollect whether I stated that in substance," said Mary. "I did not tell Dr. Suiter it was Charles Gates because it was Chester Gates that did it. I think I told Dr. Suiter that either Charles or Chester commenced firing at my father. . . I know that Chester Gates did fire at my father that morning. He shot. It was after I called Frank. Chester came in the parlor and he remained in the parlor from the time he gave me the liquor up to the time father was shot."

If Mary had set out to confuse the jury with this story, she was doing a good job. By the time she finished, it was unclear which Gates plied her with liquor, which Gates fired the first shot, and which Gates ran into the parlor. An angry Steele wanted to know why she suddenly remembered this piece of crucial evidence when she so conveniently forgot the simplest details of the murder.

From this point on, the district attorney directed his questions to the girl based upon what was recorded in the minutes of the inquest. He would prove that she had been an unreliable witness at the inquest and was also guilty of perjury at her mother's trial. When asked how many shots were fired, Mary claimed as many as twenty-one or twenty-two shots had been discharged. Steele reminded her that this was impossible, given the testimony of Frank Gates and the forensic evidence concerning the few shell casings that Dr. Suiter had presented. Mary paused and amended that number to an even dozen, claiming that these shots came from the direction of the parlor and not the kitchen.

"On the night you were arrested did you state in my presence that you saw your mother cut your father's head off?" asked Steele.

"No, sir."

"In Mr. McDonald and Mr. Marshall's presence and also in the presence of Frank Gates?"

"No, sir."

"And then afterwards state in the same conversation that you stood at the door?"

"No, sir."

"Were you playing the organ at the time your father's head was cut off?"

"I don't remember—I don't know when it was cut off."

"Which is it—you don't remember or you don't know?"

"I don't know."

"Did you, when Frank Gates described your mother cutting your father's head off, say to him, 'Frank Gates, why do you stand there and lie so?'"

"I don't remember."

"And then did you say, 'Well, it is my mother?'"

"I might have said so," answered Mary.

Steele hammered away at Mary Druse for over two and a half hours. There was nothing H. DeWight Luce could do. Because the inquest minutes had been deemed admissible evidence, Mary could not escape what she had said either privately or on the record. With each denial, she was presented with another statement she had made. She denied saying, "We planned to kill him, but no special time was set," but insisted that Will Elwood was a willing accomplice. At one point Mary claimed that Elwood had offered to drown her father in McDonald's pond.

Her denials and fabrications were so numerous that the *Richfield Springs Mercury* refused to print them, instead telling readers "Mary made wholesale denial of certain facts."

Mentally exhausted after her ordeal with Steele, Mary repeated the events of that morning one last time to the jury, as if to cry out for sympathy. Following an entire afternoon of fabrications and denials, it was interesting to note that some of what she said was true. However, most of this was to protect herself and her mother. She carefully omitted any mention of the beheading and the part she had played—dragging her father from the table with a rope around his neck.

"The job was finished," she said, "after the shots had been fired. Father was dead. I think he was. I don't know where Mother went when Father fell off the chair. I was so frightened I went into the parlor when I saw him fall. I didn't see what Mother did after that. She did not bring the head into the parlor while I was in there. I did not notice Father when I went out because I didn't like to look at him. I didn't look to see if he was dead. Nothing was said about sending for a doctor. After Father was taken into the parlor, I pinned papers up to the windows and then watched at one of the windows."

If Mary Druse was relieved to be free of Abram Steele's cross-examination, her feeling was shared by H. DeWight Luce. With the jumbled, perjured testimony of Mary Druse fresh in the jurors' minds, Luce was anxious to move ahead and introduce new witnesses who could speak favorably about his client. He hoped that his next witness, New Hartford native Mary Wakely, could stun the jury into forgetting some of Mary's testimony. And she had a story to tell that could do just that. When Roxalana was not a guest of the Griswold family, she was frequently at Mary Wakely's home.

"I considered her a very good girl," said Mrs. Wakely. Unlike the Griswolds, she hadn't lost contact with Roxalana after her marriage to Bill Druse.

"I went to the town of Warren once," she recalled, "about seventeen or eighteen years ago. Roxalana had two children; the oldest one was about two or three years old. While I was there, he [Bill Druse] put his oldest little girl in a nude condition and set her to dancing before his wife, myself, and the hired man."

It was a stunning revelation that sent a shock throughout the courtroom. When Abram Steele questioned the validity of the remark, the feisty sixty-three-year-old declared, "I couldn't repeat what I did not see."

For the next two days, Luce paraded nine Warren residents before the jury in a vain hope that sheer numbers might have an impact on the jury and make up for the weak evidence presented by some of the other witnesses. In this he was only partially successful.

Mary Northrup took the stand and described how she first became acquainted with Roxalana during hop-picking season in the fall of 1862.

"I have known her up to the present time," she said. "I considered her character good."

As for the story Mary Druse had told about leaving the Northrup home in a blinding snowstorm, Mary Northrup readily admitted that she could not recall this particular incident. She did recall, however, how Roxalana had cared for her elderly mother.

"I went off and trusted her there alone with my mother, and mother is blind. All I know about trouble between her and her husband is hearsay from her."

Mary Northrup had inadvertently supplied Abram Steele with the one word that he would use to destroy her testimony. No one save Mary Northrup had ever used the word trust in describing a relationship with Roxalana Druse, and Steele wanted to make sure no one ever would. When cross-examined, Mary Northrup was asked if her opinion of her friend had changed after she learned of the murder of William Druse.

"I have only spoken of her character previous to the last four years," she said. Then, in a direct about-face, Mary Northrup proceeded to ruin her old friend. "I heard some things against her. I heard that she stole a pocketbook from my mother. I heard the story about her breaking into the Turpening house when they were away. I heard that a peddler lost things at her house while staying there overnight on December 18 last. From the speech of people I would call her character bad."

Once again, Luce had erred. He should have stopped the cross-examination of this witness the moment she said, "I heard." Allowing hearsay evidence regarding a purported theft at the Northrup house or the Turpening residence or even the supposed loss of items from a wayfaring peddler did little to help his client's credibility. Steele had successfully erased the word trust from the minds of the jurors and replaced it with thief.

When former hired man Francis Simmons took the stand, he claimed to have intervened in a domestic squabble at the Druse farm in the summer of 1867.

"After I got to bed, Mrs. Druse called me. She wanted me to come downstairs. Mr. Druse had her by the wrist and was pushing her up, back and forth, against the wall. I told Druse to let go, and he did."

Once again, this incident had occurred a long time ago, but another hired man could make a more recent claim. James Cassidy had worked on the Stewart Druse farm. The Springfield native lived next door to Rhoda Bowen, Bill Druse's sister, and was working at the Druse farm when Stewart died in 1880. Cassidy had vivid memories of what had taken place at the funeral of his former employer.

"He was laid out in a black suit," said Cassidy.

"I object to this question," said Steele.

"Sustained."

"After he was laid out, did William Druse come in there?"

"He did."

Again, Steele voiced his objection.

"Sustained."

"After William Druse came to the house, I was called to the house."

At this moment, Judge Williams interrupted Cassidy and asked him if Mrs. Druse was also there. Cassidy said that she wasn't, and Luce was quick to explain his line of questioning.

"We offer to show," said Luce, "that after Stewart Druse was laid out in a black suit of clothes, that William Druse came to the house, that [the] witness was sent for and went into the house, and William was kicking up a row and making a fuss and wanted to take the clothes off his dead father. He [Cassidy] took the clothes off the corpse, and Bill Druse helped him, and he took them away with him. We offer to prove it for the purpose of showing the character of William Druse—an element of his character."

"The whole matter of what occurred at his father's funeral is excluded as incompetent," said the Judge, "the defendant not being there and there being no pretense that there was any transaction between husband and wife."

Luce was not pleased by the judge's decision. What did it matter that Roxalana was not present at the funeral? She wasn't present when her husband was at his neighbors' homes reading their newspapers, yet this testimony was not stricken from the record. A frustrated and disappointed Luce had no other recourse but to continue to concentrate on witnesses who could promote the image of Roxalana as an abused spouse. Once more, he had to rely on a Northrup.

The testimony of Julia Northrup was similar to that of the other Northrup women. Julia recalled how Roxalana arrived at her family's farm in 1862.

"She came well recommended," said Julia. Although she admitted that she hadn't been to the Druse house in over a year, she said it was an experience she would never forget. "I saw what they had for supper; they had mashed potatoes and butter. That was all I saw."

Encouraged by this singular description of want within the Druse household, Luce moved ahead and asked Julia if she was witness to any verbal or physical confrontations between husband and wife. Julia stated that she personally never witnessed any difficulties, but she did recall the time they left her home in the snowstorm.

"I can't state how old George was," she said.

This was good news to Luce. This admission gave credence to the previous testimony of Mary Druse. As to the rumors of Roxalana stealing from a peddler and from the Turpening house, Julia Northrup was firm on the subject—they were just that—rumors.

Of the handful of witnesses remaining, only one, Rozelle Warren, was able to add more, than "her reputation was good," or "his reputation was bad," to the court record. Warren lived about three-quarters of a mile from the Druse farm, and the fifty-year-old father of two had been a frequent visitor there. Rozelle Warren said that in all the years he had known Bill Druse, he believed that his reputation for honesty was generally good.

"I never heard of his quarreling with his neighbors," said Warren. But there was something that had always bothered him. He had on one occasion witnessed that Roxalana's face was "bee-stung very badly," as if she had been beaten.

"In forming the estimate of his character, did you take into consideration the fact that he was an infidel?" asked Luce.

"I have heard him say myself," replied Warren.

Steele sat quietly and let the question pass. What did it matter if Bill Druse was an infidel? It was common knowledge throughout Warren that he never attended church and that he worked on Sundays, but the same could be said of Roxalana. She had never made an effort to attend church either. He did, however, object to the next question.

"Did you also take into consideration the fact that you heard he had robbed his father of his grave clothes and wore them to his funeral?"

Luce tried to explain his motive for asking this question, but he was cut short by an angry Judge Williams. Luce was reminded that the affair of the funeral clothes had been previously ruled as inadmissible evidence. Ignoring this sharp rebuke, Luce moved ahead with a series of questions designed to portray Bill Druse as one of the most heartless villains of all time. He asked Warren if he was aware that Bill Druse had tossed his own mother out of her home when she was dying of cancer, and if he had heard that Bill Druse had ill-treated his own father and sister. Did he provide well for his family? Was he cruel to his farm animals?

Almost all of these questions were met with objections by Steele, and one in particular was questioned by Judge Williams. He failed to see how cruelty to one's farm animals could be equated with cruelty to one's family. The judge had ruled this as inadmissible evidence when Luce asked the same question of Van Evera, and he was making the ruling again. At this point, Luce announced that he had no further questions or witnesses. As the defense attorney returned to his seat, the judge asked if the prosecution was prepared to proceed with its closing arguments.

Steele announced that the people wished to recall several witnesses. It was his final opportunity to completely discredit Mary Druse's testimony, and he took full advantage of it by calling nine witnesses. Clarence Marshall described in detail his conversation with Mary Druse after her arrest, as did Dr. Irving O. Nellis. Both men offered rebuttal evidence that Mary had told them a completely different story than the one she told in court. Justice of the Peace Daniel McDonald did the same. According to McDonald, the girl had essentially related what had happened on that terrible December day, and it was only later that she embellished the story with numerous fabrications.

"My energies," McDonald told the court, "have not been used to convict this woman and screen Gates and Elwood. I talked with Mary for fifteen or twenty minutes. This was before she had employed counsel. Mary was at my house from Saturday evening, January 18, to Monday morning. In all that I did, I did what I thought was right. I was not working for or against the defendant. I am wholly impartial in this case."

The next several witnesses were tedious and to some extent boring. Irving Eckler, for example, offered that he could not recall escorting Roxalana and the children home from his farm, an incident Mary claimed had occurred ten years earlier.

"I don't think I could remember anything [that happened] ten years ago," said Luce in his cross-examination, "unless my woman caught me in bed with some other woman and drew a revolver on me!"

Laughter filled the courtroom. It was a rare moment of levity, a lighthearted respite from days of horrific stories and tension. A tired district attorney and an equally exhausted defense attorney approached the judge and asked if the court might be adjourned until Monday. It was already late on Friday afternoon, and both men agreed that the weekend would be sufficient time for them to prepare their closing remarks. Judge Williams was not that accommodating: the trial had lasted eight days, and he saw no reason for any further delays. He denied their request and announced that court would resume at 10 a.m. the next day, Saturday, October 3, 1885.

CHAPTER 6

The Spiritual Advisor and the Suffragette

Sheriff Valentine Brown looked out his office window at the crowd that had gathered by the Herkimer County Courthouse steps. It was a bit larger than usual, but that was to be expected; the date was October 3, 1885, and closing arguments for the Druse trial were to begin. Many, including the sheriff, expected a quick decision from the jury. It was almost 10 a.m. when Roxalana and Mary were taken from their cells and brought to his office. As he had done so many times in the past, Sheriff Brown escorted his prisoners out of the jail, past the crowd, and into the courthouse. Flanked on either side by deputies, the women walked down the aisle of the courtroom filled with reporters, well-wishers, former friends and neighbors, and the curious. Roxalana smiled graciously and seated herself in the prisoner's box with her usual aplomb. Her daughter Mary could not echo the outward appearance of self-confidence exhibited by her mother; seated beside Roxalana, she was in all respects alone. Oblivious to the circumstances surrounding the events of the past several days, Mary had perhaps fewer supporters than her mother. No one really knew if she was frightened, confused, or naively ignorant about what was soon to follow.

The atmosphere in the courtroom resembled a theatrical performance during intermission before the last act. The clamor of the crowd subsided briefly when Roxalana entered the room but quickly resumed when the jurors were escorted to their seats. As usual, Roxalana peered intently at the twelve men who would soon decide her fate.

Sheriff Brown glanced at the jury from a much different perspective. Few in the courtroom realized that both Roxalana and the jury were his responsibility. Each day of the trial, his deputies were required to escort the jury to and from the Waverly Hotel to the courthouse. Brown's sincere desire was to make the jurors as comfortable as possible during what he hoped would be their brief stay in Herkimer. The previous Sunday, for example, he had invited all twelve to attend services at the Methodist Church, and then come to his home for dinner. He also felt duty bound to protect the jury from any contact with an ever-vigilant press. Brown could easily identify local newspaper reporters, but now there were journalists representing newspapers from all across the state in town. Every large upstate paper was represented, and the New York City papers were only a click away via Western Union telegraph.

When the court was called to order, H. DeWight Luce knew he had to make his final remarks as dramatic as possible if he was to convince the jury of his client's innocence. Standing before the jurors, he made a sweeping motion with his hand, pointing directly at Roxalana.

"This is a weak and friendless woman," he declared in a voice that filled every ear in the courtroom.

He was right. Roxalana Druse was friendless, and this in itself was the weakest part of his defense. Sadly, in the twenty years Roxalana had been a resident of the town of Warren, she had failed to develop any friendships. Luce had been hard-pressed to find anyone who could come forward and say, "This is my very best friend." Those few who did step forward to say that she was a "good girl" or a "virtuous woman," were for the most part elderly individuals whose recollections dated from twenty years earlier, when Roxalana had lived in New Hartford. She may have attended the Baptist church in New Hartford, but she never attended any church in Warren. No ministers spoke in her favor to say that she was a member of their congregation. In fact, even her closest neighbors offered little insight about her life or the couple's relationship. Where was Mrs. Pett or Mrs. Eckler? Not even the Northrups claimed to be close to Roxalana.

Perhaps it was with this in mind that Luce shifted his defense strategy. In an attempt to draw strength from this weakness, Luce claimed that Roxalana became friendless when she moved to Warren and married Bill Druse—he was the real villain, she the innocent victim. It was Bill Druse who had promised to "love, cherish, and protect" Roxalana, but instead subjected her to countless cruelties, including abuse and starvation.

Luce reminded the jury that he had produced more than enough witnesses who had seen Bill Druse's violent outbursts. No one, especially his wife and children, was immune to his erratic behavior. Luce backed up this statement by reminding those present of young George Druse's earlier testimony: he could not give one instance

Rev. George W. Powell

where his father was kind to her.

"William Druse," said the defense attorney, "was a demon in human shape."

Another weak point in his defense of Roxalana was the muddled testimony offered by her daughter. Luce remarked that this was inevitable, given the methods employed by the prosecution.

"[Daniel] McDonald and [Clarence] Marshall have followed these women like human bloodhounds and have sought them night and day to try to obtain a confession from them. They did get one, but it was a made-up story, such as you, gentlemen, would tell if two imposters were trying to pry into your affairs. These two hirelings have been trying to get evidence to hang these poor women."

It wasn't only Mary's statements that were closely scrutinized but those made by her brother as well. Luce said he couldn't help but notice the inconsistencies in several statements made by the star witness for the prosecution. George claimed that he never saw his father physically abuse his mother, and then said that he witnessed her being thrashed on several occasions. Which was it, or did it really matter?

"You heard little George on the stand swearing his mother's life away," declared Luce with melodramatic flare. "The mother who cared for him so long. . . . He told his story in a studied manner, and gentlemen, he has been promised something."

Everyone present that day knew the promise was immunity from prosecution. For George it was understandable; for Frank Gates, it was not. George was for all intents an innocent bystander. He did not aid in committing the crime, nor did he willingly assist in trying to cover it up. Frank Gates, on the other hand, had grievously wounded his uncle with several gunshots yet would be forgiven in return for his cooperation at the trial.

After a brief lunch recess, Amos Prescott, Luce's assistant, rose to deliver the concluding remarks. Thus far, Prescott had played a minor role in the defense of Roxalana. He had assisted Luce in the cross-examination of several witnesses, but for the most part remained in the background throughout most of the trial.

"Men and women often do wrong," said Prescott in a serious and solemn voice. "The poor woman at the bar is no exception." There could be no question in anyone's mind that a wrong had been committed, but Prescott expressed his doubts that all the witnesses furnished by the prosecution could prove what had really happened on Hogsback Hill Road. Prescott added that he found it very difficult to accept the evidence of the forensic team of experts; the bone chips and fragments studied by Drs. Suiter and Deecke proved nothing. "It is impossible for any man to tell after bones have been burned where they belong on the human skeleton," said Prescott. "No man can tell." Besides, he continued, it was physically impossible for a frail woman like his client to reduce a human body to bits and pieces. "If this poor, unfortunate woman did what they tried to make out that she did, I think her the most remarkable woman I ever saw. I don't believe she is smart enough to do it."

For Prescott, there were too many unanswered questions in the Druse case—questions that the prosecution conveniently ignored. He found it disturbing that some witnesses were never called to testify at the trial. Mary Druse had sworn under oath that her uncle, Charles Gates, was at the farmhouse the morning of the murder; why, then, wasn't he questioned at the trial? The same could be said of Will Elwood. Both men had figured prominently in the statements made by Mary Druse. Both had been arrested, and yet neither of them was called to account for his actions during the trial.

"It is a mystery to me," declared Prescott, "why these bloodthirsty neighbors are so anxious to convict this poor woman, unless it is to hide one of their own."

Some witnesses were never called, and some could not be interviewed. Luce and Prescott were never allowed access to Frank Gates and George Druse while they were being held in the county jail. They were charged as accessories to the murder but had not yet reached an agreement with Abram Steele regarding immunity. They were suspects, the same as Roxalana and Mary. "We," said Prescott in his final statement to the jury, "have not had a fair show in this trial."

Abram Steele believed that the evidence and witnesses presented by the people left no doubt in anyone's mind as to what had happened on Hogsback Hill Road. For well over two hours, he carefully reviewed the facts of the entire case before the jury. He stressed the importance of the forensic evidence that Prescott was so quick to dismiss. It was important to consider that two physicians had reviewed the evidence, and each had reached the same conclusion: these were human remains. Adding to the credibility of these two men was the fact that a witness, Frank Gates, had led authorities to the location of these remains. Enough physical evidence was presented to show clearly that a terrible murder had taken place. From fake telegrams to fresh paint and wallpaper, Roxalana Druse had done everything in her power to cover up her crime. She was not to be pitied or forgiven for what she had done to her husband.

"No matter how bad he was," said Steele, "how little he went to church, or [whether he] worked on Sundays, how much profanity he used towards his wife, how ill he provided for his family, how many times or how cruelly he beat or pounded his wife, or how many indecent epithets he applied to her, she was not by reason of any or all of these things excused or justified in killing him. The vilest man in the world has the same right to live with the noblest and the best. The law prohibits the killing of any human being."

Days later, a reporter from the *Utica Sunday Times* would write that Abram Steele "presented the people's case in a masterly style."

Those in attendance who expected a brief recess after the two-and-a-half-hour summation by the district attorney were surprised. Despite the late hour—it was 5:20 p.m. on Saturday—Judge Williams was determined to continue with the proceedings. He addressed the twelve men who had sat patiently for the past nine days, thanking them for their honesty and their courage as part of this legal proceeding.

"You have, at more or less personal inconvenience to yourselves, sat here day after day and listened patiently to the evidence produced before you."

This had been a celebrated trial, and perfect copy for a press hungry for a good story. Judge Williams warned the jurors that their duty could not be influenced by anything that was said outside of the courtroom before the trial or while it was in progress.

"You should lay aside all feelings of prejudice or of favor for the people or the defendant," he said. "You should entirely disregard anything you may have read, or any opinion or impression you may have formed before entering the jury box. A defendant in a criminal action is presumed innocent until the contrary is proved."

The most important legal principle—innocent until proven guilty—could not be possible if the jury failed to weigh carefully all the facts presented to them. He told the jury that this, in turn, could not be possible unless all of the evidence was considered, and none of it dismissed as unimportant.

Judge Williams admitted that the most striking piece of evidence in the Druse trial was the collection of bone fragments recovered from Wall's Swamp. The interpretation of this evidence by the expert witnesses, Drs. Suiter and Deecke, was just as compelling.

"They testify in their opinion that these refuse bones are those of a human skeleton, and they can localize, that is to say, tell what part of the human skeleton some belong to," said Williams. One could not dismiss the fact that these remains were recovered with the aid of the prosecution's chief witness, Frank Gates. As credible as this seemed, Judge Williams also asked the jury to consider the evidence offered by the defense. Was the decomposed, headless corpse that washed ashore on Viele Island that of William Druse?

"You must be the judge," said Williams to the jury, "whether it [the body of William Druse] was cut up and burned there in the house or thrown in the river. . . ."

It was just as important, he told them, to consider carefully the testimony of the children. All three gave stirring accounts of the last hours of William Druse's life; there were, however, some glaring discrepancies. His instructions to the jury could not have been clearer. "The real question," he said, "is for you to determine which of these persons is substantially telling the truth."

Frank Gates and George Druse had told essentially the same story, but Mary Druse had insisted that other family members and neighbors were present. The jury also had to consider verbal attacks leading up to the physical assault. What happened that morning? Was there a heated argument about a store bill that led to Roxalana being threatened by her husband with an axe, as Frank and George recalled? Or was Roxalana attacked by a knife-wielding husband, as Mary had claimed? Was this a case of self-defense?

Judge Williams also cautioned the jury about another form of evidence. "Confessional evidence," he warned them, "needs to be considered. It is a dangerous kind of evidence. It is to be looked at carefully, considered carefully." Were some of the statements obtained by threatening the children with imprisonment if they did not cooperate, or was there a promise of immunity if they did? Did they initially make false statements, and then later recant at the trial? "All these things," he told the jury, "you are to consider."

The only thing that remained for the judge to do was to explain to the jury the definition of the crime itself. For this he quoted directly from the *New York State Penal Code*.

"Homicide," he said, "is the killing of one human being, by the act, procurement, or omission of another. Homicide is either murder, manslaughter, excusable homicide, or justifiable homicide." He paused for a moment and told the jury that they would have to decide what type of homicide took place on Hogsback Hill Road that December morning. Murder and manslaughter were crimes; excusable homicide and justifiable homicide were not. Reading once again from the *Penal Code*, the judge recited the definition of murder as "a deliberate and premeditated design to effect the death of the person."

Setting the law book aside, he looked at the jury and asked, "Did this woman, having prepared it beforehand, steal up behind the deceased as he sat at the table and shoot him and then follow it up?"

Excusable homicide was not an option for the jury to consider, and Judge Williams made this quite clear. Referring again to the *Penal Code*, he said this could occur only by "accident and misfortune, in lawfully correcting a child or servant . . . without any unlawful intent." He instructed the jury to ignore this and to concentrate on the definition of justifiable homicide. Was Roxalana, as the law stated, "the subject of some great personal injury" or in "imminent danger" at the hands of her abusive husband? Was this homicide committed by the defendant in self-defense? Once again, he urged the jury to exercise extreme caution with this issue.

"The treatment of each other by the other is a proper matter for consideration. . . . If they had always, therefore, been an affectionate and loving couple; had no quarrels, no words, but had always treated each other with kindness, she would not have been likely to believe so readily, even if such an attack was threatened. The people here do not claim that they were always a loving and affectionate couple—if they had been, there would have been no homicide at all."

Finally, the judge reminded the jurors that they had heard countless individuals testify to everything from quarrels, name-calling, and threats to thrashings and beatings, that made up the loveless marriage of Roxalana and Bill Druse. Evidence presented by both the prosecution and the defense clearly showed that this was an embattled couple.

"Now, gentlemen, you will consider all this evidence, weigh it all, and determine what the real condition of things was between these two people. . . . The guilt of the defendant should be determined by the facts and evidence presented in this case. However, Mrs. Druse could be declared innocent only if the evidence convinces you beyond a reasonable doubt. . . . You have an important duty to perform, one which calls upon you to exercise your best intelligence and judgment. You will, I have no doubt, perform this duty faithfully, honestly, and fearlessly. You will listen to no public sentiment or popular clamor that may be imagined or known to exist. You are the sole judges of the facts here. For your verdict you are answerable to no man or class of men; you are answerable to no human court or tribunal; you are answerable alone to your own conscience and to your God."

Stillness fell over the courtroom as Judge Pardon C. Williams completed his remarks. With a slight nod from the judge, the twelve men of the jury rose to their feet and were escorted to the jury room by a sheriff's deputy. It was 7 p.m., and many in the courtroom retained their seats in anticipation of a quick decision.

An hour went by, and Sheriff Brown walked slowly to the prisoner's box. He leaned toward Roxalana and whispered softly to her, asking if she would rather go back to the jail. Regardless of the circumstances, the two women had been sitting in the prisoner's box since 1:30 p.m. Both were tired and hungry.

It didn't take long for others to follow Sheriff Brown's lead. By 10 p.m. there were only a handful of people left in the courtroom, and an hour later there were hardly any. At midnight, the village bell and the Reformed Church bell tolled the hour, and ten minutes later, the courthouse bell could be heard, a sign that the jury had reached a decision. The sheriff sent word to the Druse women to prepare for a return trip to the courthouse.

The courthouse bell roused not only the Sheriff but also a great number of Herkimer citizens and others. Despite the late hour, almost 400 people made their way back to the courtroom. When Roxalana and Mary had once again taken their seats in the prisoner's box and everyone else was settled, Judge Williams spoke. Roxalana sat upright in her chair and tried to display as little emotion as possible.

"Gentlemen of the jury, have you reached your decision?"

"Yes, your Honor, we have. We find the defendant guilty of murder in the first degree."

Gasps, sighs, and shrieks filled the courtroom. As the verdict was announced, Roxalana's composed expression changed quickly to one of shock. Mary broke down and wept. Judge Williams thanked the jury and adjourned the court. Much to the disappointment of the multitude of reporters present, the judge announced that the sentencing of Roxalana Druse would take place on Monday.

When the mentally and emotionally exhausted women returned to their cells, they had no idea that their attorney was still trying to help them. When the court reconvened on Tuesday after a postponement, H. DeWight Luce made a motion for a new trial, citing irregularities with the jury. Luce charged that juror Calvin Babcock of Newport had left the Waverly Hotel and "did separate from the other members of said jury." Luce claimed that this was in direct violation of the specific instructions given to the jury by Judge Williams that "they must be kept together and should not separate until the case was finally determined and they were discharged."

Abram Steele was visibly angered by this motion and moved to have it dismissed. No less angry was Judge Williams, who quickly ruled against Luce.

The incident in question had taken place on the second day of the trial. Calvin Babcock had gone to the Allman House, a few blocks from the Waverly Hotel, but he was not alone. Deputy Dewitt Jenkins accompanied him. In a sworn statement, Jenkins said that Babcock went to the Allman house to retrieve his coat and to pay an outstanding bill of twenty-five cents for boarding his horse. Jenkins swore that Babcock did not converse with anyone about the trial.

With the motion set aside, Judge Williams ordered the defendant to stand.

"You have been, by the verdict of the jury, found guilty of murder in the first degree in having caused the death of William Druse, your husband, on the 18th day of December 1884, in the town of Warren, Herkimer County. Have you anything to say why the judgment for this crime should not be pronounced against you?"

"No," said Roxalana in a low whisper.

The Judge continued:

"The court, the jury, and the public generally have patiently waited through a somewhat lengthy trial of your case to hear and consider all the evidence given upon the one side and the other, in order that there might be a perfect understanding of the real facts in the case. The trial has shown that there is no dispute but that you caused the death of your husband and chopped the head from his body in the actual presence of your children, the one a little boy of ten years of age. And the evidence leaves but little doubt of your having then cut up the body and burned it in the stove in the house, using your little boy to aid you in bringing you from the brush lot the axe to cut up the body and shingles for fuel to burn it. These things are hardly credible, yet they are practically admitted to be true. The only defense attempted to be made for you has been that you did this killing in the lawful defense of your person, from an alleged attack made upon you by your husband.

"You have had in the trial the assistance and best efforts of able counsel, and all that could well be done has been done by them to establish this defense and secure your acquittal. The court has afforded you every opportunity consistent with its duty—sometimes trespassing upon the rights of the people— to defend yourself against this charge; but upon the evidence there appears to be no manner of doubt but that you deliberately caused the death of your husband without any justifiable cause therefore, that you stole up behind him while he sat quietly eating at the table and made the attack which resulted in his death. The jury has found you guilty of the crime and its verdict has the approval of the court, and I believe of all who have listened to the trial and heard the evidence in the case. There is no occasion now for the court to indulge in any unkindly words toward you.

"For this crime you will certainly forfeit your life. It is a sad thing that a woman should be executed, but the nature of the crime, the horrible manner in which it was committed and the body disposed of, will surely prevent the exercise of any executive clemency to save your life. You may as well realize this, and do what little you can while you live to repair the great wrong you have done your husband, your children, and yourself.

"The last duty of this court with reference to this case is now to be performed. The judgment of the law is that for the crime of murder in the first degree, of which you stand convicted, you suffer the punishment of death. This punishment will be inflicted by and under the direction of the sheriff of Herkimer County, by hanging you by the neck until dead, within the walls of the jail of the county or a yard or enclosure adjoining. While awaiting the execution of the judgment, you will be confined in the jail of the county.

The day appointed upon which the judgment must be executed is the 25th day of November 1885, between the hours of 10 o'clock in the forenoon and 4 o'clock in the afternoon of that day."

After the sentence was pronounced, Roxalana sank to her chair and sobbed hysterically. Consoled by the sheriff, she was escorted out of the courthouse and returned to her cell.

A week later, it was Mary's turn. Once again, the courtroom was filled with eager spectators. It was a scene that had been played out repeatedly, except now there was a glaring discrepancy. For the first time, the deputies escorted only Mary from the jail to the courthouse. Her mother, who had been a source of strength to her in the past, remained locked in her cell. Her mother's absence had very little to do with how Mary was perceived by the public that day. As she had done so many times in the past, the girl stared at the floor and avoided eye contact as she was led to the prisoner's box. If she had glanced upward for a brief moment, she would have seen many familiar figures present at her mother's trial, notably her cousin and her little brother.

H. DeWight Luce greeted his client, and the two shared a brief conversation before Judge Williams entered the courtroom. When the court was called to order, Mary looked up and gently nodded to her attorney. Luce rose and addressed the court. He stated that at this time his client wished to withdraw her original plea of not guilty and enter a plea of guilty of murder in the second degree.

There was hardly time for the crowd to react to this plea reversal when Abram Steele announced that the people were willing to accept the offer. The district attorney was pleased that Luce had been able to reason with his client. Another protracted trial would be fruitless. Clearly Mary was guilty of assisting her mother and had thwarted the prosecution's case with one fanciful tale after another. Steele looked upon Mary as an impressionable girl who was intimidated, if not completely dominated, by her mother.

Judge Williams asked Mary if this is what she desired. "You understand the punishment provided for that offense?"

"Yes, sir," she replied.

"You stand here convicted upon your own plea of guilty of murder in the second degree, in having caused the death of William Druse, your father, in the town of Warren, Herkimer County, on the 18th day of December 1884. Have you anything to say why judgment of the law for this crime should not be pronounced against you?"

"No, sir," she answered.

Mary may not have looked up, but Judge Williams never took his eyes off her. He made it clear that she was to be punished for the part she played in the murder of her own father. This was a horrible crime, one for which she should be, and would be, punished. Judge Williams expressed his hope that during this time of imprisonment she would change and become a better person.

"Mary, I need not refer to the circumstances under which the crime was committed. We all understand them. I have regarded it as a proper exercise of judicial power and discretion to permit you to make this plea, to accept it and to pronounce judgment against you for this degree of crime.

"The public has been disturbed long enough by the recital, publication, and consideration of the terrible details of this crime. It is well to avoid another trial, which would be necessary if this plea should not be accepted. However guilty you may be under the law of the first degree of murder, still you were a girl of eighteen years of age and acted in committing the crime in the presence and in the aid of, and under the direction of your mother. Under these circumstances, I have concluded to accept the pleas you have tendered.

"Your interest now is not in the past, but in the future; you will be sentenced here to imprisonment for the term of your natural life. In view of your age and prospects of life, this is a long time. You will very naturally look forward to a time when, by the aid of executive clemency, you may be released from imprisonment and be permitted again to be a free woman. From the nature of this case, you can hardly expect this to occur for a considerable number of years. Mere length of time will never entitle you to have or secure your release from imprisonment.

"One of the objects of your imprisonment will be to protect the public against a dangerous person. You are not now a safe person to be at large and to mingle with other people. You will never be released from imprisonment and permitted to be at large until you are so changed as to become and be a safe person at large. You must, therefore, if you would hope for, or request executive clemency, get rid of your present evil and dangerous tendencies and dispositions, and become a good, true-hearted woman. You cannot expect to deceive the public or those under whose care you are placed. If you continue to be a bad woman at heart, they will know it. If you become a good, true woman they will know that. Can you affect this change in your real character and disposition? This is the question for you, yourself, during the years of your imprisonment, to determine. That it will be a difficult undertaking, I can well imagine. That it is possible for you to accomplish this result and thus regain your liberty, I will not assume to doubt.

"Your life thus far has not been a pleasant one. Your future is largely in your own keeping. I have thus spoken a kindly word to you and have given you my judgment as to the only way in which you can expect to secure your release from imprisonment, your liberty again. I hope you may understand it and act upon the suggestion made.

"The law prescribes the punishment for this crime and leaves no discretion to be exercised by the court.

"The judgment of the law is that for the crime of murder in the second degree, of which you stand convicted, you be imprisoned in the Onondaga County Penitentiary at Syracuse at hard labor for the term of your natural life."

The words of Judge Williams resounded through the courtroom, and the sharp crack of his gavel officially ended the proceedings. One reporter noted that Mary sat silently, as he recalled, as if in "stoic indifference" to the sentence pronounced upon her. She never looked up, never spoke, and never shed a tear. Her utter lack of emotion caused some critics to question her sanity. Years later Mary would be described as feeble-minded. Some went so far as to say that she was mentally retarded.

Mary had but one request when she was returned to the cell she shared with her mother. She asked Sheriff Brown if she might be allowed to stay with her mother for a short while before being sent to the Onondaga Penitentiary. It was a request he did not deny. Neither Roxalana nor her daughter had given the staff at the jail the least amount of trouble; they were cooperative and polite. Except for the visitors who arrived to see them, one hardly noticed their presence on the upper floor of the jail. Besides, keeping Mary at the jail for a few more days would give him time to make the necessary arrangements to transport Dr. Moritz Richter to the Auburn State Prison at the same time.

After the trial of Roxalana, Dr. Moritz Richter went to trial for the murder of Fairfield professor S. Clark Smith. The Richter trial lacked the sensationalism of the Druse trial and received little notice in the local press. Dr. Deecke testified that Richter was suffering from a "chronic disease of the spine called locomotor ataxia," a neurological disorder [syphilis of the spine] that could account for his schizophrenia-like behavior at the time of the murder. His opinion was in full agreement with that of the other expert witness, Dr. A. Walter Suiter. The trial lasted five days, with the jury finding Richter guilty of second-degree murder. The sixty-two-year-old physician received a life sentence from Judge Pardon C. Williams.

On October 14, 1885, Sheriff Brown brought Mary Druse and Dr. Moritz Richter to the train depot where, not surprisingly, they were greeted by a small crowd. Brown, who was in the company of Dr. Suiter, escorted his charges on board the train with little incident and then proceeded to Syracuse. Although there were no reporters at the Herkimer station to attempt to elicit comments from Mary, this was not the case in Syracuse. A reporter for the *Utica Morning Herald* made his way to the Onondaga County Penitentiary and asked for a brief interview. The usually taciturn Mary Druse was quick to comply. In a bitter outburst, she lashed out at the judicial system, the Gates family, and her misunderstood life.

"I did not have any hand in the murder," she told the reporter, "although I was present. My mother was justified in what she did, as my father used her very brutally—sometimes he beat her with his fists and clubs. I do not deserve to be sent here and would not have pleaded guilty to murder in the second degree, only my lawyer told me I had better. The ones who should be here in my place are Charles Gates and his son. They were the cause of my father's death. My father was never jealous of my mother; neither was he a drinking man. He was only ugly by disposition."

The prison matrons brought Mary to cell number 33 and told her that her sentence of hard labor would begin in the box factory. Alone and friendless, Mary could only hope that the words of Judge Williams might come true, that someday she might receive executive clemency.

Transporting Mary Druse to Onondaga County Penitentiary and Dr. Moritz Richter to the Auburn State Prison were two of the last official duties of Sheriff Valentine Brown. Long before the Druse trial had ended, Brown announced that he would end his tenure as sheriff to run for the New York State Assembly. In a close race, Brown saw his political career end when he failed to unseat Republican incumbent John M. Budlong by 562 votes. At the same time, the town of Winfield's supervisor, Delavan Cook, fended off rival William Garlock by an even smaller margin, 236 votes, to become the next sheriff of Herkimer County.

The transition from Brown to Cook was hardly noticed within the confines of the limestone jail. The routine remained the same, as did the staff. Since many of the deputies were part-time employees of the county, all retained their positions. Staffing, supplies, paperwork, and county government were nothing new to Delavan Cook. The former town supervisor had experience in all of these particulars save one—he might have to supervise the first execution in the history of Herkimer County.

When Cook arrived at the jail in November of 1885, he was introduced to its most famous inmate. Roxalana was alone but did not experience the same solitude as her daughter. She knew most of the deputies by name, and she never ceased to receive a constant stream of visitors. She made paper flowers and dabbled in poetry, and from all outward appearances did not look or behave like a woman on death row. This façade may have begun when she became aware of the efforts of several individuals on the outside to save her from the gallows.

While her attorney, H. DeWight Luce, prepared an appeal, a local clergyman stepped forward to champion Roxalana's cause. Reverend George W. Powell had said nothing during the trial and broke his silence only after Judge Williams had sentenced Roxalana to hang. A native of Westershire, England, Reverend Powell had at one time preached in Baltimore, Maryland, and in Lockport, New York. Why the fifty-two-year-old bewhiskered minister accepted a position at the Universalist Church in the village of Herkimer is a mystery, and no one ever asked why each move he made resulted in a smaller congregation. Whatever the reason, it could not have been a lack of energy or commitment. With fire-and-brimstone zeal, Reverend Powell lashed out from the pulpit to denounce capital punishment. A master at the art of public relations, Powell announced plans to aid Roxalana and invited everyone, including the press, to attend a series of lectures he planned to present. His first was entitled "How the spirit of Mischief and Murder which is taxing the patience and pockets of our People [is] to be abated or removed."

For the next several weeks, from Middleville to Mohawk and from Frankfort to Little Falls, Reverend Powell stumped on behalf of Roxalana Druse. Following his frequent visits to the jail to consult and console Roxalana, the press began referring to him as "the spiritual advisor"—a title he took very seriously.

From the beginning, Reverend Powell realized that if he was to help Roxalana Druse, he had to keep her name foremost in the press. He never passed up an opportunity to be interviewed or to have a letter submitted to the editors. At the same time, he was keenly aware that this was only local news. If he was to succeed in saving this woman, he had to broaden the scope of his campaign. No offer of assistance was dismissed or denied.

Reverend Powell was anxious to enlist the growing suffragette movement in the state. At the conclusion of the Druse trial, Powell had invited Lillie Devereux Blake to speak at the Universalist Church. A driving force in the suffrage movement, Blake was at this time a member of the New York State Women's Suffrage Association. A confidante and friend to Susan B. Anthony, Blake never shied away from any issue that involved the cause of suffrage.

On October 23, 1885, an exhausted Lillie Devereux Blake arrived in Herkimer. This would be her last stop on a grueling five-day speaking tour of central and western New York. After speaking in Syracuse, Rochester, Ithaca, and Cortland, Blake accepted his invitation to speak in the small village of Herkimer, and the Reverend Powell was elated. When Blake arrived at the train station, she might have been a little disappointed at her reception committee. There were no crowds or reporters. In fact, not one Utica or valley newspaper mentioned her visit. Despite this, Blake was nonetheless pleased with the reception she received when she arrived at the Universalist Church.

"A fine audience greeted me," she recorded in her diary. "I spoke of Mrs. Druse, now under sentence of death; also I attacked Mr. Budlong."

The real purpose of her visit and her barnstorming tour of New York was to speak out against those assemblymen seeking reelection who had voted against women's issues. The Mr. Budlong who incurred her wrath was the same Budlong who later defeated Valentine Brown.

Blake offered quiet support for the plight of Roxalana, but nothing more. She politely refused Reverend Powell's offer to escort her to the jail to meet with Roxalana. This was a controversial issue that Blake was not prepared to embrace. The only facts she had concerning this case were those supplied by Reverend Powell. Instead, she took a more cautious approach. Blake did not want to make any public statements that might in some way jeopardize the fate of any proposed suffrage legislation. After all, there was a chance that the fate of Roxalana might resolve itself in the court of appeals—a hope shared by the prisoner as well as her attorney.

While Reverend Powell labored to rally support for Roxalana from the pulpit of the Universalist Church, H. DeWight Luce continued the fight from his arena, the courts. At his office in Rich-

Judge Pardon C. Williams

field Springs, Luce told a reporter for the *Richfield Springs Mercury* that he was preparing an appeal.

"There are a great number of exceptions in the case," he said. "Of course we will be obliged to take the opinion of the judges of the general term as to whether the errors we complain of are such as materially affect the rights of the defendant." Luce refrained from commenting on his chances of success. It was more important for the public and Roxalana to know that he was still hard at work as her counsel.

The desire to guide his client through this legal maze was admirable, but funding the mission would not be easy. In preparation for the appeal, Luce was required to furnish the courts with the transcripts and other court-related documents. One estimate placed the volume of material at close to 2,000 pages. Copying this material was the responsibility of the defendant, and Luce knew this was impossible. Of the $500.00 realized from the sale of the farm, and after debts and attorney's fees had been satisfied, Roxalana had $30.00 remaining. Luce had no choice but to ask the Herkimer County Board of Supervisors to absorb the cost of the appeal. This they agreed to do at twelve cents per page, a cost of about $240.00 of the taxpayers' money.

At about the same time, Luce had to settle the finances of his other client. In late March, he traveled to the Onondaga County Penitentiary to visit Mary Druse. When Luce arrived at the Syracuse train station, reporters eager for news about the girl besieged him. Many asked if there was indeed a possibility that she would be pardoned by the governor. Luce was realistic as well as optimistic. He told the press that it was possible, but only after Mary had served a considerable part of her sentence, perhaps eight to ten years.

Mary shared his optimism. Judge Williams had mentioned the possibility of executive clemency, but this was in the future, and Mary's thoughts were in the present. She was interested in the progress Luce was making with the appeal. She hoped too that a new trial would spare her mother's life, and perhaps Roxalana could be sent to Onondaga. Even if they were unable to speak to each other, Mary reasoned, there would be comfort in knowing that her mother was nearby. Luce assured Mary that he was doing everything possible to save her mother, but that was not the reason for his visit. He reminded Mary that although she was in prison, she was entitled to a portion of her late father's estate. Like her mother, she too was entitled to $500.00, and like her mother, she owed Luce $300.00 in legal fees.

"As an heiress," quipped the *Herkimer Democrat* at this latest development, "Mary can hardly be regarded as a success."

H. DeWight Luce filed for the appeal on the very same day Roxalana Druse was convicted, and he announced to the public his determination to fight for his client until his last breath.

"If we do not succeed in the General Term, we shall appeal again to the Court of Appeals. . . ."

Five months later on April 27, 1886, he arrived at court in Utica, New York, for the General Term to argue the case before Judges Hardin, Boardman, and Follett.

Luce introduced several key points that he felt warranted a new trial. He argued that certain testimony should not have been introduced in the trial, and testimony that could have helped his client had not been allowed. He was opposed to the introduction of evidence in the trial by Frank Gates and George Druse, but more importantly, he protested the way the district attorney had repeatedly asked the boys to describe the details of William Druse's beheading. Luce also believed that the testimony offered by Rudolph Van Evera should have been admitted. His testimony, Luce argued, would help establish the fact that if Bill Druse was abusive to his farm animals, he was just as capable of being abusive to his family. On the other hand, the testimony and statements made by Justice McDonald should have been excluded. Luce contended that the confessions of the children extracted by McDonald were given under duress. Finally, Luce believed that evidence indicating Bill Druse's erratic behavior, notably stripping the clothes from the corpse of his deceased father, was improperly excluded.

Abram Steele had stepped down from the office of district attorney the previous November, and his successor was Eugene Sheldon of Little Falls. Sheldon was just as firm as Steele was. He expressed no desire to have the ruling against Roxalana Druse reversed; she had been afforded a fair trial and found guilty by an impartial jury.

Judge George Hardin thanked the attorneys for their statements. The court, he said, would adjourn until July 1, at which time they would rule on the appeal.

When the 2:23 p.m. train from Herkimer reached the Utica station, there were no indications that its arrival would be different from any other. Hardly anyone took notice of a couple that stepped off the train and onto the platform. He was neatly attired in a suit, and she wore a long, black dress and a veil that shielded her from view. The two looked like a grieving couple who had arrived in Utica to attend a funeral service. They passed inconspicuously through the small gathering at the train station and entered a waiting carriage.

To some this might have been considered amateur theatrics, but to Sheriff Delavan Cook, it was the only way to arrive in Utica without running a gauntlet of reporters and curiosity seekers. So determined was he to avoid drawing attention to himself or his charge that he wore no badge, and Roxalana wore no handcuffs.

Their arrival at the courthouse in Utica was just as discreet. Unlike the scene in Herkimer some months earlier, there were no crowds on the steps hoping to catch a glimpse of the infamous Roxalana Druse. When they entered the Supreme Court chambers, it was a similar scene; the room was empty, except for lawyers and Roxalana. The absence of an audience may have startled her, but she seemed to regain her composure when H. DeWight Luce and Amos Prescott greeted her as she entered the room. One could only guess that "Our prayers are with you" and "Good luck" were included in the few pleasantries exchanged before the judges entered the court. Sheriff Cook led Roxalana to the prisoner's box and remained by her side. Although this was an appeal rather than a trial, Roxalana's guilty verdict required her by law to be in the prisoner's box.

The trio of judges entered the courtroom. and announced that after careful consideration, they believe there to be nothing improper or irregular in the trial of Roxalana Druse.

"Roxalana Druse," said Judge George Hardin, "stand up. Have you aught to say why the sentence of the court should not be executed in your case, and why a new day for the carrying into effect of the judgment of the Oyer and Terminer should not be named?"

Roxalana was stunned. "I have nothing to say," she stated.

"Have you anything to say to the court?" asked Judge Hardin.

"I don't think I had a fair trial." Her voice trailed off and few in the room caught her final words, which were clearly heard and understood by Judge Hardin. Her comment about not receiving a fair trial was an insult to the judicial system, and he made sure she was aware of this.

"Your trial was presided over by one of the ablest and most cautious judges of the Supreme Court of the State, who carefully saw to it that you had every right secured to you by law, under the constitution of the State. You had a very protracted trial in which you had the benefit of two counselors of this court, one of them quite distinguished as having been himself, for more than fifteen years, administrator of the criminal law of the land, who had by his ripe years and long experience, become qualified to defend you in your dire condition. He bestowed upon your case zeal, energy, and enthusiasm, and the weight of his influence, and believed you an unfortunate woman.

"Unfortunately, the evidence was overwhelmingly against you. The jurors who sat, with the responsibilities of their oaths upon them, came to the conclusion that you were guilty of murder in the first degree, and that you had taken the life willingly and deliberately of your husband.

"That verdict was received and recorded and met the approval of the judge who presided. A motion was made upon some slight irregularities, and it was patiently heard and denied. Your counsel, still loyal and devoted to your interests, however, brought an appeal to this court. That appeal, through the influence of the public authorities, was presented, at the county's expense, so far as the printing was concerned, and it was ably and carefully argued, and we patiently listened to all your counsel could say in your behalf.

"We have taken time carefully and cautiously to examine every question that was presented by your counsel, or that we could conceive appropriate to belong to an investigation of the long trial that has taken place in your case. After a deliberate inspection of the record, we are unanimous in the opinion we have this day pronounced, that you have had a fair, legal, and correct trial. By that verdict, you are condemned as guilty of the crime in the indictment. Little remains for us to do, in our calm deliberation, except to fix a day to carry into effect the sentence which was pronounced in the Oyer and Terminer in Herkimer.

"No circumstance is suggested by you in this sad hour of your life why we should stay the progress of the law. On the contrary, every consideration of public justice requires that your sentence should be executed.

We therefore, in compliance with the statute, fix the 19th day of August, 1886, as the day and time between the hours of 10 and 4 of that day, for the carrying into effect of the sentence in your case and judgment and direct the sheriff of the county of Herkimer on that day, between the hours of 10 a.m. and 4 p.m., to cause you to be executed, and that you be hanged by the neck until you be dead; and trust that a merciful Providence to be more kind to you than you have been to yourself, to your husband, to your children and to the public."

Once more, numb from the experience of hearing "hanged by the neck," Roxalana slowly sank to her chair. Earlier, Luce had told a reporter for the *Richfield Springs Mercury* that he was prepared for such a setback.

"If we do not succeed in the general term, we shall appeal again to the court of appeals, and if, after exhausting all our legal remedies we get no relief, as a last resort we shall apply to the governor for a commutation of sentence."

News of the failed appeal reached Herkimer faster than the return of Roxalana Druse and Sheriff Cook. Reverend Powell immediately contacted the *Herkimer Democrat* and announced the subject of the sermon he would deliver on Sunday: "The barbarity of judicial murder, politically called, 'capital punishment." Reverend Powell said, "All believers in this barbarous practice, with the friends of mercy and Christian charity, are invited to attend."

While Luce prepared his final appeal, Reverend Powell knew he had to awaken the conscience of the people if he was to save Roxalana Druse. By the spring of 1886, he had assumed not only the role of spiritual advisor but also that of campaign manager, publicist, guardian angel, and troubleshooter. He defended her at every turn, never missing an opportunity to champion the woman he believed was "the most friendless, desolate, and unfortunate being in all the lower world." He came to her rescue when it was reported that Roxalana had refused to pray with a visiting clergyman. (After unleashing a venomous streak of profanity, Roxalana was said to have hurled a Bible at Reverend Charles F. Edmunds as he left her cell.)

Reverend Powell attempted to defuse the situation by dashing off a quick note to the governor. The charges, he wrote, regarding the "violent language and temper" of Mrs. Druse were simply not true. Why, just the other day, Powell claimed, he had personally interviewed the jail matron regarding this incident, and according to Mrs. Waterman, "Roxalana is a quiet ,well-behaved, ladylike person and docile as a little child."

On another occasion, Reverend Powell sent a photograph of Roxalana to an acquaintance in New York City, who in turn gave it to noted phrenologist, Nelson Sizer. The author of the recently published *Forty Years in Phrenology* (1882), Sizer was largely responsible for the popularity in the United States of the study of phrenology—"a system of character analysis based upon the configurations of the skull." After carefully analyzing the photograph, Sizer concluded that Roxalana was indeed an abused woman who had seen more than her share of misfortune.

"She is not a weak woman," observed Sizer, "She appears to be a woman of great resolution and determination." Unlike the woman with a rudimentary education who had scratched out a living on Hogsback Hill Road, the woman in the photograph was, according to Sizer, of "good practical intellect" and "had a good deal of natural refinement." This is exactly what Reverend Powell was seeking. "I endorse every word of it," he remarked.

The public had to see that this was indeed a changed woman. When a stovepipe fire started in the ceiling above her cell in late fall, it was noted that Roxalana refused to leave. While the other prisoners were evacuated, Roxalana remained by her cell and assisted the deputies in a bucket brigade while awaiting the arrival of the Herkimer Excelsior Hook and Ladder Company. "The rumor that Mrs. Druse set the jail on fire is without foundation," reported the *Herkimer Democrat*.

Encouraged by the reception he received wherever he spoke and bolstered by the comments of those who shared his opinion of Roxalana as a much-maligned woman, Reverend Powell decided it was time to rally support in the form of numbers. A short while before the second appeal, he initiated a petition drive to save Roxalana from the gallows. The carefully worded petition failed to mention the crime she was convicted of, but did state "Neither justice nor the public require the death of Roxalana Druse." At his own expense, he printed and mailed petitions across the state.

One petitioner was so committed to the cause that he traveled to

Herkimer to meet the woman Reverend Powell was determined to save. Burnham Wardwell claimed to have collected 500 signatures from the citizens of Vineland, New Jersey, in support of Mrs. Druse. An avid proponent of prison reform and an outspoken critic of capital punishment, the elderly Wardwell had once spent a year in jail himself for the slanderous remarks made against a local sheriff.

Wardwell spent several hours visiting Roxalana, and the next day, before he left Herkimer, he arranged for a small press conference at Loveland's store on Main Street.

"Yesterday, I mingled my tears with [those of] Mrs. Druse," he told the small crowd. "She weighs 102 pounds. She is very gentle in appearance and is in very poor health. I cannot think the safety of New York, the command of God, or the teachings of Jesus require the shedding of her blood."

Wardwell left Herkimer but never forgot his meeting with Roxalana. The two exchanged several letters and Roxalana, from all indications, genuinely enjoyed his company.

"I have had many calls since you were here," she wrote, "and all seem to be in sympathy with me, especially one of them, a playmate in my youth who I did not remember, said we do not intend to let you die if a petition would save you." The petitions would have to save her—because the courts would not.

On October 13, 1886, H. DeWight Luce argued his final appeal for Roxalana Druse before the Court of Appeals. Thirteen days later the court handed down its decision: there was no doubt that, given the evidence presented, the deceased, William Druse, came to his end at the hands of the defendant, Roxalana Druse.

The Court of Appeals upheld the decision reached earlier by the General Term. The court agreed that District Attorney Abram Steele had acted properly in allowing Frank Gates and George Druse to recall particular incidents of the murder and that Judge Williams had protected their legal rights as witnesses. As to the evidence offered by Van Evera that Bill Druse was cruel to his farm animals, the court ruled that this was third-person hearsay evidence and agreed with the lower courts that it was inadmissible evidence. Finally, all the judges agreed that the evidence presented indicating Bill Druse had "robbed his father when in the coffin" was completely irrelevant. The judges were unanimous in their decision; Roxalana's execution was rescheduled for December 29, 1886.

Almost a year ago, Luce had boasted that if he failed in the appeal process, he was prepared to take the case directly to the governor and ask for a commutation of sentence. Now Luce needed a miracle to save Roxalana Druse. He needed petitions, letters, and above all, he needed Reverend Powell.

Roxalana was devastated when she learned of the failed appeal. Unschooled in the legal system, she knew at least that there could be no more appeals. Mrs. Waterman, the jail matron, did her best to reassure Roxalana that she was not alone or forgotten. Reverend Powell was expected at any moment. In the meantime, Sheriff Cook had arrived outside her cell door and asked if she might want to leave her cell for a few moments. The distraught woman did not question the sheriff and was ushered into another cell by Mrs. Waterman. Cook feared that after hearing the news of the failed appeal, Roxalana might try to harm herself. While deputies searched her cell for any items that might be used in a suicide attempt, Roxalana was searched by Mrs. Waterman. The jail matron presented her with a new dress, and then carefully examined the discarded dress.

Roxalana was permitted to return to her cell, but the ever-vigilant Mrs. Waterman was always nearby. Outwardly depressed, Roxalana was somewhat heartened by the arrival of her spiritual advisor. The two prayed and then talked quietly about the future. Ever the optimist, Reverend Powell told her not to give up hope. Petitions were arriving daily at the governor's office, and he was in constant contact with the governor. He promised her that would go to Albany to beg for her life.

This was no idle boast. Through his clerical connections and his membership in the Philadelphia based Universal Peace Union, Reverend Powell was able to reach out to hundreds of people with his petitions. With less than two months remaining before the scheduled execution, he had to step up the intensity of his campaign to convince the governor that Roxalana deserved to live. He was convinced that the petition drive, the letters of sympathy, and the discovery of new evidence in the Druse murder would force the governor to reconsider the sentence.

Indeed, letters and petitions to save Roxalana had been arriving at the governor's office sporadically ever since she had been convicted in October 1885. Now exactly a year later, with all appeals exhausted, the volume of material reaching the governor's desk increased considerably. The task of wading through this odd assortment of material fell to his secretary, William Gorham Rice.

A native of Albany, Rice rose through the political ranks after graduating from Albany Academy in 1875. His first appointment as assistant paymaster to the National Guard came from then Governor Samuel J. Tilden. In 1883, Rice became the private secretary to Governor Grover Cleveland. When Cleveland won the presidency, Rice remained in Albany and continued his duties as private secretary to the next governor, David B. Hill of Elmira.

For months, Rice had been sifting and sorting Druse related mail. Petitions with as many as a hundred names were now joined by some with as few as ten or even five names. Letters, postcards, and telegrams with postmarks from all across the nation found their way to his office. From the most illegible scrawl to the finest Spenserian script, the voices of the people crossed gender and economic lines in their effort to either save or condemn Roxalana Druse.

From Port Jervis, New York, Albert Huntington Jr. wrote, "You might think it strange that a small boy of twelve years of age should ask for a woman's life, but she is a mother and I have got a mother." He closed his letter with an apology to the governor for writing such a brief letter: "It is time to go to school." Others echoed the sentiments of young Huntington. "Can you think of your own mother and not change the sentence?" wrote an anonymous correspondent.

A "friend to women" from Brownsville, Texas, informed the governor that this crime would never have happened in his part of the country. "I am an old man and have been a close observer for seventy years and can say that our southern women are not apt to kill good husbands."

And of course there were more than a few melodramatic letters to the governor written in the style of one Miss Maggie MacDonald: "Anything, Dear Governor, but the shameful spectacle of a woman's death on a gallows."

Signatures of prominent attorneys from the New York City boroughs as well as that of the mayor of Brooklyn graced the petitions submitted by the law office of Elbert, Ludlam, and Wakeman. "Every fact which has come to light shows very plainly that she is to be hung rather because of the manner in which she, in her crazed horror, disposed of the body—isn't that so?"

Others raised the same point. Adelphia Child expressed the concern that just because Roxalana had "disposed of the body in a revolting manner" should not have any bearing on the sentence imposed upon her by the courts.

Early on it became apparent to Rice that the driving force behind most of these letters was Reverend Powell. Petitions sponsored by church groups began arriving in Albany almost on a daily basis. A church congregation from Ithaca sent a petition with one hundred names, and another arrived from New York City with two hundred names. From Auburn, Jacob H. Harter, minister, lecturer, and reformer, offered his petition of twenty-three signatures. Another disgruntled church elder voiced his protest uniquely, expressing his thoughts on the back of the printed sermon he had delivered the previous Sunday.

Another member of the clergy went so far as to suggest that spiritual salvation was more necessary in this case than hanging. "It is evident that Mrs. D. does not realize the sinful condition and extreme danger of her soul," wrote E.D. Peape. "She should be allowed ample time —that is, the rest of her life—for a repentance sufficient to lead her to ultimate salvation, through the merits of the blood of the lamb." Peape recommended that the leading clergymen of the day, Thomas Dewitt Talmage and Edward Beecher, be allowed, as he wrote, "to pray with her to their hearts content."

Rice also discovered a few correspondences that were not so much pro-Roxalana as they were anti-capital punishment. Leading this crusade were many of the petitions circulated by the Universalist Peace Union. Reverend A.A. Miner, pastor of the Universalist Church in Boston for thirty-eight years, declared, "It is barbarous to hang a woman."

During this time, Roxalana rocked away the hours in her cell entertaining a seemingly endless parade of well-wishers. Those who came to visit gazed upon a jail cell adorned with lithographs, paper flowers, and pictures. A reporter for the *New York World* described her as slight in stature with thin lips, a prominent nose, and thick brown hair. Charming and amiable, Roxalana expressed hope that public opinion would succeed where the appeals process had failed. "I have the sympathy of ten thousand women, and ten times that number would sympathize with me if they knew the facts of the case. I am aware that there has been a petition circulating among the people of adjoining states, but I do not know whether it will help me or not."

When asked about the role Charles Gates had played in the murder, an angry Roxalana became very defensive. "I have nothing to say concerning Gates, either against him or for him. I don't want to hear his name mentioned. I don't want to say anything about him at all. I don't think it is right to keep me shut up while the guilty party is running around sunning himself. If I had anything to do with the murder, I was not a principal in its execution."

The reporter noted that the most peculiar object in her cell was a cigar- box lid on which she had painted in red: You was not there. Judge not. For you do not know it all. And on the reverse: Judge not. You do not know it all.

At the same time, Reverend Powell was working to convince the governor's office that the people in Herkimer County were a generally forgiving group. "Public opinion in this community has undergone a great change," he wrote. "Three months ago nearly everyone said she ought to hang. Now the sentiment is all the other way."

To prove his point, he enclosed with his letter a petition with the names of one hundred prominent citizens of the village of Herkimer and an additional petition containing fifty names from the city of Little Falls obtained by H. DeWight Luce. The spiritual advisor discovered that petitions from rural Herkimer County were not as plentiful as from the villages. Forty-six-year-old Sara Burgess of Cedarville apologized to Reverend Powell for the meager dozen signatures she obtained, claiming, "The feeling is bitter against Mrs. Druse." It was a feeling shared by the residents of Warren, as the minister would soon discover.

Reverend Powell forwarded one local letter to Governor Hill that had been published recently in the *Herkimer Democrat*. "The sweet womanly letter speaks for itself," said Reverend Powell. "It appeals to all hearts with the force of sympathy and truth." The author of the letter stated that at one time, she too had been in favor of capital punishment. However, after carefully considering the "mitigating circumstances" surrounding the Druse murder, she was forced to change her opinion. The real villain, she claimed, was Bill Druse. He had brought about his own demise because of the brutal treatment he had inflicted upon his loving wife. This was clearly a case of justifiable homicide, and she hoped that the governor could at least see his way to commuting the sentence to life imprisonment. The author of the letter was none other than Julia Northrup.

Reverend Powell conveniently omitted the fact that Julia Northrup was not only one of Roxalana's oldest friends but also a key character witness at the trial. The publication of the Northrup letter caused quite a stir, especially in the town of Warren where opinions regarding the fate of their infamous neighbor were sharply divided. The publicity the town received after the murder was anything but complimentary. Halfway through the coroner's inquest, a reporter for the *Utica Morning Herald* had little good to say about Roxalana, her family, or anyone else in Warren. "The whole party certainly cannot be rated very high even for the town of Warren," said the reporter, "where it is told that voters are bought like cattle." Now, months after the trial, the resentment of certain residents surfaced once more with the publication of this letter in support of Roxalana from Julia Northrup. Those who wanted to forget Roxalana were furious at its publication and just as upset with the actions of its author. For weeks, Julia Northrup had gone door to door in an effort to collect signatures on behalf of her friend. For her efforts, she collected twenty signatures and managed to arouse the animosity of the previously silent "anti-Druse" neighbors, who began now to circulate their own petition:

"We the undersigned, citizens of the town of Warren, Herkimer County, and neighbors of the late William Druse, hereby appeal to you in behalf of the broken-hearted sister and relatives of said William Druse, who have borne their grief in silence, trusting in the justice of the law to deal out proper punishment, but fearing the letters written and the statements made in behalf of the murderer by her friends, might have some bearing on public sentiment, we do desire to inform you that many of these are false, that any letter written or statement made by Julia Northrup who is Roxy's associate, are incredible; that the murderer and her daughter had for a long time kept a disorderly house and made their home so hideous that Mr. Druse was often forced to go to the neighbors and spend much of his time, and occasionally enjoy a good meal, which they would not prepare for him at home; that he was an honest and temperate man, that no such brutal treatment by him to his family was ever known by us as has been reported; that he was never heard to express a word against his family; that to kill him had long been talked of by them. The murder was premeditated and without provocation . We the undersigned, citizens, earnestly appeal to you in the name of public justice and in the name of private safety, not to interfere with the sentence of Roxy Druse, but to permit a speedy execution and rid the world of a miserable nuisance and give the public a rest from this incessant subject that has long crowded the columns of the newspapers."

Roxalana was stunned when she learned of the harshly worded document and even more upset to discover that so many people, fifty-three, had signed the petition. It took a little while for the news to reach Julia Northrup, who had relocated to Washington, D.C., but when it did, she exploded in anger. "I have just learned that there has been a base fraud in getting names to a petition asking for the speedy execution of Mrs. Druse," she wrote in a letter to Governor Hill. "It is said to [have] come from fifty or so prominent citizens of Warren, Herkimer County. I shall take immediate measures to investigate it as the perpetrators there ought to be punished."

Northrup suspected that the motivating force behind the petition was the first person whose signature appeared there, Justice of the Peace Daniel MacDonald. It probably didn't help matters when she discovered that her own brother, Chester, had signed it as well after previously signing her petition.

The "Warren Petition" came from the pen of thirty-one-year-old David E. Mixter. In a cover letter to Governor Hill, Mixter explained that many people had been influenced by the false statements made by Julia Northrup. The fifty-three signatures, Mixter said, are a "true sentiment of the people who reside nearest the scene of the tragedy. I write on behalf of the few remaining persons who bear the Druse name who are good respectable people and deserve much sympathy for the terrible disgrace that has been cast upon their names." It was a painful reminder to Mixter that the aunt who had raised him and with whom he had resided with for over twenty years was named Laura Druce.

A short while after the Warren Petition arrived in Albany, Herkimer County Democratic leader Sam Earl lent his support. Enclosing a copy of the Warren Petition as it appeared in the local papers, the Herkimer County attorney added in his letter to Governor Hill his own thoughts. "I will take the liberty to add also that I well knew William Druse in his life and that I know he was a harmless, good-natured man. His only fault was his shiftlessness."

The Warren Petition did have another effect—it helped break the monotony of the pro-Druse letters that William Gorham Rice had been accustomed to reading. Although the majority of the material delivered to his desk fell into the "commute the sentence" or "free her" categories, a few letters cried out for blood.

Charles Garlick of Saquoit, New York, couldn't understand why there was such an uproar over this issue. "She has had a fair trial," he wrote, "and [was] found *guilty* in the *first degree*; let her hang. I think this is the voice of the people."

Esther Esty of Ithaca, a forty-nine-year-old widow, agreed. She couldn't resist using medical imagery in her assessment of the Druse case. "You have *diagnosed* that case correctly and your prescription and treatment is equally admissible and effective."

Whitman Clarke could not understand how anyone could be

sympathetic toward Mrs. Druse. "The she devil ought to be hung years ago."

Thomas Howell of Canandaigua agreed, especially since she had fed her husband "to the hogs."

Of all the letters that arrived at the governor's office, few exhibited the intense hatred of that submitted by J.A. Jones of Brooklyn. "No husband can feel safe if women once get to believe that they can't be hanged for murder. The she devil Mrs. Druse ought to be burned alive for it or boiled alive as she did to her husband's body, hanging is too easy a death for such a horrible and deliberate crime. . . . The great pressure for her pardon or commutation of sentence comes from those nuisances to society, the 'women's rights females.'. . . These females have done and are doing more harm to this country than fifty business panics or ten wars combined. I shall breathe a prayer of thankfulness to God when I hear that the murderess Mrs. Druse has suffered the full penalty of the law and her abominable soul has been summoned for eternal punishment."

In truth, the "women's rights females" were not quite as vocal as Jones had suggested. For the most part, the suffragettes were cautious about their association with the Druse affair. Few letters from prominent members of the women's suffrage movement reached the desk of the governor. They never staged any large demonstrations or rallies in support of Roxalana. Only one, Lillie Devereux Blake, had ever been to Herkimer, and she hadn't take the time to visit Roxalana.

Blake found it less problematic and a lot safer to protest the unveiling of the Statue of Liberty that autumn than to publicly denounce the execution of Roxalana. Two days after the failed appeal, Blake and a contingent of hardy suffragettes boarded a smelly cattle barge in New York Harbor. Braving the cold, wind, and rain, they set out to protest the symbol of liberty in the form of a woman. How could this image grace a land where women had so few rights? Pleased with the newspaper publicity they received for this action, Blake was worried how these same papers might interpret the suffragettes' stand on the Druse case.

Now with less than two weeks remaining until the scheduled December execution, the New York Suffrage Association broke their silence. At the December meeting, Association President Lillie Devereux Blake tactfully approached the issue, hoping that it would not divide their group. A resolution was introduced that stated it was unjust to hold women accountable to any laws made by men, laws which they "had no voice in framing."

Naturally this resolution caused a great deal of excitement among the group, and it didn't take long for one member to voice her disapproval. "I am opposed to this resolution," she said. "I think our association as a body cannot afford to express sympathy with a crime like this. I have deep sympathy for this unfortunate woman, and I hope she will not be hanged, but this association should be governed by reason and not by sympathy."

Mrs. Anna Garlin Spencer was just as straightforward. "If it is right to hang a man, it is right to hang a woman." Renowned author, feminist, and soon to be ordained Universalist minister, Spencer stressed that the real issue in the women's rights movement had always been equality and not exemption. "We should be unworthy of the suffrage we ask if we claimed exemption from the consequences of crime because of our sex. We want to be considered responsible beings, and this is the very life basis of our agitation."

The resolution failed, and another was quickly introduced. The new resolution condemned the practice of capital punishment and asked the governor to commute the death sentence imposed upon Roxalana to life in prison. This resolution passed, signed by all in attendance, and was sent with little fanfare to the governor's office. As a group they did nothing more to help Roxalana.

In the end, few of the suffragettes saw the fate of Roxalana in a more pragmatic way than Lillie Devereux Blake. If the sentence was commuted, the suffragettes could claim a victory because their voices were heard. And if the sentence of death was carried out, what then? "Will this wretched woman be martyr to our cause?" confided Blake to her diary. "Surely if men hang us, they must let us vote."

CHAPTER 7

"The law must be permitted to take its course."

Deputy Sheriff Bartlett Manion slowly walked the horseshoe-shaped corridors of the jail. He peered into each cell, said an occasional "Good night," and gently tugged at each cell door. A busy, noisy place during the day, the twilight hours brought a variety of new sounds. A sneeze, a cough, the rustle of blankets—all made one forget that this was indeed a jail.

Manion and Jailer Harry Brown lived at the jail so they were in constant contact with the prisoners, and complaints or requests usually went to either man. The sheriff too was mindful of the needs of the prisoners under his care, but he relied on his deputies to see to them. His primary concern was the daily operation of the facility, and this entailed keeping a meticulous record of any expenditures associated with it. There were instances when local physicians were called to the jail to care for sick inmates and times when local merchants had to bring in clothing. There were requisitions for food and, as the winter months approached, it was necessary to keep a supply of coal in reserve, along with a few cords of firewood. A sudden snowstorm could make village roads impassable and delay coal shipments for several days.

In 1886 the year-round operation of the jail cost the taxpayers of Herkimer County $6,762.02, or roughly 5 percent of the entire county budget. However, this did not include the salaries of the sheriff and his staff. Deputies, like Bartlett Manion, earned $2.00 a day. He augmented his salary by performing a variety of duties at the sheriff's office. An issued subpoena earned him an additional twenty-five cents, and if he issued a warrant, he could collect fifty cents. An arrest entitled an officer to one dollar, while escorting a prisoner to the courthouse for trial earned an additional two dollars.

As an elected county official, Sheriff Cook was entitled to a salary of $1,000 per year. On paper this seemed like a paltry amount, given the responsibilities of the office, but he was permitted the same opportunities to make extra money as his deputies. Whether it be a summons, a warrant, a subpoena, or a request to be reimbursed for a travel expense, the voucher had to be approved by the Board of Supervisors before the taxpayers' money could be spent. Simply put, if you didn't keep accurate records, you didn't get paid.

The sheriff was also required to keep a daily logbook showing how much money was spent on each prisoner. As the year 1886 drew to a close, one name stood atop the list. The whitewashed cell on the third floor of the jail had been home to his longest-serving prisoner, Roxalana Druse.

In the first week of December 1886, H. DeWight Luce requested and was granted an audience with Governor Hill. With the execution of Roxalana scheduled to take place four days after Christmas, Luce knew that this would be his last opportunity to speak on her behalf. The governor acquiesced but insisted on hearing from Eugene Sheldon, Herkimer County's District Attorney, as well. Hill's comments had been guarded up to this point, but he knew the day would arrive when he would have to come forward and issue a statement. Given the amount of publicity the Druse case had received, Hill could ill afford to ignore it. Although commutation, clemency, or execution were all within his power as governor, the political implications of his decision had to be considered.

"Nine out of ten who are asking it [clemency] are your political enemies," warned Dr. J. Densmore Potter. "You will gain nothing and lose much."

One anonymous letter writer felt much the same way: "If you pardon that woman, you would never stand a chance of being elected to the Presidency of the U.S."

And there were those who felt otherwise. "I am not a crank," wrote R. Meridith about the pardoning power of the governor. "Exercise it—you will win thereby 1,000,000 votes for President."

For the forty-three-year-old governor, the prospects of a White House bid did not seem all that remote. After all, his predecessor had become the current president. If Grover Cleveland made the decision not to seek a second term, many Albany insiders considered Hill a good choice to succeed him. Could the fate of Roxalana Druse change the course of his career? It was difficult to predict how an emotional public would accept the outcome of the Druse affair. Few seemed to recall that when Grover Cleveland was sheriff of Erie County, he had faced a similar challenge. In 1872, Patrick Morrissey was convicted of killing his mother. As Morrissey stood on the gallows with a noose around his neck, it was Sheriff Cleveland

Governor David B. Hill

who had stepped forward and sprung the trap. A short while later, he performed a similar service when he hanged local gambler Jack Gafney for the murder of a fellow cardplayer. If these two hangings hadn't damage the career of a future president, how could hanging Roxalana Druse harm David B. Hill's career?

Luce arrived in Albany by train from New York City, not Herkimer. At the conclusion of the Druse trial, he accepted a position with a New York City law firm. This change in location increased his income but didn't change his relationship with his clients. He could have easily abandoned Roxalana after the final appeal, but he refused to give up on her. Luce made numerous trips to Herkimer to visit Roxalana, to Onondaga to see Mary, and a few to Utica to argue the appeals. If there was the slightest chance he could save Roxalana, he was willing to try. Luce never submitted one voucher to the Herkimer County Board of Supervisors to recoup any money for expenses incurred on these trips.

"This woman," Luce told Governor Hill, "has been living for twenty years in a place called home, but which was no home; for the past two years she has been incarcerated in the jail in Herkimer, and she will tell you herself that she has fared much better there than she ever did at home."

It was a singular point that no one could argue. Her life was vastly better in jail. She wore clean clothes, ate decently prepared meals, and entertained plenty of visitors. The only physically demanding labor she endured was to sometimes wash her own clothes. Two years had passed, he said. Why then couldn't her remaining years be spent in jail out of the way? "If Mrs. Druse had a kind husband, she would have made a kind and affectionate wife."

Herkimer County District Attorney Eugene Sheldon reviewed for Governor Hill the harsh details surrounding the murder of William Druse. "For atrocity," he said, "the crime of Mrs. Druse hardly has a parallel in the county and certainly in the state."

Hill listened carefully to both attorneys. He did not wish to discuss with either of them the merits of Roxalana, the law, public opinion, or anything else for that matter. He simply thanked them for their comments and assured them that his decision would be forthcoming.

Of the hundreds of letters that his secretary opened and filed, only one was important, and it had not yet arrived. Hill was waiting for a response to a letter he had written earlier in the month, and Rice presented it to him a few days before Christmas. Bearing the postmark Watertown, New York, it was a seven-page letter from Judge Pardon C. Williams.

The venerable judge could not comprehend the public outcry about the fate of Roxalana Druse. In his letter, he dispelled once and for all the myth or rumor that a miscarriage of justice had taken place in his court. These were premeditated actions on the part of the accused, as well as that of her daughter. The evidence presented at the trial clearly indicated that the shots fired at Mr. Druse, regardless whether they were fired by Roxalana or Frank Gates, were not fatal. William Druse's own daughter had placed a rope around his neck, and then pulled him from his chair. Lying helpless on the floor, he had uttered, "Oh, Roxy, don't," before he was beheaded by his wife.

"Mr. Druse was still alive," wrote Judge Williams. "In reply to your request that I give my opinion of the minutes of the application for executive clemency, I must say I am aware of no reason why the application should be granted. If the penalty of death is ever to be inflicted as punishment for murder, first degree, it seems to me it should be in this case. The courts have all carefully considered this case."

The letter from Judge Williams sealed Roxalana's fate in the mind of Governor Hill. On December 22, 1886, Hill issued a prepared statement in response to the petitioners, politicians, clergymen, and critics. He reminded everyone that this was not a simple case of a domestic dispute gone awry. "It is a clear case of murder in the first degree," he said. "The evidence shows clearly that the killing was most brutal and atrocious in its character."

Hill wondered if those who had been so quick to sign the petitions had bothered to look at the facts surrounding this case. Unlike the interview he'd had with Luce a few days earlier, Hill not only gave a brief description of the events leading up to the murder but also described it in graphic detail, inspired most likely by the letter he had recently received from Judge Williams. Using Bill Druse's chilling last words—"Oh, Roxy don't"—Hill described the beheading, and how Roxalana tried to cover up the crime, threatening the two boys if they did not cooperate. The boys obeyed her and helped spread rumors about the disappearance of Bill Druse. It was sad, thought Hill, that later on that evening the two boys sat and played checkers, "thus showing the unconcern and utter lack of feeling of the whole family."

The public seemed to forget that the facts presented at the trial pointed to a clear and deliberate act of murder. When Reverend Powell assured the governor that forthcoming information would shed new light on the crime and possibly change everything, Hill remained unimpressed. According to the minister, "A gentlemen detective in this case hopes soon to make it clear to your Excellency that other parties, who for some reason have never been brought to trial, are more guilty, that she was a tool of others." As far as Hill was concerned, this was an act of desperation. Plenty of time had elapsed since the trial, and thus far no one had come forward with any new information.

The governor also cautioned the public regarding the oft-repeated claim of "mitigating circumstances" that said Roxalana was a victim of abuse for many years. A careful review of the testimony given by reliable witnesses clearly showed that both parties were capable of initiating quarrels—quarrels that might be viewed by some as a motive for murder rather than an excuse. "There does not seem to be any ground whatsoever for the exercise of executive clemency," said Hill, "unless it is the sole fact that the defendant is a woman." The law made no such distinction. As governor, he had no power to change the law and every responsibility to enforce it.

Hill assured the public that it was very difficult for him to ignore the Druse case. "I have been besieged with arguments and petitions of every description in favor of this application." He categorized those who cried out for clemency into four groups. First, there were those who were against capital punishment. For their benefit, he stated again that the law had existed long before he took office, and he was obliged to enforce it.

Second, to that minority who objected to capital punishment in the case of women, Hill imparted a simple civics lesson. The law as it now stands, he explained, does not make a distinction between men and women. This group should not waste its time petitioning the governor, but instead should focus its efforts on the legislators who make and amend the laws.

The third group, the suffragettes, also presented a weak case for clemency. The arrival of the Suffrage Resolution came as no surprise, except that it came in the mail and not hand delivered by Lillie Devereux Blake. Hill felt compelled to respond to this group's claims that women should be exempted from laws that they did not formulate. This was ludicrous; if women were exempted from these laws, then why not minors, Indians, and immigrants? All of these are held accountable for laws they did not make. "The law of our state," explained Hill, "made by men is simply in harmony with the law of the Almighty. It provides for equal punishment for all classes of its people and will remain this way until the legislature deems otherwise." The suffragettes, who fought long for equality, could not argue with Hill's logic.

Finally, there was one group who had great sympathy for Roxalana but not many facts. "They are individuals," Hill reasoned, "whose sympathies have been naturally aroused by the erroneous statements which have been spread concerning the ill-treatment sustained by her at the hands of her husband, and which statements do not seem to be corroborated by the evidence produced at the trial." While he never came out and named the source of this erroneous information, it was clear that he was referring to Roxalana's most vocal crusader, her spiritual advisor.

Hill pointed out that the statement that his predecessor, Grover Cleveland, granted executive clemency to Morrisville murderess Mrs. Haight in the shooting death of her husband because she was a woman was absolutely false. Her advanced age, ill health, and possible psychological state at the time of the commission of the crime saved her from the gallows, but not from spending the rest of her life in prison. She was presently at Onondaga Penitentiary in a cell next to Mary Druse. Hill maintained that his office had to maintain consistency; if he interfered in one case, he must do the same others. "A commutation in this case [Druse]," said Hill, "would furnish a precedent for all others." This would mean that the most recent husband killers would make a similar application to his office because of their gender, including Mrs. Wileman of Cattaraugus County, whom a jury found guilty of putting arsenic in her husband's pie, and the same could be said for Hattie Penseyres of Buffalo, recently convicted of second-degree murder in her husband's death.

Executive clemency or commutation were not options Hill was prepared to endorse. The sympathies of the public were one thing, but no one else associated with the case, except her attorney, endorsed her application. Not one member of the jury who had convicted her had contacted his office to express a desire to see her sentence reduced or reversed. "The district attorney appears and strenuously opposes it. The able and impartial judge who presided at the trial does not favor it. . . . Much as I would personally be gratified if I could see my way clear to grant this application, I cannot do so as the law now stands and am compelled to deny it," he declared.

The only thing Hill could do was to postpone the date of the execution—December 29. Because of its proximity to the holidays, he changed the date to February 28. The postponement would appease some, but more importantly, it would grant the legislature time to act if they deemed it necessary to change the existing laws that did not differentiate between the sexes for the punishment of a capital crime. There was always the possibility that the public could pressure lawmakers into amending the law. If they failed to act, there would be no other choice but to carry out the judgment, and Hill said so in the conclusion to his ten-page address.

"If the legislature, upon which the responsibility for the enactment of the laws mainly rests, refuses to modify the present law, it must be enforced as it now exists, and unless it shall be changed in the meantime, the case is closed so far as my official action is concerned, and on February 28 next, the law must be permitted to take its course."

Unaware of the Governor Hill's decision, Reverend Powell had every reason to believe that he might yet save Roxalana. On December 4, 1886, Frank Mondon escaped the gallows when he pled guilty to second-degree murder in the death of John Wishart. Mondon now joined Dr. Richter as a convicted felon who had escaped the death penalty in Herkimer County. Surely, thought the minister, if these men could spend the rest of their lives in prison, there was no reason why the same could not be extended to a woman. Once more he cried out for public support in his melodramatic style. "I ask in the name of justice that all humane persons in the county will lend their influence by signing their name to a petition to the Governor, with thousands of the best men and women from all parts of the state, to have the sentence commuted to imprisonment for life. You can do this by calling at my house in Herkimer, or by sending your name and residence on a slip of paper to put on our list. Pause and think of the ghastly and awful scene of a woman being suspended in midair—and think that the punishment by death nothing more than judicial murder."

The lobbying efforts of the spiritual advisor continued unabated for the next several weeks. Even the announcement of the governor's decision not to interfere did not dampen his spirits. When the *New York Times* published Hill's entire address under the byline "Two Months to Live," Reverend Powell optimistically interpreted this as "Two Months to Be Saved." After all, hadn't Hill said that this respite would give the legislature an opportunity to review the existing laws on capital punishment? Encouraged by this hint of possible legislative action, Powell was determined not to let Roxalana's cause slip from the minds of the public, especially during the Christmas season.

Knowing that it would take several days for the valley newspapers to print the entire text of the governor's address, Reverend

Powell arranged to have one of Roxalana's letters printed in the *Herkimer Democrat.*

Herkimer
December 24

Dearest Daughter,

... thought I would write you a line. Governor Hill has given me a stay until 28th of February. Judge Prescott came in the morning, also Mr. Luce this afternoon, and assured me they should still fight for me & kind Mr. Cook came in and said the paper was served on him this morning to stay the execution until the 28th of February as I have above stated. Georgie has been here today. I bought him a pair of skates for a Christmas present. Mr. Sheriff Brown was here to see me yesterday. I was glad to see him; he gave me still great encouragement. The governor seems to be in my favor still does not want to take the whole responsibility upon himself. It seems however there is no use to give [up]. We must keep up good courage and hope for the best for the prospects are as favorable as ever only we must watch and wait and pray.

... Mr. Powell was in to see me last night,

From your mother in life or death
Mrs. Druse

The Christmas Eve letter may have tugged at the heartstrings of some, but others doubted its authenticity and its authorship. It would be difficult to have a letter travel from Herkimer to Syracuse and back to Herkimer for publication in the *Democrat* in just four days.

The gift of skates for George was touching indeed. He was the most likeable of anyone associated with the trial, but where did Roxalana get the money for them? What little money she did have came from selling paper flowers to her visitors. The surrogate records show no such transaction, nor did the records in the sheriff's office. If the skates were purchased at all, it was probably by Reverend Powell. It was he who was guiding her pen as well as her thoughts, and now he was attempting to sway public opinion. Governor Hill never said that he was "in favor" of Roxalana—these were Powell's words. It wasn't until several days later that the people of Herkimer, as well as the entire state, would hear what the governor really had to say when his address appeared in print.

Standing firmly behind Governor Hill, the *New York Times* denounced the crime as one done "in the most brutal and blood thirsty fashion." An editorial titled "Can a Murderess Be Hanged?" praised Hill for not attempting to circumvent the law because of the convicted murderer's gender. He was right, they claimed, not to interfere, since no new evidence had been brought to alter anyone's perception that there had been a miscarriage of justice. "The question has remained a local one," said the *Times*, "and in the neighborhood where the crime was committed, there has been no feeling on the subject that has had any effect on the part of the judge, the jury, or the prosecuting attorney." The newspaper harbored doubts that the legislature would make any changes in the law to help "that atrociously guilty woman."

With lawmakers poised to meet sometime after the first of the year, Reverend Powell may have attempted to influence their decision by "discovering" a vital piece of evidence. In a letter to the *Herkimer Citizen*, he claimed to have startling new information that would radically alter everyone's opinion concerning the murder and Roxalana.

"You refer at once to the mutilation of her husband's body and say such a woman is incapable of love. Then she is to be pitied. But I have it from her lips and her handwriting," said Powell in an attempt to silence a few critics suspicious of the last letter to appear in print, "and I believe what she says, for I have never discovered the slightest attempt at prevarication—that the body was not cut up, nor burned, nor given to animals. This is all a mistake. There is a man living who knows where the body is."

News of this latest development caused more than a few people to take notice. Many who had followed the Druse case for the past two years were waiting for just such a moment. Since Roxalana had never taken the stand in her own defense and had not made any public statements after the trial, some believed that she would one day come forward with a confession, a missing piece of evidence, or both.

Roxalana didn't mince any words in her exposé which appeared in the *New York Star*. She freely admitted that some of the events leading up to the murder were indeed true. The story of Frank Gates rising early, making the fire too hot, the argument regarding the store bill, the board cut by the axe, and the threats made by Bill Druse were all true. Then, her story veered sharply from the testimony presented at trial.

Her husband, Roxalana recalled, not only threatened her with an axe—he actually drove it into the cupboard door she was standing near. "The marks are still there," said Roxalana. Her husband removed the axe from the cupboard door and tossed it toward the woodstove. It was only after he returned to the kitchen table and sat with his back turned toward her that she went to the cupboard and removed the loaded pistol that was wrapped in newspaper. Hiding the weapon between the folds of her dress, Roxalana said she did manage to pour her husband a cup of tea in spite of this frightening experience,

According to Roxalana, her husband was sitting at the kitchen table skinning a herring with a large pocketknife, and she was seated directly across from him. After one sip of tea, Bill Druse suddenly exploded in anger. It was not the tea he was accustomed to, and he accused her of spending money they did not have. As the volume and intensity of the argument grew, Roxalana ordered the two boys out of the house. The altercation continued, and her husband reached across the table and grabbed her by the wrist. He then raised his free hand, brandishing the knife, and swore, "Goddamn you—I'll cut your throat."

Wrestling free of his grip, Roxalana produced the revolver and fired a single shot, striking her husband in the neck. "I shot him in self-defense," she said. This was a face-to-face confrontation in which she feared for her life and it was not the cowardly act of shooting a defenseless man in the back, as was portrayed repeatedly at the trial.

Wounded, Bill Druse slumped in the chair, momentarily resting his head on the table. Blood flowed from his neck onto the table and dripped onto the floor. Horrified at what she had done, she stepped back and let the revolver slip out of her hands. "I screamed and almost fainted away. I remember saying, 'God, what shall I do,'" recalled Roxalana.

The two boys heard the gunshot and returned to the house just in time to see Bill Druse rise from his chair and move toward Roxalana to exact his revenge. Suddenly three men burst into the house. By a singular coincidence, Charles Gates, Will Elwood, and another man whom Roxalana couldn't remember had been walking past the farmhouse when they heard the screams and the shot. Charles Gates, she claimed, picked up the revolver and fired three more times at Bill Druse, thus killing him.

The body of Bill Druse was dragged into the parlor but never cut up. Gates and Elwood returned the next evening with a wagon and took it to an undisclosed location. It was Gates who suggested to Roxalana that the alibi about having gone to New York was plausible, given the fact that her brother was a tugboat captain in New York harbor.

In the past, Roxalana said, there had been friction between her husband and all three men. It was just a fortunate coincidence that they had happened by Hogsback Hill Road on that day. She could never recall the name of the third man with Gates and Elwood, but Roxalana was convinced that they were her saviors.

Reverend Powell hoped that the release of this confession would convince people that not all of the facts had been presented at the trial, but the howl of protest he envisioned never occurred.

The one person in Herkimer County who was the most upset was the man who had said the least about Roxalana after the trial, and this was Abram Steele. After stepping down from the office of district attorney, Steele divided his time between his law practice and civic endeavors in the village of Herkimer. Like everyone else, he remained interested in the Druse case, but he never made any official statements. With the publication of this "confession" in the *New York Star*, with the headline "Her many stories," Steele felt compelled to break his silence . This was a personal affront; it gave people the impression that he had failed to investigate the facts surrounding the murder thoroughly.

Why was this confession released to a New York City tabloid and not to the district attorney's office in Herkimer ? Granted, Roxalana had not taken the stand in her own defense—as was her right—but she did plenty of talking before the coroner's inquest. In fact, she gave several versions of the murder, all of which conflicted with the statements given by Frank Gates and her son and daughter. The only part of the confession that Steele agreed with was that the body parts had not been fed to the pigs. He wasn't sure how that rumor started, but he had a pretty good idea. "All I know about that," he said, "is what I have read in the papers."

This confession was nothing more than shameless, eleventh-hour grandstanding. Steele reminded the public not to be blinded by Reverend Powell's sympathetic rhetoric. Pity the woman or not, this was a vicious murder. "She then cut his head off with an axe, rolled the head up in a paper as she could not bear to look at his face, took the body into the parlor and cut it up with the clothes on, and then put it in the stove in parts, then when she came to put the intestines in the stove, they put the fire out and she had to send for matches," he reminded them.

He asked the public to dismiss this latest confession. "Mrs. Druse has already given three different versions of the murder," said Steele.

Equally irritated by this confession was former coroner, Dr. Irving O. Nellis. "I trust this is the last time I will be called upon to make reference to a subject more nauseating to me than to the public in general," he said. Nellis believed that the real mastermind behind this ploy was not Roxalana but Powell. In a sarcastic and bitter letter to the editor, Nellis lost patience with the minister and with his cause. "Dr. Powell has stamped other things as lies which have proven to be quite the contrary. We do not reflect upon the integrity of this learned divine, but only claim that men are liable to be mistaken. When I know that I am mistaken in this matter, I will cheerfully acknowledge it. Until then, I have nothing more to say, unless others see fit to relieve me of that responsibility."

No one questioned or argued with either the former district attorney or the coroner, for both possessed the credibility that the allegations in this confession lacked. The local press was equally unmoved by these latest claims; they brushed aside the comments and never investigated a single claim. Days passed, and not one person stepped forward to demand an inquiry.

Although the confession failed to stir the masses as Reverend Powell had intended, he still held fast to the belief that the legislature would act favorably on behalf of Roxalana by amending the existing penal law. When a reporter from the *Little Falls Evening Times* was granted an interview with Roxalana, he was impressed by her calm demeanor as the days that preceded the legislative vote and her own execution drew near.

"I am still hopeful," she told the reporter regarding the pending bill. "In the few days I have left, I don't want to read any more of the falsehoods of reporters who come and see me, only to go away and write things which I never said at all, or else distort and misconstrue my words."

About the same time this interview took place in Herkimer, the New York State Assembly held another discussion in Albany. Floyd Hadley of Franklin County introduced the long-anticipated bill that would revise the penal code. Ever since Governor Hill had postponed the execution, critics of capital punishment had been waiting for this moment. Hadley announced that he was introducing the bill "by request." Almost immediately, people began speculating that he was doing this on behalf of the governor, but Hadley denied it. He said he had no real sympathy for Mrs. Druse but felt compelled to introduce the measure on behalf of several reputable citizens of the state. The Hadley Bill, also called the Druse Bill, provided that women convicted of first-degree murder be imprisoned for life and be thereafter exempt from capital punishment.

One of the most fervent, if not eloquent, supporters of the measure was the chairman of the committee, Charles D. Baker of Steuben County. Baker worked the floor trying to draw support for the measure and insisted that he was not doing this at the governor's behest. He believed this was a moral question and one of the most important he had ever addressed. "Not only the weal and woe of the immortal soul of Mrs. Roxalana Druse is concerned," implored Baker, but "a broad principle is involved in this question. Let us wipe capital punishment from our statute books, especially in the cases of women. In many foreign countries capital punishment has been abolished altogether. And it is a fact that crimes in these countries have materially decreased."

Baker went on to say that in his opinion, capital punishment should be reserved for those cases that involved treason, a federal crime. "I concede that the State has the right to inflict the death penalty," he said. "But I do not concede the expediency of it. As a Christian nation, we have arrived at a time when women should be exempted from bearing the penalty. We shrink from the idea of the disgusting and demoralizing spectacle of a woman led to the gallows and executed. Such a spectacle has a most demoralizing effect upon the community in which it occurs. It lowers their moral standing."

This clear moral condemnation of capital punishment would have been loudly cheered and applauded by Reverend Powell had he been there, for these were essentially the same things he had been saying for months. But Powell was not there, and angry legislators who were present did not wish to see the penal code changed for the sake of Roxalana Druse or anyone else.

Frederick W. Kruse thought that the argument presented—that if women are not permitted to vote they should not be hanged—was a weak one and would earn his "no" vote. The legislator from Cattaraugus County maintained that it was not consistent to hang men but not women.

William F. Sheehan of Erie County said that he would never support the measure and urged his fellow lawmakers not to, and Frank B. Arnold of Otsego County said that he was not in favor of the measure either. The law should not be changed to reflect different punishments for men and women, he declared, adding, "What is sauce for the goose should be sauce for the gander."

A powerful ally in defeating the measure was Patrick McEvoy of Herkimer County. Passage of this measure would enable a woman to get away with murder. "We must be consistent," he said. "To exempt women from the death penalty and hang men would be radically inconsistent. Such a law would have a tendency to increase the number of murders. It would encourage bad men to conspire with bad women to put a third person out of the way."

Other legislators voiced opinions ranging from the Bible's admonition to "turn the other cheek" to those who sarcastically supported women's rights—one lawmaker steadfastly declared that all women were entitled to all the rights that men had, and this included the death penalty. In the end, Baker did not have the support necessary and the "Druse Bill" was soundly defeated 72 to 30. For Reverend Powell, the lopsided vote was a particularly cruel blow. Had the bill been narrowly defeated by one or two votes, he could say that the issue was controversial enough to demand intervention by the governor. The vote ended all speculation.

"This determines the fate of Mrs. Druse," said the *New York Times*. "The Legislature will not interfere, and her execution must take place on the 28th inst."

With the public unmoved by the last-minute confession and the legislature's refusal to amend the penal code, Reverend Powell made a final journey to Albany to see Governor Hill. His visit was brief, and he returned to Herkimer, noted one newspaper, "very discouraged." He went at once to the jail to visit the woman he had fought so long and hard to save. It was a difficult reunion. No Bible passages or poetry could make what he had to say any less painful. Every avenue had been explored, each option considered, and the answer was always the same. Her last day on Earth, he told her, would be February 28th. There was a brief moment of silence, the eerie stillness that often follows a great calamity. Roxalana trembled, sat down, and slowly began to weep. Powell did his best to console her and suggested that they pray. When they had finished and he was about to leave, he made her a promise: he would not desert her in her final days.

Having failed in his attempt to save Roxalana's life, Reverend Powell was now more determined than ever to vindicate her in the minds of the public, the politicians, and the press. In what little time remained, he would personally write the last chapter in her life. He would show everyone that Roxalana was a confused, misguided woman, deserving of pity rather than scorn. A kind and loving mother, she had grown despondent and depressed with each day that passed on Hogsback Hill Road. From her jail cell, she wrote: "From the window where I sometimes sit, I can overlook a part of three streets. The Dutch Reformed Church and the city of the dead; and sometimes I wish I and my dear children were lying there, out of this world of sorrow and trouble."

How could one doubt upon reading this passage that this woman was truly deserving of sympathy? Or was she? When these lines appeared in the *New York Star*, its editor claimed to have received them from a "good woman" who had befriended Roxalana. Days later, the *Herkimer Democrat* reprinted the same passage with a mild rebuff: "It reads well but lacks the importance of truthfulness."

In fact, the editor of the *Star* had long been sympathetic to Roxalana's plight. Not only had he circulated petitions on her behalf, but on one occasion he wrote to Governor Hill asking that she be entitled to "the mercy of the law." In all probability, the *Star* received the lines not from a good woman but a good man, and that was Reverend Powell.

For the *Herkimer Democrat*, it wasn't all that important where the *Star* obtained the letter. Like Reverend Powell, the *Herkimer Democrat* had plans for Roxalana Druse. In what little time remained, the paper set out to gather old information and new interviews for a special "execution" edition. It was with this in mind that a reporter paid a visit to Abram Steele.

With the exception of a few guarded comments relevant to the latest "Druse confession," Abram Steele said very little about to Roxalana Druse. The *Democrat* was eager to hear from the prosecutor who had successfully tried Herkimer County's most famous case, but the headline-hungry press received very little in the way of sensationalist copy from Steele. He did not brag, gloat, or revel in Roxalana Druse's fate. He preferred to underscore the seriousness of the entire affair in a brief statement. "No greater dread can be conceived," he said, "than to know for certain that a party must die at a given time. The punishment of death is the most dreadful of all punishments. . . ."

This was a horrible crime. During the time Roxalana was incarcerated, she had been vilified by her enemies and sanctified by her supporters. Each effort to save her, and there were quite a few, began with hope and ended in despair. Nothing, it seemed, could save her, not even the eleventh-hour arrival of three physicians.

In mid-February, Governor Hill sent a team of doctors to Herkimer to examine Roxalana Druse's mental state. Arriving unannounced at the county jail, the trio was led by Dr. Judson B. Andrews of the Buffalo Insane Asylum. Joining him were Dr. Charles F. MacDonald of the Asylum for the Criminally Insane at Auburn and Dr. Lewis Balch of the New York State Department of Health. If the governor harbored any doubts or suffered any pangs of conscience, these were set aside when he read the report of the visiting physicians. The doctors were in complete agreement with the investigation conducted earlier by Dr. Charles Gray and Dr. A. Walter Suiter: "Roxalana Druse was sane at the date of the commission of the act for which she was convicted and is now sane."

This report finally convinced Governor Hill. He set it aside and sent a message to Reverend Powell, informing him that there would be no reprieve. The execution would take place with no further interference or communication from his office.

No one knows in what manner Reverend Powell related this news to Roxalana. Perhaps he thought it wise to disregard it altogether. Roxalana, he noted, was growing more nervous and agitated with each passing day. What possible good would it do to present her with more bad news now? Besides, he was facing his greatest challenge as a clergyman. Unlike comforting the terminally ill who could die within days, he had to prepare Roxalana to die on an exact date. Abram Steele was right—this was dreadful.

There was nothing more he could do except to be a constant presence at the jail. His daily visits, he hoped, would be a source of strength, inspiration, and comfort to his friend. Some may have found fault with his tireless lobbying efforts, and a few may have even questioned his motives. But his actions, noted the *Herkimer Democrat*, were consistent "with charity and a Christian spirit, and commendation of those who believe in the creed of the church."

Reverend Powell wasn't the only one who possessed this Christian spirit; Mrs. Powell joined him on many of his visits. Although overshadowed by her husband, Hannah Powell played an equally important role in consoling Roxalana during her last weeks. The jail, after all, was a world of men. With the exception of the matron, Mrs. Waterman, and the sheriff's wife, Mrs. Cook, Roxalana had enjoyed little female companionship since Mary's departure some seventeen months earlier.

Not every member of the cloth shared Powell's opinion that Roxalana was a misguided soul deserving of compassion and God's mercy. Some, like Reverend Henry Parkhurst of Richfield in Otsego

County, openly criticized Powell's motives as well as his methods.

"Mr. Druse was an inoffensive, peaceable, honest man, very slack in business," recalled Reverend Parkhurst, who saw Druse as a harmless man whose personality was in stark contrast to that of his wife. "Mrs. Druse was a surly, quarrelsome, vengeful person. I refrain from rehearsing the facts of one of the most brutal murders ever committed. This is the sentiment of every unbiased person that is familiar with the facts in this case. The jury confirms the statement; the judge sanctions it; the Court of Appeals endorses it; and the sentence for the crime is again pronounced. We ask what use have we for a judge or jury? What use have we for Courts of Appeal?"

What bothered Reverend Parkhurst most was Mrs. Druse's obvious lack of remorse. How could anyone offer her sympathy when she never expressed it toward others she had hurt? "Shall we not show mercy to the penitent? Yes, indeed," he said. "But is Mrs. Druse penitent?" After speaking to those who had visited her at the jail, he didn't believe she was. "The Bible says that no murderer hath eternal life abiding in him. We ask for law and justice."

The press constantly reminded the public that Herkimer County had never experienced a public execution, and neither the sheriff nor his deputies had ever witnessed one either. Still, there was always the possibility that the governor would change his mind and grant a last minute reprieve, as a previous governor had a dozen years earlier.

In 1875, Albert and Lodici Friedenburg were arrested in the town of Ohio for the particularly gruesome murder of Orlo Davis, a relative. Davis, labeled "imbecilic" by the press, had been brutally beaten to death with an axe. A jury found both the husband and wife guilty of murder, and the judge sentenced them to be hanged behind the jail. At the last minute, as the gallows was being assembled, then governor of New York Samuel J. Tilden commuted both sentences to life in prison after reviewing "new testimony." The unfinished gallows was disassembled, and the timbers placed in storage in the attic of the jail.

Cook knew about these old timbers but didn't entertain any thoughts of reconstructing the gallows—this wasn't necessary. In mid-December, a portable or "galloping" gallows had arrived from neighboring Oneida County. This type of gallows could be easily assembled and as the name implied, just as easily transported. When it arrived at the jail for the scheduled February execution that had been postponed from December, Cook ordered the contrivance stored out of the way in the basement. He saw no need to assemble and display the gallows until the last possible moment. First, he did not wish to satisfy the morbid curiosity seekers who would undoubtedly compare it to the guillotine. And second, there was the outside chance that the governor would have a change of heart and commute the sentence at the last minute, as in the case of the Friedenburgs.

A last-minute reprieve would take a miracle, and even Roxalana did not think that it was possible. Alone in her cell, she had slowly come to terms with her own mortality. To her spiritual advisor she made few requests; Reverend Powell had done so much for her that she asked but two favors. She wanted to see her children one last time. He assured her that he would do his utmost to fulfill this request. She then asked that her funeral be held immediately following her execution. To this request, Roxalana received his solemn promise.

Her insistence on a funeral following her execution may not have been motivated entirely by her sudden embrace of religion. Roxalana may have feared that her remains might meet the same fate as those of her late husband and become the object of scientific inquiry. There were still many who believed that unclaimed remains, especially those of convicted felons, became the property of the medical profession. This rumor had its origins in—of all places—Herkimer County.

W. H. Tippetts in *Herkimer County Murders* was quick to point out that the first murder in Herkimer County had been committed by a woman. According to Tippetts, she was executed for the murder of her husband around 1798. After her execution, a group of medical students supposedly made off with the corpse and brought it to a small island in the West Canada Creek. After stoking the fire beneath a large cauldron, they proceeded to boil the flesh off the body until only a skeleton remained.

Part of this macabre tale is true. Pomroy Jones in his book *Annals and Recollections* notes that Sylvia Wood, also known as Sylvia Brown, was indeed convicted of murdering her husband, Major Wood, on April 29, 1798, in the town of Augusta, which in those days was part of Herkimer County. According to eyewitnesses, Sylvia Wood and her common-law husband were at a local tavern in a highly intoxicated state following an Election Day gathering. Words were exchanged, and in no time the confrontation between the two became physical. "While her husband was attempting to restrain her," recalled Jones, "she seized his gun and inflicted a fatal wound."

A tavern full of witnesses, many who liked him but disliked his wife, testified at the trial. Sylvia Wood was convicted and sentenced to be hanged behind the county jail on June 29, 1798 between the hours of 10 a.m. and 2 p.m. The presiding judge in the case ordered that her body be delivered to Dr. Amos G. Hall for the purpose of dissection. "Upon the morning of her execution," wrote Jones, "she was found dead in her cell in the Herkimer jail, having hanged herself with the expectation that she could thus evade the whole of the sentence. In this, however, she was mistaken, for science had its *subject*."

Although this had taken place in the late 1790s, few people in Herkimer County needed a reminder that it wasn't all that long ago when medical students at nearby Fairfield College had been suspected of robbing graves for the purpose of securing cadavers. This, plus the fact that both coroners, Dr. Nellis and Dr. Suiter, had graduated from Fairfield, fueled the public's speculation that this is exactly what would become of the remains of Roxalana Druse.

Reverend Powell helped ease Roxalana's fears by once more pledging his word that her body would not be violated by either grave robbers or the medical profession. He would personally see to every detail of her funeral. When he spoke to reporters, he was only too happy to tell them that Mrs. Druse had confided in him and expressed her wish that she not be laid to rest beside her beloved daughter Nellie at the farm on Hogsback Hill Road. Although she had loved her daughter dearly, the farm and Warren itself were the scenes of a great many tragedies in her life. The kindly minister avoiding mentioning that Roxalana was responsible for at least one of these tragedies. Furthermore, who could say if the new owners of the farm would permit her to be buried there?

What Reverend Powell announced next took reporters and everyone else by surprise. He planned to have the funeral, including the public viewing of the remains, at the Herkimer County Courthouse. County officials were furious with him. With every effort on the part of the sheriff's office to de-sensationalize the upcoming execution, they felt sure that Powell's latest announcement was a ploy to try to make a public statement about capital punishment. There was no way they would allow him to lionize Roxalana in the very building where she had been condemned. He need not concern himself with an autopsy, for there would be none, and there would be no public funeral. Any remarks he wished to make could be delivered at Oak Hill Cemetery.

With his plans somewhat altered by the officials of Herkimer County, Reverend Powell had no recourse except to announce that he would preach a sermon at his church the following Sunday. Having failed to choreograph a funeral, he tried to redeem himself by staging a family reunion.

With only four days remaining in February, Reverend Powell made a hurried trip to the Onondaga Penitentiary to meet with prison officials. The prison chaplain confirmed for Powell what he already knew in his heart—during her fifteen-month incarceration, Mary Druse had been a model prisoner. Her demeanor had changed little since leaving the Herkimer County Jail. She remained the quiet, somewhat withdrawn girl whose loyalty to her mother never wavered. Mary had few visitors, and the sight of Reverend Powell was indeed a welcome one. She was aware of all that he had done to help her mother and was thankful for the visit, but she did not share his optimism about the prospects of being reunited with her mother. She too had tried and failed. On Christmas Day she had sent a Western Union telegram to Governor Hill requesting permission to visit her mother before her December 28 execution date. Her request had been denied.

Now it was Reverend Powell's turn. With typical dramatic flair, the spiritual advisor begged the governor to allow mother and daughter to be reunited. "We know of no other way to bring this about unless you will give your permission. The Superintendent would gladly comply with the pleading desire of this unfortunate woman. I pray you will grant this small favor. P.S. Please do not deny this last tearful, dying cry." Like Mary's telegram, this request went unanswered.

To many who had followed the Druse trial, Mary seemed like an unwilling accomplice who was under the influence of a domineering mother. George, on the other hand, was seen as a harmless little boy. The press warmed to him during the trial, and after it was over he was never bothered him for an interview, even as the execution date drew near. Because his name was not in the news, however, it should not be assumed that he was disinterested in his mother's fate. George didn't have a Reverend Powell to champion his cause, but he did have a neighbor step forward, and that was Charles Garline. A fairly successful dairy farmer who had at one time been the town assessor and constable, Garline had known the Druse family for years. In his letter to Governor Hill, he spoke on behalf of young George:

"At the request of George Druse, son of the condemned, I write you on his behalf. He lives here in our place with his aunt, a sister of the deceased Druse. He hopes of your saving his mother from the gallows, and I hope and trust you will let her go to prison for life. Those parties from the town of Warren that petitioned you to let her hang will regret it. There was two sides to the trouble in the family and she got the best of him. Please do not let her be hung. If you would like to see the boy I will call down to your chamber with him.

Judge Robert Earl of the Court of Appeals, J.W. Vrooman, Clerk of the Senate, and Hon. J.W. Husted, Speaker of the Assembly, are friends of mine and you can confer as to my standing if you Choose. Please let me hear from you.

Truly Your Friend
C.D. Garline

At noon on Sunday, February 26, George Druse arrived at the county jail. He hadn't seen his mother since the trial and had not spoken to her since they were all arrested two years ago. Since then, he had been living with his aunt and uncle, Phoebe and Newton Chamberlain, on their farm in Miller's Mills.

The reunion between mother and son can best be described as bittersweet. Roxalana beamed at the sight of her little boy and how he had grown. Now twelve years old, George was fit and healthy. What the two spoke of will forever remain a mystery, as the sheriff's deputies stepped aside and respected the moment. One reporter surmised that George "visited and chatted as any boy might do who had been apart from his mother for a short time and expected to see her again in a few days."

As George was about to leave, his mother presented him with a gift—a camp chair. Clutching it with both hands, he walked out of the cell toward the waiting deputies. He looked back one last time and quietly said, "Good-bye, Ma."

CHAPTER 8

"Weep not for me dear child..."

As the last week of February drew near, the execution scheduled to take place behind the jail at the corner of Main and Church Street was the most talked about event in the village. The ever-vigilant Sheriff Cook took every precaution and saw to each detail of the impending execution. Although it was not one of his official duties as a law enforcement official, he began by placating the press. He arranged to have one of the six Western Union Telegraph lines drawn to the jail and another to the Herkimer County Courthouse. Cook expected representatives from the *New York Times*, the *New York Journal*, and the *New York World*, as well as Utica and valley newspapers to send dispatches immediately following the execution.

The sheriff was also mindful that crowd control in and around the jail was a serious matter. In late December or early January, Cook may have asked as many as fifty individuals to attend the hanging . No one knows if these invitations were extended for political reasons or if he simply took it upon himself to ask whomever he chose. What is known is that the passage of the McMillan Bill forced the sheriff to rescind these invitations. This recent amendment to the penal code limited the number of people that could be present at an execution to twenty-eight.

Invitations to the macabre spectacle were extended to the highest county officials. County Judge Rollin H. Smith, District Attorney Eugene Sheldon, and County Clerk A.T. Smith were asked to attend, along with the coroners, Dr. A. Walter Suiter and Dr. Cyrus Kay Jr. Reverend Powell and fellow Universalist minister S.R. War were joined by coal dealer J.H. Huyck and Herkimer merchant C. Munger. H.P. Witherstine, whose paper was poised to report the execution in a special edition, was asked to attend, as was West Winfield banker, H.P. Wheeler. The only person from the town of Warren who was extended an invitation was Abram Tilyou, a farmer. He had been less vocal about the Druse case than many of his

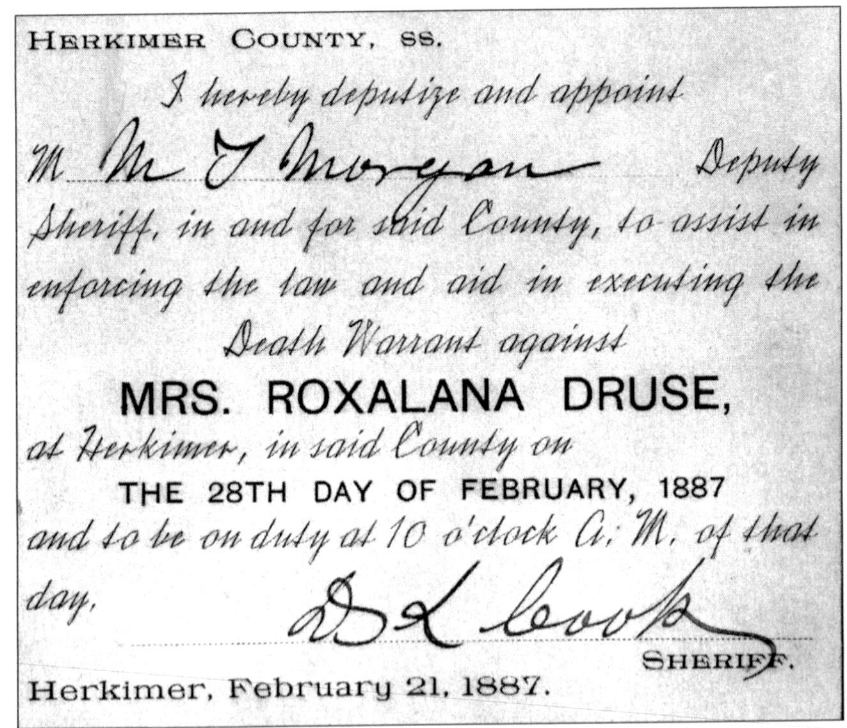
HERKIMER COUNTY, SS.

I hereby deputize and appoint

M M T Morgan Deputy

Sheriff, in and for said County, to assist in enforcing the law and aid in executing the Death Warrant against

MRS. ROXALANA DRUSE,

at Herkimer, in said County on

THE 28TH DAY OF FEBRUARY, 1887

and to be on duty at 10 o'clock A. M. of that day.

D L Cook

SHERIFF.

Herkimer, February 21, 1887.

An inviitation pass to the execution.

neighbors and had not added his signature to the infamous Druse petition. Aside from farmers and businessmen, the only other group that would be well represented at the execution was the medical profession; four more physicians would join Drs. Suiter and Kay. Finally, Abram Steele was probably extended an invitation. It is not known whether a woman was asked to witness the hanging.

Sheriff Cook did not know what to expect from any gatherings outside the jail while the execution was underway, but he didn't want to take any chances. On the morning of the execution, the Remington Rifle Corps from nearby village of Mohawk surrounded the building, with orders not to let anyone within 200 yards of the jail.

As to the placement of the gallows, Cook had few choices. Given the narrow confines of the jail yard, he instructed his deputies to tuck the device near the east corner of the jail. He knew that it would be almost impossible to hide the gallows entirely from those who wanted to see the hanging, but he did his best to discourage them. On Sunday, February 27, one day before the execution, the deputies began assembling the gallows. Sometime after the governor's final decision, Cook had ordered his deputies to paint it white. He never offered an explanation about this, but some said he did it out of respect because it was a woman who would be hanged. Others speculated that the gallows was whitewashed to hide the eleven notches carved into the wood on the main upright.

Unlike the "trap door" gallows commonly associated with justice west of the Mississippi River or the "drop panel" gallows reminiscent of the Lincoln assassination, this one required a counterweight. When the weight was released, it would jerk the victim upwards with such force as to break his or her neck. The rope to be used for the execution had been in the sheriff's office since it was purchased from the Adams Brothers Company on December 23 for ten dollars.

While Deputy Bartlett Manion uncoiled the rope and prepared to run it through the gallows, other deputies dragged out the 213-pound counterweight forged in Herkimer by the C.H. Warburton Foundry. Manion spent a good part of Sunday afternoon dropping and re-dropping the counterweight. Each time the weight was released, it took up the rope's slack. Surely this was enough to snap the neck of a woman who now weighed less than 100 pounds.

Every particular of the events of the next few days came under Cook's umbrella of authority. Every detail, however trivial, concerned him. When Rome, New York, resident A.R. Davis contacted Cook via telegram stating that he had a petition signed by many prominent citizens asking for the imprisonment of Roxalana for life, Davis asked for time. "Will you postpone matters until the last hour of your official limit? Please answer at once to Oneida, N.Y."

Unlike the governor, who never responded to the petitions or communiqués that reached his office, the sheriff felt compelled to reply to this last minute request and had it printed in the *Herkimer Democrat.* "I am assured by Governor Hill he will not interfere. The postponement would avail nothing and might seriously complicate matters. I regret I cannot grant it," he responded. There were other telegrams to be sure, and a few of these Cook ignored. Some came from individuals asking if they could be present at the execution; some came from those who volunteered to perform the service of releasing the counterweight free of charge.

The only detail Sheriff Cook could not control was the unpredictable Mohawk Valley weather. The last several days had brought bitter cold, and now it was beginning to snow. This shift in the weather, while unpleasant for those longing for spring, pleased the sheriff. The least bit of wind would create snowdrifts over the roads leading into the village, making it difficult for anyone trying to get to the jail. If the snow continued, some village residents might even stay home. Cook was overjoyed when the board of trustees of the village schools announced that, despite any bad weather that might arrived, the schools would remain open that Monday. It was indeed unfortunate, they said, that eighteen months earlier some students had skipped school to watch the trial of Roxalana Druse.

The drop weight used at the execution.

Sunday, February 27, was a busy day for Reverend Powell. His day began in Herkimer where he conducted services at the Universalist Church. The sermon was brief if not predictable. He reminded his congregation that he had no regrets for the part he played in assisting Roxalana. She was, in his opinion, "a poor fallen, friendless creature" in need of his help. From the pulpit, he admitted that his methods were not accepted by some, but he assured his flock that he would have done the same for anyone. From Herkimer he traveled north to Middleville to conduct services at the Universalist Church there, and then it was back to Herkimer to preach at a funeral service. It was a long day, but Reverend Powell knew that the much greater challenges lay ahead.

At about 7:30 p.m., the minister arrived at the jail with a few women from the church choir. Sheriff's deputies escorted the small party through the corridor and directed them to the new cell occupied by Roxalana. A few days earlier, she had been moved from the third floor and her room stripped of its contents. The box organ had been shipped to Onondaga Penitentiary for Mary, and the sewing machine was returned to Mrs. Cook. In addition to the change in cell accommodations, Under-sheriff A.M. Rice noticed a change in Roxalana. Her hearty appetite disappeared suddenly, and she wasn't her usual talkative self. Not only had she refused breakfast, she also refused to visit with Rice. She turned away from one who had befriended her with a solemn "I can't talk." Rice understood and walked away.

The deputies set up chairs outside of Roxalana's cell for Reverend Powell and his choir, but did not unlock her cell for the spiritual advisor as they had done for George. The minister remained outside her cell all evening and did his best to comfort her. After leading the choir in "Nearer My God to Thee," Reverend Powell began his prayer: "Blessed are the poor in heart for they shall be comforted. . . .Go to God with a sweet, forgiving spirit. Whatever unkind feeling others may have against you, have no hatred toward anyone. . . . In my Father's house are many mansions, and He has gone to prepare the way for you. Fix your mind upon the Holier and brighter world. . . . In everything in life there seems to be a match for, except one, and that is death. It is your fate to pass over to the other side, but you will be happier and better, where there is nothing but glory and hope; something brighter and more beautiful for you."

He paused for a moment, and then asked Roxalana to think back to Nellie, the child she had lost. "If you were assured that you would see that darling child, would it not afford you great joy?" he asked her.

"Yes," she replied, and then asked the choir to sing "On that Beautiful Shore" and later, "Open Wide the Gate." They prayed and sang for about an hour, and the choir was about to leave when a deputy stepped forward and whispered to Roxalana. It was late and she was very tired, but he asked if she would like to receive a visitor—H. DeWight Luce had just arrived from Albany.

Escorted to her cell door by a deputy, the dour expression on Luce's face betrayed his innermost thoughts and feelings. He had recently seen Governor Hill and was personally assured by him that there would be no last minute reprieve. Luce briefly reviewed the trial, the legal process, and the appeals. He did his best to explain to her that he had done all the law would allow but had failed. For this he offered his heartfelt apology.

It was late in the evening when Luce and Reverend Powell left the jail, but not too late for the local reporters waiting for a story. Luce told them that he had spoken to Roxalana, and at this late hour, she expressed no ill will toward anyone. "She is fully prepared to go and is calm and composed. If the people of this state want to hang her, she is brave enough to die, although she says she does not deserve such a fate." Luce paused and added, "She is the bravest woman I ever saw."

Reverend Powell agreed with Luce, but he could not pass up

the opportunity to offer the press a premature eulogy. "She is reconciled to her fate," he said, "but not to the manner of death. She would not mind death so much, but the thought of hanging in an enlightened country like this is awful. Mrs. Druse has been greatly misrepresented by the reporters. She is not a heartless, unfeeling woman. On the contrary, she is as affectionate and as devout as one could ask. She has just given me two letters, and here is one, probably the last she will ever write. Look, is it not touching?"

By sheer coincidence, Reverend Powell had not one but several copies of Roxalana's "last letter," and he was only too happy to distribute copies to the press.

Herkimer, N.Y.
Feb. 27, 1887

Dear Mrs. Sheriff Brown
Dear Kind Friend,

Remembering your many deeds of kindness that time cannot erase, and wishing to sincerely thank you for your still continued favors, have therefore taken the liberty to write you a few lines. Never shall I forget the night I came to this place, or your expressions of sympathy, besides your desire to make us as comfortable as possible under the circumstances, and ever after while you all did all you could for our comfort and to cheer our sad hearts crushed with sorrow. I was your prisoner I know, but you treated me with great respect, and all of our friends that came to visit you have often spoken kind words and expressed their sympathy for me. However, my prayers will be that for this kindness you will pass many pleasant hours away, certainly with a clear conscience, if nothing more. Feeling that you have been kind to all, harsh to none, to yourself and Mr. Brown, I am even more thankful than words can speak for this last kindly call and gentle good-bye. I humbly ask one more favor: only that you will not forget and write a line to them occasionally. If it is not my sad lot to die on Monday, it will be a great comfort to me in my dying hours and thousands of friends would willingly save my life had they the power to do so. I have parted with my dear boy today. Oh, it is hard to say good-bye forever. Must this be! Is this truly so or am I dreaming? Can I ever see his dear face again or hear his voice? And my dear Mary wrote, "Oh, mother, how can I be reconciled to your terrible death, and I know I shall soon follow you." These were her words written in her letter to me—a farewell letter, a dying woman comparatively, with so many enduring words of pity, and deepest love and affection for me while so near to the end of a long life of suffering and sorrow.

I am nearing the river's brink
For I hear the loud angry waves roll,
In the deep abyss I fear I shall sink
And fierce waves o'er me will roll.
But again my spirit may rise
And soar to that world of light
Where no parting is known or tears in the eyes
Among loved that are happy and bright.

Excuse this writing for I am so nervous and I can hardly write.
Write me, good-bye
Mrs. Druse

The letter was reprinted in many of the local papers; it even made its way via telegraph to the editorial offices of the *New York Times*, which printed it the next day. The article, titled "Roxie Druse's Last Sunday," took the liberty of correcting a few mistakes, the letter and poem being "extremely faulty in punctuation and spelling."

The entire piece was panned by the *Times*: "She considers herself something of a poetess, though the belief did not develop into action until she had been in prison for some time. She is by no means the only prisoner who has attempted to find relief in verse."

No one, not even the *Times'* editors, ever questioned the authorship of the letter, but certain passages almost assuredly flowed from the pen of Reverend Powell. It is doubtful that Roxalana's rudimentary education could have afforded her a poetic style steeped in the imagery of romanticism.

Reverend Powell bade the reporters a good night and then reentered the jail. As he approached Roxalana's cell, he could hear her sobbing. Mrs. Waterman, the matron, was there with Deputy Bartlett Manion and ex-Sheriff Valentine Brown. Roxalana cried on and off until the sedatives she was given had taken effect, and she drifted off to sleep at about 11:30 p.m. Despite the sedatives, it was a restless slumber. Seated outside her cell door, Mrs. Waterman noted that Roxalana's breathing was heavy at times, and in her delirium she was heard to murmur a few phrases: "women hang and Gates go free. . . he thinks he is better than I am, but they will find out . . . they think they got Bill's bones . . . they have got dog bones. . . . he ain't to blame."

At 1 a.m. she woke with a start and asked Mrs. Waterman for a lantern. The startled matron asked if there was something wrong. "No," said Roxalana. She wished only to read her daughter's letter again. Mrs. Waterman summoned a nearby deputy who brought a lantern. Roxalana unfolded Mary's last letter and read it several times before setting it aside. Mrs. Waterman heard Roxalana say, "Oh dear, oh dear." It was then that she asked for writing paper. Into the early morning hours, Mrs. Waterman sat outside the cell as Roxalana composed farewell letters. She wrote the first letter to George and the second to Mary:

I shall have this letter buried with me if I die, but hope that a kind, tender one from above will whisper softly in the Governor's ear and let me live.

Dearest child,

If no such message comes do not grieve for me; be brave for I have suffered everything but death for what others ought to, and if I die I shall be at rest. Weep not for me dear child, for life has so little pleasure at best, and none for me. It is nearly 3 o'clock at night. I have willed my body to Mr. Powell and he will take care of it. He will write you in a day or two. He brought the choir here this evening to sing for me. They sung several nice pieces and I enjoyed it very much. I am more thankful to them and the Reverend Mr. Powell for kindly asking them to come as well as the thousand other favors he has bestowed upon me. He will be a friend to you as well as to me when I am gone. In time of need, Mrs. Powell is just as kind and is a very pleasant lady.

Good-bye my Dearest, Dear girl and may some flower spring up in your life's pathway to obscure the darkness that clouds it. Farewell is my last dying word, is all I can say to my Dear daughter that I love so well.

Mrs. Roxalana Druse

This last letter to Mary was published in the *Herkimer Democrat* the following day. With hints of a reprieve by the governor and the continued effort to implicate others in the crime, the letter appeared suspicious. It had all the trappings of Reverend Powell's influence. And there was something else—for all the sentimentality associated with these touching letters, it was odd that she closed each one with the unaffectionate "Mrs. Druse."

It was almost 6 a.m. when Roxalana set her pen aside. In addition to her children, she had written to the two sheriffs she had known and their wives, whom she regarded as friends. She also wrote a note to Sarah Rice, the wife of the under-sheriff. Her last letter was addressed to Deputy Bartlett Manion.

Roxalana had said nothing more to Mrs. Waterman after asking for writing paper and now, without a word, set herself down on her cot. The matron noted that at first she seemed restless again but then slept soundly for an hour. At 7 a.m. she awoke and put on the dress made for her by Maggie Clark. Local gossip suggested that the dress would be tasteless and gaudy, but these rumors were quickly dismissed. The floor-length black satin frock had a small bit of white ruffling about the neckline and hem. The *Herkimer Democrat* noted that the dress was "made for the occasion."

After she had dressed, Roxalana brushed her thick brown-black hair. After a few strokes of the hairbrush, she carefully cut a few locks and slipped them into the letters she had written only a few hours earlier. When this was done, Mrs. Waterman told her that Reverend Powell had arrived with Deputy Superintendent Terry and Chaplain Durston of the Onondaga Penitentiary. Remarkably composed until now, Roxalana's eyes swelled with tears, and she sobbed at the sight of her spiritual advisor.

The superintendent tried to calm Roxalana, telling her that Mary was well cared for and well thought of at the penitentiary. For the past sixteen months, she had worked in the box factory. He echoed what H. DeWight Luce had said earlier—she need not worry about Mary; from all accounts, she appeared to be a model prisoner. Chaplain Durston told Roxalana that Mary was deeply affected, very distressed and agitated. On the day of the execution, Mary was told she did not have to work, but Chaplain Durston said she preferred to keep busy. "I shall miss my mother," she confided to a matron. "Oh, no one can understand how great a comfort she has been to me all these days of imprisonment, and how can I live without her?"

For a moment these words calmed Roxalana. The bouquet of roses, the Chaplin said, was a gift from Mary. She stared at the roses, perhaps remembering the conversation she'd had with Mrs. Waterman regarding her fondness for flowers, whether real or the paper ones she made in jail. Deputy Superintendent Terry then reached into his pocket and produced a letter. Roxalana set the bouquet aside and wept as she read the last note she would get from her daughter.

At the penitentiary, Mary remained unrepentant. She had harsh words for those who were "involved" in the murder and even suggested that her brother could speak on their mother's behalf. She believed that her mother could save herself if only she would speak. "Oh, why doesn't she say something? She could say something," Mary had said.

With her life running out in a few short hours, Roxalana did have something to say. She asked for paper, and with the assistance of H.P. Witherstine, she drafted the following final statement, which the editor of the *Herkimer Democrat* promised to publish after her execution.

I, Roxalana Druse, in my last moments, do hereby solemnly swear and affirm that my daughter, Mary Druse, who is now confined in the Onondaga Penitentiary, had nothing whatsoever to do with the killing of her father, William Druse, or with the disposition of his body. This statement I have repeatedly made and always adhered to it at the inquest and since my confinement. My daughter, Mary Druse, is absolutely innocent and was no way connected with her father's death.

Mrs. Roxalana Druse

Subscribed and sworn before me, this 28th day of February 1887

H.P. Witherstine
Notary Public

Witness,
G.W. Powell
O.W. Waterman

By affixing her signature to this document, Roxalana all but guaranteed that Mary would one day receive a pardon. Stating that she was completely innocent wasn't the truth, but trying to save her daughter from a life in prison was Roxalana's most noble act. Everyone would remember the murder on Hogsback Hill Road, but few would recall the love she had for her daughter.

By 11 a.m. the Remington Rifles were in place, and the sheriff was told that the snow had been removed from the walkway to the jail and the area immediately surrounding the scaffold. Throughout the morning, reporters hoping to gain admittance to the courtyard had been arriving at the jail, only to be detained at the sheriff's office. Leaving an armed deputy to guard the entrance to the cell area, Cook informed his staff that it was time. He led the quiet procession of Under-sheriff Rice, Deputy Bartlett Manion, and Jailer Harry Brown to Roxalana's cell. Reverend Powell had just finished praying with Roxalana when Cook announced that he was required to read the death warrant issued by Judge Pardon C. Williams on November 8, 1886, aloud.

After hearing the chilling words, "hanging the said Roxalana

Druse by the neck until she be dead, within the walls of the jail . . . ," Reverend Powell offered yet another prayer and what encouragement he could. When the prayers ended, Roxalana said good-bye to her faithful companion, Mrs. Waterman, and thanked her husband, Orsenus, for his assistance as well. Clutching the bouquet of roses, Roxalana leaned on Powell's arm and together they walked out of the cell for the last time.

The somber procession walked through the narrow halls down a set of stairs, past the kitchen, and toward the only door that led to the courtyard. Still clinging to the reverend's arm, Roxalana entered the courtyard and beheld the gallows for the first time. She stopped and stared for a moment at the white gallows, trimmed now with black crepe, and then glanced at the group of men assembled there to watch her die. She hesitated once more as they neared the gallows. Cook and Rice gently eased her to the platform and placed her directly beneath the noose. At that moment, the sun broke through the clouds, bathing the entire courtyard in light that seemed all the brighter reflecting off the new-fallen snow.

Cook and Rice stepped aside and once more Reverend Powell offered prayers. Kneeling with Roxalana on the gallows, his voice boomed across the yard as if he were preaching in a large cathedral, while Roxalana's voice trembled with fear.

"Almighty and most merciful Father, we lift our sad, sorrowful hearts to Thee as we stand beneath this deep and awful gloom." The prayer was all Powell—a vigorous combination of religious fervor and theatrics. The spiritual advisor had but a small congregation, but he made the most it. "We commend this sorrowful soul to Thy unrelenting love with the full assurance of faith and hope that Thou wilt receive her into Thy Kingdom of Peace. . . ." There was pity: "Oh, most merciful Father, pity and bless the dear sorrowing child. . . ." and the usual condemnation of capital punishment: "Pity all those mistaken souls who have driven us in the spirit of retaliation and vengeance under the shadow of this terrifying instrument of death. And may Thy disapprobation rest upon all the torturing instruments of death that are not in accord with the Divine Spirit of love and forgiveness."

The managing editor of the *Herkimer Democrat* was unmoved by this last "sermon." H.P. Witherstine printed it the next day but not before labeling it "very pathetic."

When they had finished praying, the two stood, and Sheriff Cook

The gallows

asked Roxalana if she had anything to say. The previous day, H. DeWight Luce had told reporters he thought it highly unlikely that Roxalana would offer any last words as she stood on the gallows. Still trembling, tears streaming down her face, Roxalana looked to the one person who had been her voice for the past sixteen months. Reverend Powell had plenty to say, and he lashed out a final time, using his pulpit voice to denounce capital punishment once more.

"And now I wish to speak for myself, not to you only, but to the

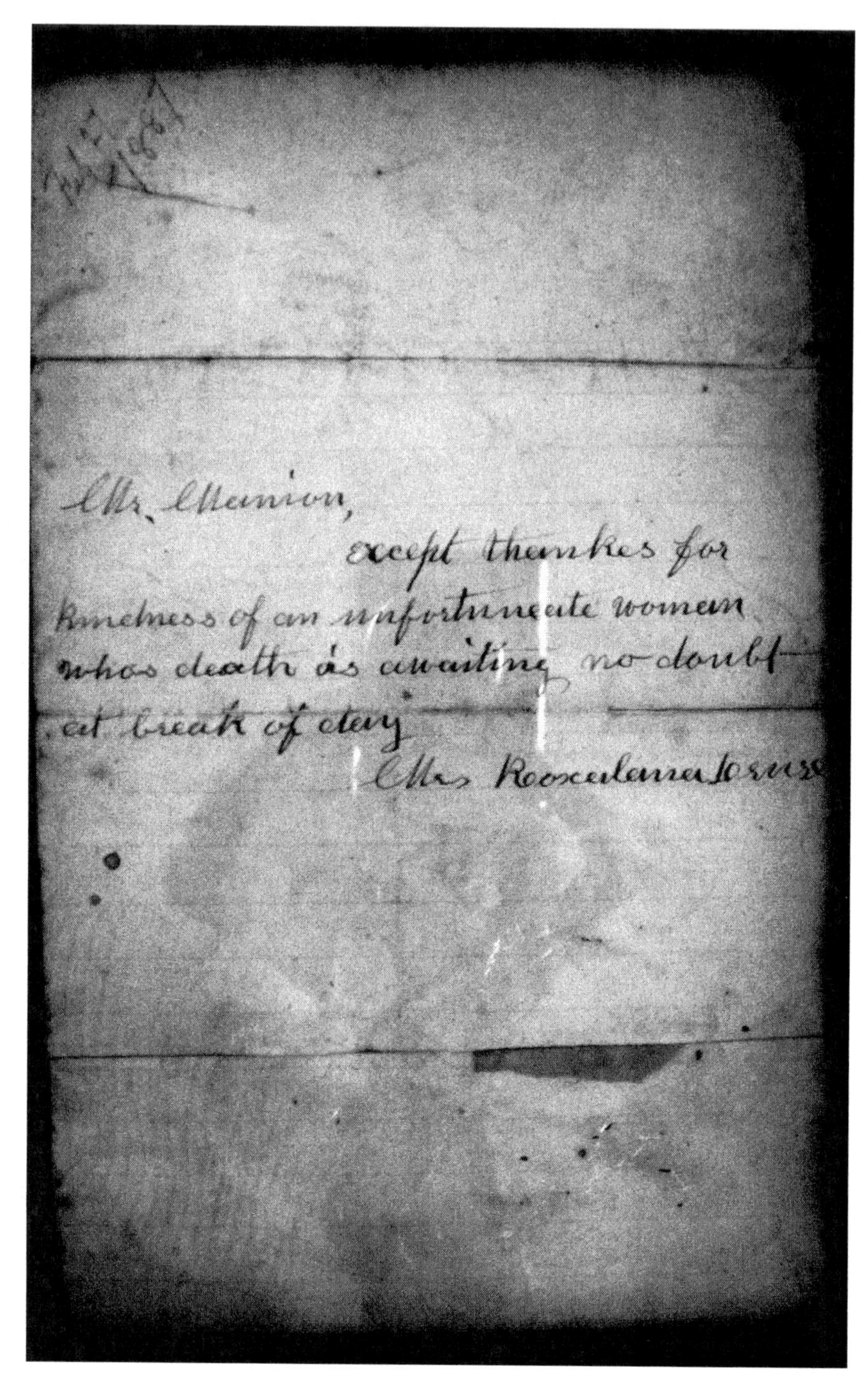
Mr. Manion,
except thankes for
kindness of an unfortunate woman
whos death is awaiting no doubt
at break of day
Mrs Roxalana Druse

Roxalana Druse's Final Letter

whole world. I have led up on my arm this sorrowful child of the Earth to the fatal spot, and stand by her side as her true friend in trouble, but I am not here as party to this ghastly scene. I have no manner of sympathy with it. It seems to me out of place with the civilization of our Christian religion, and I can but hope that the human people of our beloved land will from this dark day sweep the law of punishment by death into everlasting oblivion."

Powell wasn't finished yet. With a dramatic flair, he took Roxalana by the hand and intoned, "Go to thy fate, trembling child of sorrow, Go to thy loving Father, God! Go to thy compassionate Brother, Jesus, and to the side of thy angel who has gone before. Go bravely in the strength of hope and faith, that there will be a place for thee somewhere above these dark and dismal shadows. Go, penitent and bleeding heart, the transit from Earth to Heaven will be but short. Go! While we can say go, the angels say come! And may the grace of our Lord, Jesus Christ, the love of God, and the fellowship of the Holy Spirit of truth and power go with and remain with you forever."

He gently released her hand, stepped aside, and said, "Amen."

Cook nodded his head and Deputies John McKinley and Cyrus Ballou stepped forward and placed themselves on either side of the condemned woman. While one lashed her legs together, the other tied her wrists. Her hands were not tied behind her back but in front, enabling her to keep her hold on the roses. When the black hood was lifted and placed over her head, she let out a terrible shriek, and then cried out once more when the noose was placed about her neck. Cook dropped his hand—the signal for Ballou to release the pin. Warburton's counterweight fell and hit the gallows platform with a loud bang, and Roxalana's body shot upwards in one violent motion. Dr. Cyrus Kay noted the time. It was 11:50 a.m.

When five minutes had elapsed, Drs. Kay and Suiter stepped onto the platform and made a horrible discovery—Roxalana still had a pulse! Her neck had not been broken and she was still alive. At 11:56 her pulse was 96, a minute later it was 126 and then 140. At noon her heart was still beating; Roxalana was slowly strangling to death. At 12:03 the pulse in her right wrist ceased, a minute later her heart stopped beating.

The lifeless body remained suspended in air for another fifteen minutes while a wagon containing her coffin was brought into the inner yard. It was only after lowering her body into the coffin that the hood was removed. Sadly, it revealed the bouquet of roses crushed now between the rope and her neck. The coffin lid was nailed shut and the wagon was led slowly out of the yard. It traveled down Main Street and turned left onto German Street toward the vault at Oak Hill Cemetery over a mile away.

Very few people braved the bitter cold on that final day of February to witness the slow funeral cortege. As it passed along German Street and then up to Oak Hill Cemetery, many residents remained indoors and some, like Charles Warburton whose foundry produced the dropweight for the gallows, elected to take their families out of town. When the procession arrived at the cemetery, the coffin with the remains of Roxalana Druse was brought to the vault where it would remain until a spring burial could be arranged. Before the door was locked, Reverend Powell stepped forward to offer yet another prayer. Sheriff Cook then locked the vault door and placed the only key in his pocket. When he returned to the jail, he discovered that his deputies had already dismantled the gallows for its return to Oneida County. The rope used had been cut up into souvenir lengths.

The following Sunday, Reverend Powell preached his eulogy sermon. He condemned capital punishment, lauded Roxalana as a "woman of a loving disposition," and called her husband's atheism a catalyst to the crime. Both the *Herkimer Democrat* and the *New York Times* noted that his remarks were well received by a large audience.

CHAPTER 9

"I'll haunt you. . . ."

Throughout most of that February 1887, Lillie Devereux Blake watched events unfold from Albany. She greatly anticipated the results of the Municipal Suffrage Bill being discussed in the assembly at the same time the Hadley Bill was introduced. The defeat of the Hadley Bill had left no doubt in her mind what would happen to Roxalana. "Feel much less hopeful. That wretched woman will surely hang tomorrow," she recorded in her diary. On February 28, she wrote: "Made me sick by the thought of that unhappy Mrs. Druse."

Her depression was short-lived, however, and Blake quickly regained her feminist zeal. She attacked not only the governor's remarks but also the law and the base hypocrisy of a trial by one's peers. Had Roxalana been a man, she never would have been convicted, no matter how brutal the crime—and Blake could prove it. All one had to do was look at the Unger murder trial held in New York City that same February.

On January 21, 1887, Edward Unger, a onetime sea captain and present day sausage peddler, savagely beat a man to death with a hammer after a heated argument involving money. August Bohle, the unfortunate victim, was his business partner. No one knows for sure how many blows Unger inflicted because Bohle's head had been wrested from his body with a shaving razor. Unger then packed Bohle's headless body in a steamer trunk and made arrangements to ship it to Baltimore. After tossing Bohle's head into the East River, Unger spent the rest of the day mopping up blood in his apartment. Days later, Unger's oft-repeated claim that his business partner had gone to Chicago came under suspicion when a trunk oozing with blood was discovered at the train station. Unger, not among the greatest criminal minds, had neglected to remove his name from the trunk, thus giving the police their man. A week later, he was placed under arrest and charged with the murder of his business partner.

Blake saw direct parallels with the Unger and Druse murders.

The murder of Bohle was no less brutal than that of William Druse. Both murderers attempted to cover their crimes by disposing of the body, Roxalana by cremation and Unger by railroad freight. Roxalana claimed her husband went to New York; Unger claimed that Bohle had gone to Chicago. When arrested, both confessed. Before the coroner's inquest, Roxalana admitted that she had killed her husband, and Unger made a similar confession before his inquest even convened. At their respective trials, both entered pleas of not guilty and later were found guilty of murder. The only differences were their genders and sentences. Roxalana was hanged—Unger went to Sing Sing Prison for twenty years.

Remembering Governor Hill's remarks about women not being held accountable for laws they did not help enact, an angry Blake made her feelings known.

"It is monstrously unjust to hold women to a full responsibility before the law and yet deny them full privileges in law. Women's only equality in law is at the gallows and in prison—not at the polls. Were it not for the comparison of Mrs. Druse's case with Unger's, I would say that she got a just sentence. But Unger was tried by a jury of his peers, and Mrs. Druse was not. Would a jury of women have hanged Mrs. Druse? Why should she have not been tried by a jury of her peers?"

Blake pointed out that Unger, surrounded by his weeping children, gave a tearful performance when he took the stand in his own defense. He even perjured himself, claiming that his son had disposed of Bohle's head (his son had an alibi and took the stand to testify that he hadn't), and then had the audacity to beg the court not to separate him from the children he so loved.

"I do not know the legal points in her trial, but I do know the facts. You men have feelings for your sex, and no doubt such feelings influenced the Unger jury. Would Unger have consented to a jury of women to decide his fate?" argued Blake.

Blake was not alone in her criticism of the apparent double standard that existed in the legal system. "Mrs. Druse fully earned her fate," announced the *New York Tribune*, in the next breath asking why similar crimes involving men received lesser punishments. "The crimes of Unger and Rourke were not a whit less black than the brutal murder of Druse."

On the day Roxalana Druse was hanged, New York City policeman William F. Rourke was sentenced to life in prison for the fatal shooting of fellow officer Roundsman Montgomery. It certainly did

THE GIBBET AS AN ENGINE OF REFORM.
The ignorant offspring of church and state must suffer for the shortcomings of its parents.

This cartoon was sent to Governor Hill after the execution.

appear that men were getting away with murder, prompting the *New York Sun* to question capital punishment. "We are by no means satisfied that the infliction of death is the best method of dealing with the murders, but we are clear that no difference should be made between men and women when they are guilty of that dreadful deed."

Yet there were those who hailed the execution of Roxalana Druse as a mercifully quick end to an ugly crime. The *Brooklyn Eagle*, after reviewing the caseand the appeals, concluded that the execution was justified. "There are some crimes occasionally committed by women which are of so extraordinary and outrageous a character that no punishment except the death penalty seems adequate to meet them. . . ."

The *Troy Telegram* went so far as to suggest that the inevitable hanging of Roxalana Druse was a relief to everyone, including the victim. "To such a woman, imprisonment would have been an unending torture," noted the *Telegram*. "The state, by mercifully hanging her, cut short her imprisonment. In doing that it shocks the whole community."

The widespread shock of hanging Roxalana Druse did pass eventually. When Dr. Cyrus Kay recorded the death certificate and filed it with the clerk's office in the village of Herkimer, he wrote that the forty-three-year-old woman had died of "asphyxia (judicial hanging by the neck)." Her fifteen-minute ordeal on the gallows did, however, shock the legislature into action. On June 8, 1888, a bill was passed making electrocution the preferred means of execution in the state of New York. Thus, Roxalana Druse became not only the first (and only) person to be executed in Herkimer County but also the last woman to be hanged in the state of New York. On April 6, 1890, William Kemmler had the dubious distinction of being the first person to die in the electric chair at Auburn Prison. Kemmler had murdered his wife—with an axe.

The only other shock delivered to the community was the amount of money expended on the Druse trial. At a time when the average worker was fortunate to earn a dollar a day, the trial and execution were indeed costly. It appeared that anyone who had the slightest connection to the case promptly billed the Herkimer County Board of Supervisors for services rendered. Neighbors from Warren who had housed and fed Roxalana, Mary, George, and Frank Gates submitted vouchers, as did several deputies who served subpoenas. There was also a bill from Thorpe's Hotel for the inquest. All through the summer of 1885, bills arrived. By the time the trial began in September, the county had already spent in excess of $1,000. The cost of housing Roxalana at the county jail for 774 days amounted to a staggering $3,150.18, and one must not forget that Mary was at the jail for almost ten months before her transfer to Onondaga Penitentiary.

Even the execution was expensive. The "galloping gallows" from Oneida County came with a hefty rental tag of $500.00; no one asked if there was a carpenter in Herkimer who could make a similar contrivance for less. Deputies in attendance in the jail yard were paid $2.00, and Deputy Ballou received $125.00 for pulling the pin that dropped the counterweight to hang Roxalana. Both physicians submitted bills of $25.00 to record the pulse of a strangling woman; the county saw fit to pay them $5.00 each for this service. Mrs. Waterman received $382.60 for the hundred nights she remained outside of Roxalana's cell, while Herbert Paul received $2.00 for shoveling the sidewalks prior to the execution. Harness maker James Suiter, father of Dr. Suiter, billed the county $2.00 for the leather straps used to bind Roxalana's wrists and legs, and W.B. Howell charged only $2.00 to make a simple pine casket. Finally, on March 8, 1887, the Board of Supervisors paid the last bill when Sheriff Cook had Roxalana's former cell whitewashed at a cost of $2.50.

The total cost to the taxpayers—almost $10,000—remained the most expensive legal case in Herkimer County until the Gillette–Brown "American Tragedy" murder in 1906. It was no wonder, then, that when Mary Druse pled guilty to second-degree murder, her plea was hailed as a cost-saving measure by a county that wished to avoid another expensive trial.

Even after the last bill was paid, it wasn't an easy task to forget about the Druses. Shortly before her execution, Roxalana Druse told a reporter from the *Herkimer Democrat* that if she were executed, she would exact a unique revenge. "By J- C- ," she announced, "if I am hung, I'll haunt you all in my night clothes." No one knows if she made the remark in jest, perhaps for the entertainment of her jailers, or if these were the words of a frightened woman who was measuring her life not in days but in hours. In time, Roxalana did seem to haunt the citizens of Herkimer County.

H.P. Witherstine, for instance, ensured that Roxalana would continue to haunt the public for a long time. The owner and editor of the *Herkimer Democrat* saw to it that a special "IT IS OVER" edition hit the streets of Herkimer within two hours of the execution. Roxalana had sold newspapers when she was alive, and she sold even more after she was dead. Witherstine claimed that sales of his newspaper reached somewhere between 9,000 and 10,000 copies. The *Utica Globe* reported a similar surge when they released their special edition. Accustomed to a circulation of between 80,000 and 90,000, the Globe reported that sales reached 121,087 copies for its coverage of the Druse execution.

During the years that followed, Mohawk Valley newspapers never missed an opportunity to print any story related to the crime—from the trivial to the absurd. The press went so far as to suggest that Roxalana haunted some people and cursed many more. The tale of the "Druse curse" began with the untimely death of Charles Pett. Several days before the execution, the court-appointed guardian for George and Mary died from the effects of inflammatory rheumatism. The story of the curse might have ended there, except for a series of unfortunate—if not bizarre—events.

On July 27, 1909, the *Utica Daily Press* reported that seventy-one-year-old Reverend George W. Powell committed suicide by drinking carbolic acid. Roxalana's former spiritual advisor had been a resident of the Masonic Home in Utica for almost a year with his wife, Hannah. On the morning of July 26, Mrs. Powell noticed that her husband had not risen for breakfast and immediately called for a nurse. A doctor was summoned to their room, and a quick inspection revealed that an empty bottle of laudanum and carbolic acid had been hidden under Powell's mattress. For the rest of the morning, the spiritual advisor drifted in and out of consciousness. He died later that day, and after his funeral at the Masonic Home, he was buried on the grounds of the hospital.

About a year later, Lucy Gates died. The sister who was not called as a witness at the trial was also the same sister who never visited Roxalana while she was in jail. Lucy died from a broken neck after tumbling down a flight of stairs at her home in Jordanville.

When the press couldn't locate an unfortunate soul to perpetuate the curse, they simply altered facts or omitted minor details. People were surprised to learn that Adam Bellinger, a purported member of the Druse jury, had been committed to the Utica Insane Asylum. Newspapers neglected to mention that Bellinger did not serve on the jury but instead had been one of the 360 potential jurors interviewed.

There were times, however, when the stories reported generated a great deal of excitement and required immediate investigation by the authorities. In March 1887, a Troy, New York, newspaper reported that a cadaver at the Albany Medical College bore a striking resemblance to Roxalana Druse, right down to the rope burns about her neck. In no time at all, the curious descended upon the college, hoping to catch a glimpse of the infamous murderess. The *New York Times* reported that at least fifty locks of hair had been snipped from the corpse's head. The tale of the nearly bald corpse with suspicious rope marks on its neck reached Herkimer, and local papers asked if it was possible that Roxalana's corpse had been spirited away to Albany. One newspaper, the *Dolgeville Herald*, even described how this could have been accomplished and hinted boldly at the physician who might be responsible.

With rumors of body snatching now appearing in print, Sheriff Cook organized a posse and led it to the vault at Oak Hill Cemetery. Inserting the key he'd had in his possession since the last day of February, Cook unlocked the vault and stood before the pine coffin. The lid was pried off and, one by one, those who had witnessed the execution peered into the coffin. All agreed that the frozen body with its wilted bouquet of roses was Roxalana Druse.

Cook ordered the coffin nailed, shut and after all but a few deputies departed, he made arrangements to bury the body. He chose the location of the grave, and in order to insure secrecy, he never submitted a bill to the county. Unmarked, its location remains a secret to this day.

For a time, Roxalana did haunt Governor David B. Hill. Weeks after her death the specter of Roxalana appeared in the governor's office in the form of letters— emotional and dramatic in their content, as one might expect. Some writers, like A.C. Moore of Bay City, Michigan, vented their anger in the harshest terms possible: "You are mean, a brute unworthy to be called a man . . . this is not the fourteenth century."

And there were a few who invoked Biblical images in their condemnation of Hill. An anonymous writer from Utica likened him to a modern day Pontius Pilate, and F.M. Jones of New York City wrote, "'Tis only the ignorant and unfettered, the rabble that cry, 'Crucify! Crucify!' as they did in the days of Nazarine."

Within two months, the letters ceased. Hill's part in this human drama failed to mar his political career, as some might have suspected. He successfully campaigned for governor once more and was eventually elected to the United States Senate. In 1894 he attempted to retake the governorship but was swept aside by Levi P. Morton. Hill continued to remain active in Democratic politics in the Albany area, at the same time maintaining a lucrative law practice. He died on October 20, 1910, at his home, Woolfert's Roost, near Albany.

Hill's private secretary, Colonel William G. Rice, remained active in New York politics and eventually became a member of the State Civil Service Commission, retiring in 1938. Rice saved every correspondence relating to the Druse case and diligently filed these apart from the David B. Hill Papers. The Druse Papers remained separate and might have stayed "missing" or forgotten had it not been for a Cooperstown graduate student doing research for his master's thesis in 1967. William G. Case was perhaps the first person since Rice to view the entire collection of Druse material. Dick Case has been a feature writer for the *Syracuse Post Standard* for over thirty years.

Judge Pardon C. Williams enjoyed a long and distinguished career as one of the premier jurists in the state of New York. When he retired in 1912, he was a judge in the Appellate Division of the State Supreme Court. Judge Williams died at the age of 83 at his home in Watertown, New York, on January 18, 1925.

For the rest of his life, Abram Steele shunned the publicity associated with the Druse trial. He served for six years and lost only three cases, and his remarkable tenure insured his rise in the county's political ranks. But the district attorney had other plans. Although eminently qualified to serve as a county judge, Steele preferred civic pursuits. For the remainder of his life, he devoted all of his energies to a wide variety of civic projects in the village of Herkimer. When he died on March 28, 1910, the village he loved honored his memory by naming a street after him.

Although Reverend George W. Powell had garnered most of the publicity in his attempt to save Roxalana Druse, the efforts of her defense counsel are noteworthy and commendable. H. DeWight Luce did everything he could to help his client, although her situation was truly hopeless. He had attempted to change the location of the trial, dismiss evidence, and discredit witnesses. Even the failure of the appeals did not stop Luce from personally entreating Governor Hill on several occasions. Luce continued to practice law in New York City until his retirement in 1911. He returned to Richfield Springs and died in 1919, never having granted an interview regarding the part he played in the Druse affair.

In sharp contrast to Steele and Luce, the stoic and often humorless Dr. A. Walter Suiter never tired of his association with the case. Suiter was keenly aware that his forensic sleuthing, in addition to his oral testimony at the trial, was the key to the prosecution's case against Roxalana. He wasn't modest about telling the medical community or anyone else how important his testimony was, and he wasted little time in doing so. In February 1887, as Roxalana was awaiting execution, he published a paper for the New York State Medical Society leaving no doubt in anyone's mind that his interpretation of the bone chips was vital to this case. With a title that took an entire breath, *Some Points of Medico-Legal Interest in the Scientific Investigation of the Case of the People versus Roxalana Druse, Together with an Exhibition of Specimens Representing the Corpus Delicti*, Dr. Suiter gave a brief synopsis of the crime and explained how he had interpreted each bone fragment. The paper was so well received that he embarked on a limited speaking tour of upstate New York. His fame came with some notoriety though; for years he had to defend himself against recurring rumors that he had made off with the body of Roxalana Druse. "It would not surprise us," reported the *Dolgeville Herald*, "if the bones of Mrs. Druse would not be found in the possession of some Herkimer County doctor."

Upon his death in 1925, Dr. Suiter's home was presented to the Herkimer County Historical Society to be used as a museum, in accordance with provisions he made in his will. The Queen Anne style brick mansion, a familiar sight to Roxalana Druse as she was escorted from the jail to the courthouse, maintains a collection of Druse memorabilia to this day.

Frank Gates stayed in Warren where he worked on his father's farm for many years. On January 2, 1891, he married Josephine Sitts of Jordanville. The couple remained on the farm, raised four children, and cared for Charles after the death of his wife, Lucy. When Josephine died in 1928, Frank Gates left the family farm and moved to Utica where he embarked upon a career as a painter and paperhanger. He died at the age of 75 at St. Elizabeth's Hospital on December 27, 1950, and was buried beside his parents at the Jordanville Cemetery.

Mary Druse, the occupant of cell number 7 at the Onondaga Penitentiary remained steadfast in her oft-repeated claim that she was innocent of all wrongdoing, stating, "I never had a hand or act or part, in any way, in the tragedy." Immediately following her mother's execution, Reverend Powell had paid Mary a visit. His arrival was expected—and not without fanfare. The *Syracuse Standard* announced his arrival as "the spiritual advisor for Mrs. Druse and the apostle of the maudlin sentiment which has been wasted on that murderess."

It was time for yet another confession from Mary. She had always insisted that Charles Gates and his son Chester killed her father and that her mother was innocent. She never denied that her mother and father had been "fussing" before breakfast and that the bill from Chet Crim's store was part of the reason. She went on to explain that when their argument escalated into shouts, threats, and screams, the boys were sent out of the house. None of this was startling information; it had been established previously in the court testimony of her brother and her cousin. What followed, however, was a bit far-fetched.

After her father had threatened her mother with the axe, "he struck the [pantry] door with the axe once or twice," Mary said. Then her father sat down at the table and proceeded to skin a herring with his knife. "It was a three-bladed jackknife," she recalled, "almost new. He always kept his knife sharp." Questioning the store bill, he drew his knife and threatened to skin Roxalana. Frightened by this violent exchange, Mary ran from the house and called for the boys. Suddenly she remembered hearing gunshots coming from the kitchen. She ran back into the house to discover her father lying face down in a pool of blood. Standing behind him holding a pistol was Chet Gates, or it could have been Charles Gates. She just couldn't remember. "Chet always carried a revolver," she said.

Mary claimed that she wasn't surprised to see either of them in the kitchen. Charles had been there earlier on the pretext of borrowing a sleigh. When her father had refused his request, angry words were exchanged. The only way she could account for their sudden appearance in the kitchen was that they must have been hiding in the barn.

With her father grievously wounded and her mother having fainted dead away in a nearby rocking chair, Mary made an incredible announcement. "Pa," she said, "I'll go [for help] just as soon as I get through with Ma." It was bizarre to think that her first priority was to bathe her mother's forehead with camphor and water, while her father lay bleeding and groaning for help. Mary further claimed that she was physically restrained from leaving to seek help by Chet Gates, a cousin about whom she said, "I stood in fear of more than anyone else."

There was no beheading, no dismembered body, no incineration. "Not to my knowledge," she said. The body was wrapped up in an old quilt, dragged into the parlor, and later that day taken from the farmhouse by Chet, his father, and Will Elwood, who happened to stop by that afternoon. These men made off with her father's remains.

"My father abused me shamefully," Mary recalled, "but I did not want to see him murdered. People say I had no love for him. They don't know all. Long, long ago, when I was a little girl, father was kind to me, and all through his cruelty afterward, I remembered that kindness and loved him for it."

This latest confession about a crime that many would just as soon forget drew an instant and angry response from the editorial desk of the *Syracuse Standard*: "If any more maudlin letters of condolence and sympathy arrive in the mail, he [the superintendent of Onondaga] should exercise his authority and throw them unread by the girl into the stove. The sniveling gossipmongers who come to her with messages from her dear, dying mother should have the door of the penitentiary slammed in their faces. Nothing like the disgusting travesty of religion that was permitted at Herkimer prior to and during the execution of the wretched Borgia, her mother, should be repeated in Syracuse on any pretext. . . . The posey and gumdrop nonsense should end at once, lest it be ordained that killing is no murder."

The *Herkimer Citizen* was equally unmoved but slightly less harsh in its assessment of the latest effort on the part of Reverend Powell. "Mary has never been able yet to tell the truth. In this matter, she has made several confessions and no two of her stories agree and are so contradicting that no credence can be given them. Efforts to secure her release from prison are well enough; they should not be made at the expense of the truth. Nor is it necessary to malign the dead."

For the next few years, the girl who worked in the box factory was all but forgotten. She adapted well to prison regimen and from all accounts was a model prisoner. On June 1, 1893, Mary and the other female prisoners were transferred to the women's section at Auburn Prison. She appeared a little apprehensive about the move at first but adjusted quickly to her new surroundings. Because her behavior had been so exceptional at Onondaga, Mary was assigned to the infirmary.

At Auburn she granted no interviews, received few visitors, and—perhaps for the first time in her life—made many friends. Her name was mentioned occasionally in the press, but she did not seek this attention. Well-meaning individuals attempting to draw support for a governor's pardon were quick to resurrect the new confession, and thus open up old wounds. Some, like the *Utica Morning Herald*, were eager to point out that Mary too had been a victim. Charley Pett, Mary allegedly told the *Herald*, "talked to Ma and told her it would be the best thing I could do to testify to [being] guilty as having helped her in the murder of my father. My guardian coaxed me up and I promised him I would do as he said. He told me it was real nice in prison, and people would bring us presents and we would have lots of company and no one to scold us, and Ma would be happy, and it would save her being hung. My guardian said my lawyer would get all my money and have Ma and I both hung. I was terrified and I did not know who to trust, so I listened to the guardian, but he was the one that stole my money after all and Georgie never has received one cent of his share from the sale of the farm."

One Boston attorney, convinced that this naïve young woman had been coerced into pleading guilty, argued that this revelation in itself entitled Mary to a pardon. He argued that her guardian, Charles Pett, and her attorney, H. DeWight Luce, made off with the majority of the Druse estate. Mary was indeed penniless, but not because of the dishonesty of her lawyer or her guardian. After liens and claims, there wasn't that much of an estate left to divide.

Efforts to secure her release from prison began as early as the fall of 1887, when a group of Rome, New York, citizens circulated a petition asking the governor to pardon Mary. The petition received little support because there were those who believed that she should serve more than just two years of a life sentence. In December of 1890, Abram Steele said that he personally had no objections to Mary receiving either a pardon or a parole from prison. "I cannot say that I consider Mary Druse a vicious person," said Steele. "But I thought her of weak mind and easily influenced." Amos Prescott, who had assisted Luce with Roxalana's defense, agreed, stating, "I sincerely hope that Mary Druse will soon receive a pardon."

Roxalana Druse had advised her daughter to trust and confide in her only true friend on this Earth, Reverend Powell. Unfortunately for Mary, the spiritual advisor who had lobbied so hard for her mother and comforted her during her last days ceased to be of any help. There were no petitions for Mary, no sermons, and no visits to the governor on her behalf. She would have to look elsewhere.

In the summer of 1895, Mrs. Ada Springer Sherman began a petition drive on Mary's behalf. The New York City shopkeeper who specialized in making wax flowers had heard of Mary's talent for making paper flowers. She visited Auburn on several occasions and contacted the governor's office regarding a pardon. Mrs. Sherman spent a considerable amount of time and effort trying to secure a pardon for Mary. When it eventually arrived, she was quick to claim the credit, but the pardon, in fact, had come from an unlikely source.

"I said to Mary when I sentenced her," said Judge Pardon C. Williams, "that if she changed her character and became a good woman, she might after some years hope for executive clemency." This same judge who had urged Governor Hill not to commute Roxalana's sentence was offering a different opinion to the current governor, Levi P. Morton, regarding Mary's future. "I do not advise or object to a pardon, but leave it to your own judgment upon the nature of the crime, the circumstances that Mary was a girl acting under the direction of her mother, and the behavior of Mary while in prison and her present disposition."

Mary Druse was released from Auburn Prison on June 25, 1895.

Her pardon did not come without its share of controversy. On August 11, 1895, the *New York Times* reported that several New York City judges were opposed to it. The harshest critic of the pardon was Judge John Goff. "In the Druse case, of course, we revolt at the thought of liberty for such a woman, but it is very possible that her confinement should not be in a penitentiary. This suggests a fault in our system. They do these things better in England. When one has at any time become so irresponsible morally or mentally as to commit an atrocious crime, then a repetition of the atrocity should be made forever impossible by confinement for life. Such people should be taken care of by the state for the rest of their lives. Which one has ever been insane enough to do such a horrible a thing as Mary Druse did, she has enough insane tendency to require that she be locked up in a criminal insane asylum for the remainder of her life. . . . We don't need Mary Druses in our midst."

Fortunately, not everyone condemned Mary Druse, and few looked upon her as a threat to society. The nine years and eight months she had served profoundly affected the twenty-nine-year-old. "Those who have observed her closely," reported the *Herkimer Democrat*, "say they doubt if Mary Druse will live more than a year." There was speculation that she was suffering from the "grippe" (influenza) or consumption (tuberculosis).

Mary Druse sought refuge with Mr. and Mrs. John Rhue, a couple who had visited her in Auburn. At their home she slowly regained her strength and contemplated the future. She turned down Mrs. Sherman's generous offer to relocate to New York City. Mrs. Sherman promised to give Mary "a practical business education" at her shop while giving her the opportunity to change her name, thus ensuring her a certain degree of anonymity. Mary remained at the Rhue house for a short while and spoke with only one reporter from the *Syracuse Herald*. There were no more confessions or accusations; a very tired Mary Druse refused to speak of the past. "It is very hard," she told the reporter, "for a woman in my position to decide what to do to earn a living without attracting unpleasant attention and criticism. I am tired of that and I think I have had my share. I want the past to bury the past."

In 1899 Mary Druse married John Ganon, a harness maker and native of Watertown, New York. Where and how they met is not known. It is known that for a while, the couple resided at 411 East Fayette Street, Syracuse, and that Mary earned a living as a domestic. This union was short-lived, however, and evidently unhappy.

Mary was separated from her husband when she signed his death certificate on July 6, 1915; John Ganon is buried at St. Agnes Cemetery in Syracuse. A short while later, Mary fell ill and succumbed to pneumonia on August 30, 1915. She is buried in an unmarked grave in the family plot of her employers, the Brose family, at Oakwood Cemetery in Syracuse.

George Druse never visited his sister while she was in prison, nor did he attend her funeral. "Little Georgie" remained with the Chamberlain family in Miller's Mills for a few years, and then secured employment with the Remington Arms gun factory in Ilion, New York. On September 16, 1896, he married Mabel Clara Johns of Frankfort, New York. Their only child, Florence, was born there on July 19, 1900. George remained with Remington Arms until after World War I. In 1920 he relocated to Utica where he obtained a position as a machinist with the Savage Arms Company.The following year, for reasons unknown, he moved to another part of Utica and abruptly dropped his last name. He was known as George William Stewart until he died of a heart attack at the age of 68 on January 3, 1944. Upon his death, his wife Mabel altered his death certificate. In place of his parents, Roxalana and Bill Druse, she inserted the names of her own parents. George, his wife Mabel, and their daughter and son-in-law are all buried at Crown Hill Cemetery in Utica, New York.

CHAPTER 10

Postscript

A short time before her execution, the story of Roxalana Druse entered the realm of myth and legend. For this, history can thank her spiritual advisor, for no one twisted facts or concocted stories on her behalf quite like the Reverend George W. Powell did. Many people regarded him as the "keeper of the flame" when it came to Roxalana Druse. He did his best to convince the public, and perhaps himself, that an injustice had taken place when she was executed. He inspired many others, and his disciples for a short time contributed to shaping this legend. They wrote letters, circulated petitions, and collected signatures. Some were creative and, like Roxalana, turned to verse.

In mid-October of 1885, a week after Judge Pardon C. Williams had passed sentence on Roxalana Druse, a series of poems began appearing in the *Frankfort Registrar.* Purportedly composed by two individuals, the poems argued the merits of Roxalana's trial and execution. One of the poets, known only as J.S.S., sympathized with her plight. The other, known only as "A," believed that justice had been served. These two battling bards attempted to tell the story of Roxalana in simple singsong verse:

Roxy Druse,
There is no use,
To plead her cause
Before our laws.

Every other day, a new poem appeared in the *Registrar* defending or attacking a poem printed in the previous edition. This continued for weeks, spurring reactions from readers. Before long, editorials from an individual calling himself "Steel Pen" began to appear, along with more poems. The poems printed in the *Registrar* were often quite clever. In addition to "Roxy Druse got the noose," there was "This is to Roxy—get hung by proxy." In the end, the poets failed to preserve her memory for posterity. None of these simple sing song verses had the jump-rope jingle rhythm of "Lizzie Borden took an axe," which appeared five years later.

Roxalana failed to be immortalized in poetry. In fact, the public perception of her was quite vague almost from the beginning. Reverend Powell had a lot to do with this, but we can also thank her defense attorney. In an effort to shield her from the press, H. DeWight Luce instructed his client to guard her words and refuse to grant lengthy interviews to the press. Here Luce proved very successful. During the two years Roxalana served in jail, she granted few interviews, and only one—the interview conducted by Drs. Suiter and Gray—offered any insight about her true personality. Her few friends from her New Hartford days presented scant information about her at the trial, as did her neighbors in Warren. None of these ever came forward after the trial to offer any additional information. Roxalana did not take the stand in her own defense, in itself perhaps a wise move on her attorney's part; but that too leaves a mystery. Fragmentary evidence presented by witnesses at her trial suggested that Roxalana was in an abusive relationship, but this was not enough to sway an all-male jury. Although Luce did his best to portray her as pitiable, there was something lacking. No one stood up to declare love or deep affection for Roxalana. Neither her sister Lucy nor her brother Amon made public comments about her before, during, or after the trial. No one, save her daughter Mary, expressed any love for her. Her demeanor, her appearance (no photograph exists), and her personality are forever shrouded in mystery. All that is known for sure is that even though some believed she was arrogant, mean-spirited, and vengeful, she was also very scared and lonely as she stood upon the scaffold.

In time the county had other murder trials, but this one remained different from the rest. Anyone else who was convicted of murder in Herkimer County was sent to a state prison for life or executed at a state prison. Roxalana will forever remain "the woman hanged behind the jail." This, and erroneous statements such as "she chopped up her husband and fed him to the pigs" and "they hung her from that hook behind the jail" helped sustain the legend of Roxalana Druse.

Generations later, questions remain:

Where was Roxalana's cell?

When she was brought to the jail in January of 1898 with her children and Frank Gates, they were most likely brought to the attic, the third floor. This section of the jail was reserved for women, children, and those considered by the authorities to be of a non-threatening nature. When Frank and George were released and Mary transferred to Onondaga, Roxalana remained on the third floor for quite some time. With a rocking chair and a sewing machine furnished by the sheriff's wife, and a small box organ that Mary left behind, Roxalana was relatively comfortable. Here she entertained visitors and passed many hours with her poetry and making paper flowers. A careful inspection of the attic area to this day reveals the charred wood from the chimney fire she helped extinguish. A few days before her execution, she was moved to the first floor of the jail.

In 1898, the interior of the jail was completely renovated. The limestone cells were replaced with steel walls, floors, and bars. It is much easier to direct a visitor to the cell of convicted "American Tragedy" murderer, Chester Gillette, than it is to locate the original cell occupied by Roxalana Druse.

Did she make the dress that she wore to the gallows?

Although she had access to a sewing machine, whether she used it is not known. A quick look at the Board of Supervisor minutes for 1885, 1886, and 1887 reveals a number of clothing purchases for Roxalana. For years, it was assumed that the dress she wore to her execution was made by Mrs. Fred Griffin. One of the many people who befriended Roxalana, Mrs. Griffin billed the county $1.50 for the calico dress she made for Roxalana. A calico bonnet for this dress is in the collection of the Herkimer County Historical Society. The black dress presented to her three days before her death was made at a cost of $5.00 by Maggie Claire.

Where is Roxalana Druse's grave?

This question, one of the most frequently asked about Roxalana, is also one of the greatest mysteries in the case. After the Albany medical student hoax, the body of Roxalana was removed from the vault at Oak Hill Cemetery and buried immediately. The exact location of her final resting place will never be known as the record book for the Oak Hill Cemetery for the year 1887 is missing. In the early 1960s, Herkimer undertaker James F. Burns said that she was buried in the middle of one of the many roads in the cemetery to prevent anyone from visiting or desecrating her grave. Later, in 1973, Jim Parker of Ilion, New York, claimed to have located a cast-iron grave marker in Cedarville bearing the name Roxalana Druse. Like the burial records from Oak Hill, this too has gone missing.

What became of William's bones?

Physical evidence used in a trial is kept by the district attorney for as long as he deems necessary. The forensic display that many considered the single most important piece of evidence used to convict Roxalana Druse was given to Dr. A. Walter Suiter by District Attorney Eugene Sheldon. For over fifty years, the bones of Bill Druse remained in a dust-covered box labeled "Exhibits A and B" in the basement of Dr. Suiter's home. After the doctor died and before his estate was transferred to the Herkimer County Historical Society, the vacant mansion was burglarized. The doctor's sister, Mary Grace Suiter, was aware of the bones in the basement and feared that they might be stolen in a future burglary. In 1935 she arranged to have them interred at Oak Hill Cemetery.

What became of the pistol?

While no one knows what happened to the axe used in the crime, we do know that Eugene Sheldon presented the nickel-plated pearl handled .22 caliber seven-shot revolver to Sheriff Delavan Cook after the execution. Cook in turn gave it to his friend, Conservation Officer Wilbur Strough. For years, Strough had the weapon on display in the window of the O'Rourke and Hurley Drugstore in St. Johnsville where, according to the *Richfield Springs Mercury*, it "attracted considerable attention."

And the gallows?

The "galloping gallows" was returned to Oneida County where it remained an object of curiosity. In time, the contrivance was purchased by Joseph Wagner, proprietor of the Union Hotel. No one knows if the timbers were burned or sold as souvenirs, but as late as 1972, the *Observer Dispatch* claimed that the dropweight was still in Utica.

Is the Druse house still standing on Hogsback Hill Road?

Scarcely anything remains on Hogsback Hill Road today to remind the casual visitor that this was once the scene of a dreadful tragedy. The house that once belonged to Charles Pett still stands, and so does his wagon house where Frank Gates was first interviewed. The Druse house has long since disappeared. A few years after Roxalana's death, the new owner, Jeremiah Eckler, reportedly had the farmhouse lifted from its foundation and moved to his farm. Whether he used it as a storage shed or a chicken coop, we shall never know. In the late 1930s, *Utica Press* reporter H. Paul Draheim visited the property and discovered that a tree had taken root in the center of the old foundation. As the years passed, the property changed hands several times. Today the entire area has been landscaped, and a beautiful home sits on the site formerly occupied by a rough-hewn farmhouse.

Did Roxalana go to the gallows to protect her children?

Was it possible that a fantastic miscarriage of justice really did take place? Years later, it was suggested that William Druse's real murderer was his own daughter, Mary, and that Roxalana covered up the crime and accepted the blame to protect her. Mary perjured herself so many times during the trial that it was difficult for anyone to believe anything she said. In addition, Reverend Powell claimed that besides Charles Gates, Chet Gates, and Will Elwood, others were involved in the murder.

Given the evidence, it is difficult to accept that Roxalana was a martyr for her children. After her release from prison, Mary and her brother George had plenty of time to tell their side of the story but neither ever did. Both desired and achieved a certain degree of anonymity.

Would Roxalana be convicted if this crime took place today?

District Attorney Abram Steele was praised for conducting a thorough investigation of the crime before it was brought to trial. In an effort to piece together a weeks-old crime that had occurred on Hogsback Hill Road, Steele subpoenaed countless individuals. Today the investigation would be conducted in much the same way and, in all probability, the results would be the same.

A modern police investigation would require warrants to search the crime scene, regardless of the fact that the inhabitants of the house had vacated the premises. And instead of having amateur sleuth Dr. A. Walter Suiter dismantle the farmhouse floor and make off with the stove, a team of trained investigators would be present to gather the evidence.

It is interesting to note that not one photograph of the crime scene was introduced as evidence or used by Steele to assist in his investigation. Today multiple photographs would be taken of the interior and exterior of the farmhouse and used by investigators to reconstruct the crime. Photographs, an accurate floor plan of the farmhouse, and the testimony of a ballistics expert would help investigators corroborate the testimony of Frank Gates. Was he standing in the kitchen when he fired the pistol at his uncle? Did he miss and strike the wall?

The most crucial piece of evidence, the bones of the deceased, today would be sent to a forensic laboratory for DNA analysis, severely weakening the argument presented by defense counsel H. DeWight Luce. It would not matter what part of the human skeleton the bones represented because DNA testing would determine who the bones belonged to.

In addition to the physical evidence presented at the trial, Roxalana Druse's sanity was questioned from the moment the crime was announced in the local press. Was this a case of temporary insanity or some other psychological aberration? A short time after her arrest, Roxalana was interviewed by one of the most preeminent psychologists of the day, Dr. John Perdue Gray, who declared her sane. Several days before her execution, another team of psychologists interviewed her and came to the same conclusion. In a twenty-first century courtroom, there would be a very good chance that Roxalana would be declared mentally incompetent and placed in the care of a mental institution. The study of the human mind has expanded tremendously in the one-hundred-plus years since this crime. *The Diagnostic and Statistical Manual of Mental Disorders*, published by the American Psychiatric Association, contains a litany of mental disorders that would benefit the defense. Mental illnesses such as schizophrenia, depression, bipolar disorders, post-traumatic stress disorder, might be used to explain Roxalana's actions.

Perhaps the saddest part of the entire episode is the lack of psychological help offered to the children who witnessed this horrible act. Not once during the trial or its aftermath did anyone step forward to express concern for the children who must have been traumatized by witnessing this brutal murder. Counseling would be readily available for the children if this crime occurred today.

Although the term was not in vogue in the 1880s, H. DeWight Luce could not convince a jury that Roxalana was a victim of "battered wife syndrome." This would be a plausible defense tactic in a modern-day case. Even though no police or social services records of spousal abuse existed, a defendant could claim that there was abuse and that she feared for her life or feared another attack was imminent. The only way to do this would be for the defendant to take the stand and attempt to convince a jury that she had been repeatedly abused. A perfect example of this can be found in State of Maine v. Anaya, a case that mirrored the Druse murder.

In this case of "battered wife syndrome," the prosecutor argued that Linda Anaya did not fear her boyfriend, since she never attempted to leave him. "Although the prosecutor concluded that the couple had a 'bizarre' relationship that involved fighting and knife-wielding, he suggested that the repeated abuse was simply part of a 'loving game' in which the couple routinely engaged." The defense attorney argued before the jury, as had Luce one hundred years earlier, that the defendant believed that "she was always in imminent danger of grave physical harm whenever she was in his presence." The prosecution therefore made the case that Linda Anaya's actions were not so much defensive as they were vengeful. In the Anaya case, like the Druse case, the jury handed down a guilty verdict. They were not convinced that the defendant was a victim of abuse.

A few mistakes were made during Roxalana's trial, but little would change if it were held today. Evidence and eyewitness testimony would still be the determining factors in one's guilt or innocence. Judge Pardon C. Williams made sure the jury received as much information as possible in order for them to reach a verdict. Today, however, he would be faulted on how he addressed the jury at the close of the trial. "Mrs. Druse," he said, "could be declared innocent only if the evidence convinces you beyond a reasonable doubt. . . . You have an important duty to perform, one which calls upon you to exercise your best intelligence and judgment." Here Judge Williams infers that, in addition to the evidence presented at the trial, the jurors would have had a better opportunity to render a verdict if Mrs. Druse had testified. Not testifying places a burden on the defendant and would be viewed as a "reversible error" in a modern court.

In the end, the fate of anyone on trial rests with the jury. For decades, feminists argued that the absence of women on a jury was a great injustice to the legal system. Despite the passage of the 19th Amendment, women did not serve on juries in New York until 1937 and even then only on a voluntary basis.

What doomed Roxalana was not the evidence presented at her trial, or the lack of psychological profiling, or an all-male jury. The defendant herself made the greatest mistake. Roxalana Druse could have escaped the noose by pleading guilty in exchange for a life sentence, as her daughter had done. Instead, she gambled, lost, and paid the ultimate price.

SOURCES

The most important piece of documentation relevant to the Druse murder is the trial transcript. Printed excerpts of the trial were needed to present to the New York State Court of Appeals and they remain an invaluable source of information regarding not only the details of the murder but also offer a rare glimpse into the life Roxalana Druse led befoe she married Bill Druse. The transcripts allow the people to speak. Here, friends from her past, neighbors she had known and even her own children describe circumstances in their own words. Unless otherwise noted, all quotes were taken from these transcripts and all the images are from the Herkimer County Historical Society collection.

Census records, too, were helpful. The Town of Marshall Census of 1850 provided scant information about the Teft family. Interestingly, it listed her as Roxanna, not Roxalana. More importantly, the Town of Warren census records offer a fairly good description of the farm on Hogsback Hill Road. A careful examination of the data in the census records from 1860 to 1880 clearly indicates that the Druse farm was facing serious hardships. The contents of the farmhouse are listed in documents located in the Surrogate's Office in the Herkimer County Office Building. These documents, prepared by the court, also list the names of those who had liens against the Druse property.

Every warrant, subpoena, voucher and any other expense relevant to the Druse case was recorded in the *Board of Supervisors Minutes* by the Herkimer County Sheriff's Department. As detailed as these expense accounts appear, it's impossible to determine the actual number of deputies needed to maintain the jail. Since numerous accounts indicate that both the jail and the courthouse required constant maintenance and repair, it's safe to assume that many were required.

Newspapers farthest away from the, "scene of the crime," generally did the poorest job of relaying the news to their readers. A careful examination of the local press, notably, *The Richfield Springs Mercury, The Herkimer Democrat, The Little Falls Evening Times,* and The *Ilion Citizen,* indicates that their coverage of the trial was far more accurate than that of the metropolitan newspapers. In almost every instance, the court transcripts and the local press reports were exactly the same.

The Druse murder was the subject in only two books prior to the turn of the century. Before the trial, Tippetts garnered most of his information regarding the Druse murder from the local press for his *Herkimer County Murders*. The first pamphlet to appear after the execution was, *Mrs. Druse and Maggie Houghtaling, An Innocent Woman Hanged, The Truth Revealed at Last.* It was in this rare publication that Lillie Devereux Blake offered her opinions regarding capital punishment, and the apparent inequity of the law.

The lack of diary entries and letters by the principal characters in the Druse story is disappointing. The avalanche of letters, both pro and con received by the Governor's office, offer no real facts about Roxalana. They merely support her efforts to live, or damn her for all time. At the time of this publication no other firsthand accounts of this murder have surfaced. Perhaps the general public as well as the polititians wanted to forget the dreadful affair once and for all. With the exception of Dr. Suiter, none of the principal characters involved in this tragedy ever wrote about it. Rev. Powell eulogized Roxalana but did little after that. He never lectured or wrote about the woman he had tried so desperately to save.

BIBLIOGRAPHY

Manuscript Collections

Lillie Devereux Blake Papers. Missouri Historical Society, St. Louis, Missouri.

Roxalana Druse Papers. Herkimer County Historical Society, Herkimer, New York.

Roxalana Druse Papers. County Surrogate's Office, Herkimer, New York.

David B. Hill Papers. New York State Archives, Albany, New York.

Dr. A. Walter Suiter Papers. Herkimer County Historical Society, Herkimer, New York.

Newspapers

Auburn Dispatch
Brooklyn Eagle
Dolgeville Herald
Frankfort Register
Herkimer Citizen
Herkimer Democrat
Herkimer Evening Telegram
Ilion Citizen
Little Falls Evening Times
New York Star
New York Sun
New York Times
New York World
Norway Tidings
Richfield Springs Mercury
Schenectady Evening Star
Syracuse Herald
Utica Daily Observer
Utica Daily Press
Utica Morning Herald
Utica Observer Dispatch
Utica Saturday Globe
Utica Sunday Tribune
Watertown Daily Times

Primary Sources

Herkimer County Census for 1865. Herkimer County: Clerk's Office.

Herkimer County Census for 1870. Herkimer County: Clerk's Office.

Herkimer County Census for 1875. Herkimer County: Clerk's Office.

Herkimer County Census for 1880. Herkimer County: Clerk's Office.

Oneida County Census for 1850. Oneida County: Clerk's Office.

Oneida County Census for 1880. Oneida County: Clerk's Office.

Otsego County Census for 1855. Otsego County: Clerk's Office.

Otsego County Census for 1860. Otsego County: Clerk's Office.

Otsego County Census for 1865. Otsego County: Clerk's Office.

Otsego County Census for 1880. Otsego County: Clerk's Office.

Board of Supervisors of the County of Herkimer for the year 1885. Frankfort, NY. Register Book and Job Print, 1885.

Board of Supervisors of the County of Herkimer for the year 1886. Weaver and Munger Publishers, Ilion Citizen and Herkimer Citizen, Book and Job Printers, 1886.

Board of Supervisors of the County of Herkimer for the year 1887. Steuben and Co. Publishers, Little Falls Journal and Courier Book and Job Printers, 1887.

Hill, David B. Public Papers. David B. Hill, Governor 1886. Albany, NY. Argus Company Printers, 1886.

Jones, Pomroy. *Annals and Recollections of Oneida County.* Rome, NY. Published by the author, 1851.

The People of the State of New York, Respondent, against Roxalana Druse, Appellant. Supreme Court, General Term. 1886. Herkimer County: Clerk's Office.

Suiter, Dr. A. Walter. *"Some Points of Medico-Legal Interest in the Scientific Investigation of the Case of the People v. Roxalana Druse, Together with an Exhibition of Specimens Representing the Corpus Delicti,"* Boston Medical and Surgical Journal, Vol 116, 1887.

Secondary Sources

Carter's Directory of Little Falls, Herkimer, Mohawk, and Ilion for 1886–7. New York: Carter and Company, 1886.

Case, Richard G. *"The Druse Case: A Folklore Study of Murder."*

Master's thesis. Cooperstown Graduate Program, 1967.
——*"The Hanging of a Murderess,"* Legacy: Annals of Herkimer County. Herkimer County Historical Society, 1987.
Diagnostic and Statistical Manual of Mental Disorders, 4th. Edition Washington, DC: American Psychiatric Association, 1994.
Dieffenbacher, Jane. *This Green and Pleasant Land: Fairfield, New York.* Town of Fairfield, New York, 1996.
——*"Murder in Middleville,"* Legacy: Annals of Herkimer County. Herkimer County Historical Society, 2004
Eckler, A. Ross. *The Eckler-Ackler-Ackley Family.* Morristown, NJ. 1970.
Farrell, Grace. *Lillie Devereux Blake: Retracing a Life Erased.* Amherst and Boston University of Massachusetts, 2002.
Frasca, Ralph. *The Rise and Fall of the Saturday Globe.* Susquehanna University Press, 1992.
Gordon, Ann D., ed. *The Selected Papers of Elizabeth Cady Stanton and Susan B. Anthony,* Vol. 4. Rutgers University Press, 1997.
Hardin, George A., ed. *History of Herkimer County, New York.* Syracuse, NY: D. Mason, 1893.
Hearn, Daniel Allen. *Legal Executions in New York State: A Comprehensive Reference,* 1639–1963. Jefferson, NC: McFarland & Company, 1997.
Jackson, Marilyn M. *"Oh, Roxy, Don't,"* Courier Magazine, June, 1954.
Mrs. Druse's Case and Maggie Houghtaling: An Innocent Woman Hanged. The Truth Revealed at Last. Philadelphia, PA: Old Franklin Publishing House, 1887.
Oakes, R.A. *Genealogical and Family History of the County of Jefferson New York, Vol. 1.* New York and Chicago: Lewis Publishing,1903.
Peck, Ada Marie. *A History of the Hanover Society.* Deansboro, NY: Berry Hill Press, 1995.
Pinkerton, Matthew Worth. *Murder in All Ages.* Chicago: A. E. Pinkerton and Co., Suite 803, No.215, Dearborn Street, 1898.
Steber Directory of the Villages of Herkimer, Mohawk, Ilion, and Frankfort, 1909–1910. Utica, NY: Directory Publishing, 1910.
Tippetts, W.H. *Herkimer County Murders.* Herkimer, NY: H.P. Witherstine, Steam Book and Job Printers, 1885.
Walter, George W. *Sinners and Saints. Stories of Upstate NewYork.* Sherburne, NY: Fay Edward Faulkner Printing, 1973.

List of Illustrations